KEITH GIFFEN WRITER PAT OLLIFFE PENCILS

JOHN STANISCI INKS HI-FI COLORS

PAT BROSSEAU JOHN J. HILL TRAVIS LANHAM LETTERS

52 AFTERMATH

THE FOUR HORSEMEN

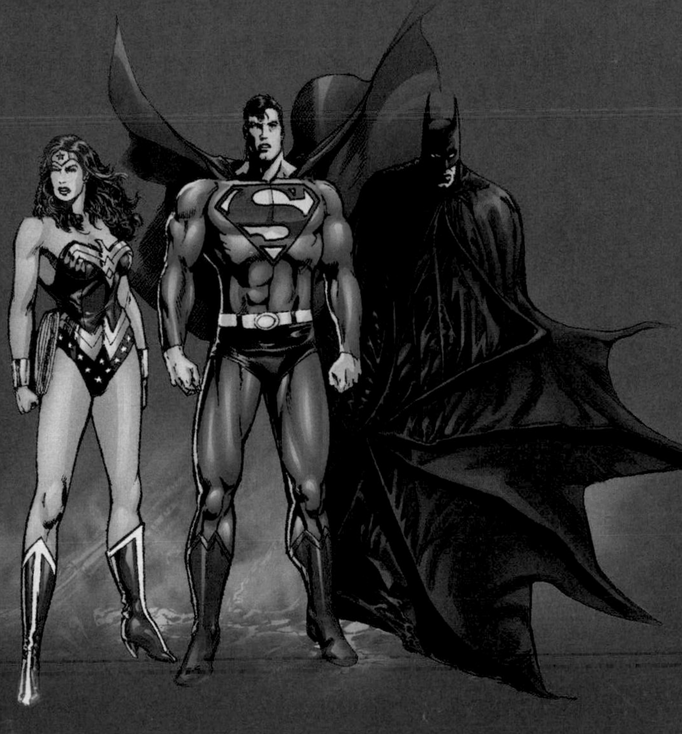

DAN DIDIO *Senior VP-Executive Editor*   MICHAEL SIGLAIN *Editor-original series*   HARVEY RICHARDS *Assistant Editor-original series*
BOB HARRAS *Editor-collected edition*   ROBBIN BROSTERMAN *Senior Art Director*   PAUL LEVITZ *President & Publisher*
GEORG BREWER *VP-Design & DC Direct Creative*   RICHARD BRUNING *Senior VP-Creative Director*   PATRICK CALDON *Executive VP-Finance & Operations*
CHRIS CARAMALIS *VP-Finance*   JOHN CUNNINGHAM *VP-Marketing*   TERRI CUNNINGHAM *VP-Managing Editor*
ALISON GILL *VP-Manufacturing*   DAVID HYDE *VP-Publicity*   HANK KANALZ *VP-General Manager, WildStorm*   JIM LEE *Editorial Director-WildStorm*
PAULA LOWITT *Senior VP-Business & Legal Affairs*   MARYELLEN McLAUGHLIN *VP-Advertising & Custom Publishing*   JOHN NEE *Senior VP-Business Development*
GREGORY NOVECK *Senior VP-Creative Affairs*   SUE POHJA *VP-Book Trade Sales*   STEVE ROTTERDAM *Senior VP-Sales & Marketing*
CHERYL RUBIN *Senior VP-Brand Management*   JEFF TROJAN *VP-Business Development, DC Direct*   BOB WAYNE *VP-Sales*

Cover illustration by Ethan Van Sciver   Cover color by Hi-Fi   Publication design by Brainchild Studios/NYC

52 AFTERMATH: THE FOUR HORSEMEN
Published by DC Comics. Cover and compilation Copyright © 2008 DC Comics. All Rights Reserved. Originally published as
52 AFTERMATH: THE FOUR HORSEMEN 1–6. Copyright © 2007, 2008 DC Comics. All Rights Reserved. All characters, their
distinctive likenesses and related elements featured in this publication are trademarks of DC Comics. The stories, characters and
incidents featured in this publication are entirely fictional. DC Comics does not read or accept unsolicited submissions of ideas,
stories or artwork.

DC COMICS 1700 Broadway, New York, NY 10019
A Warner Bros. Entertainment Company.
Printed in Canada.   First Printing.   ISBN 13: 978-1-4012-1781-5

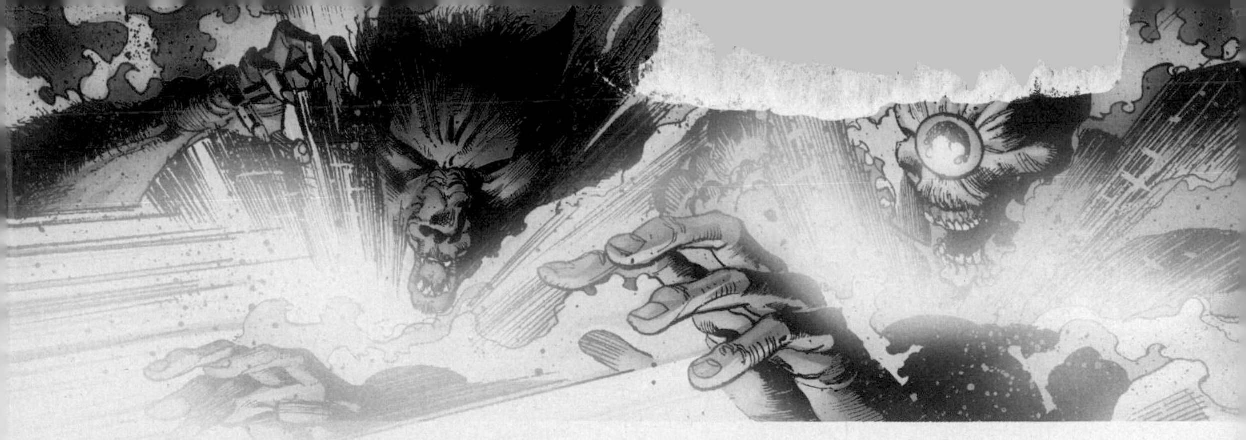

52 AFTERMATH

THE FOUR HORSEMEN

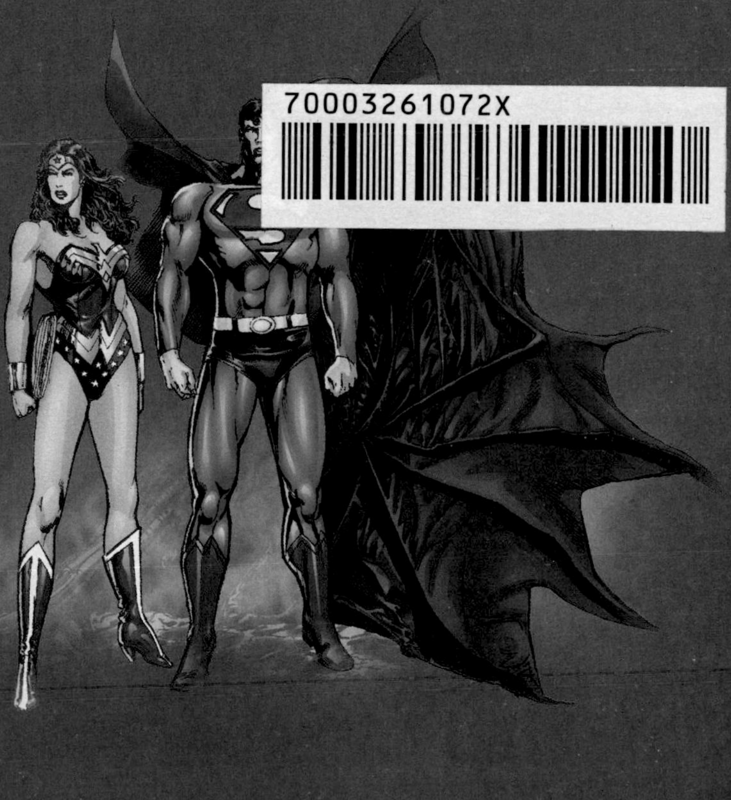

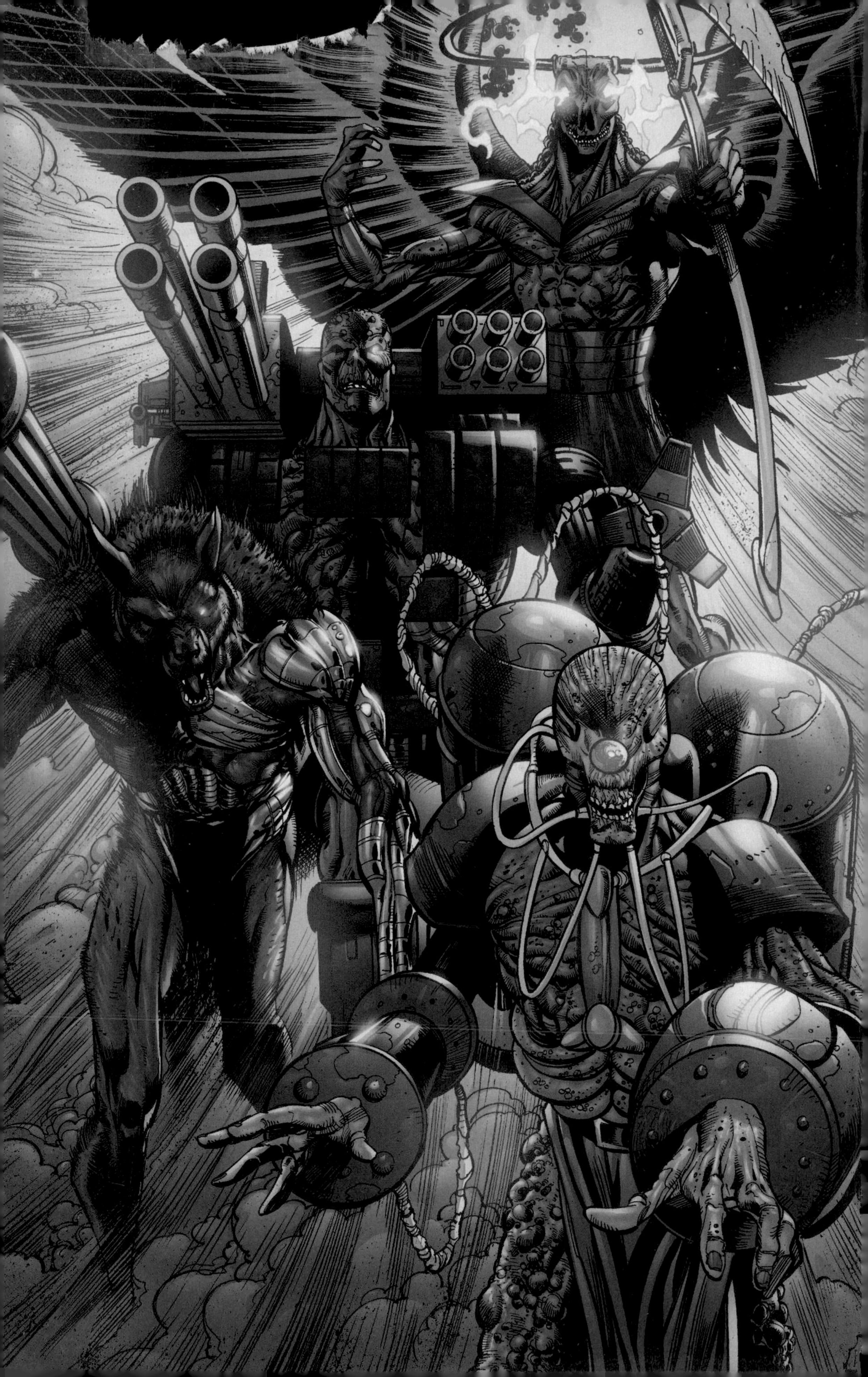

RESURRECTION

Cover art by ETHAN VAN SCIVER

CHAPTER ONE

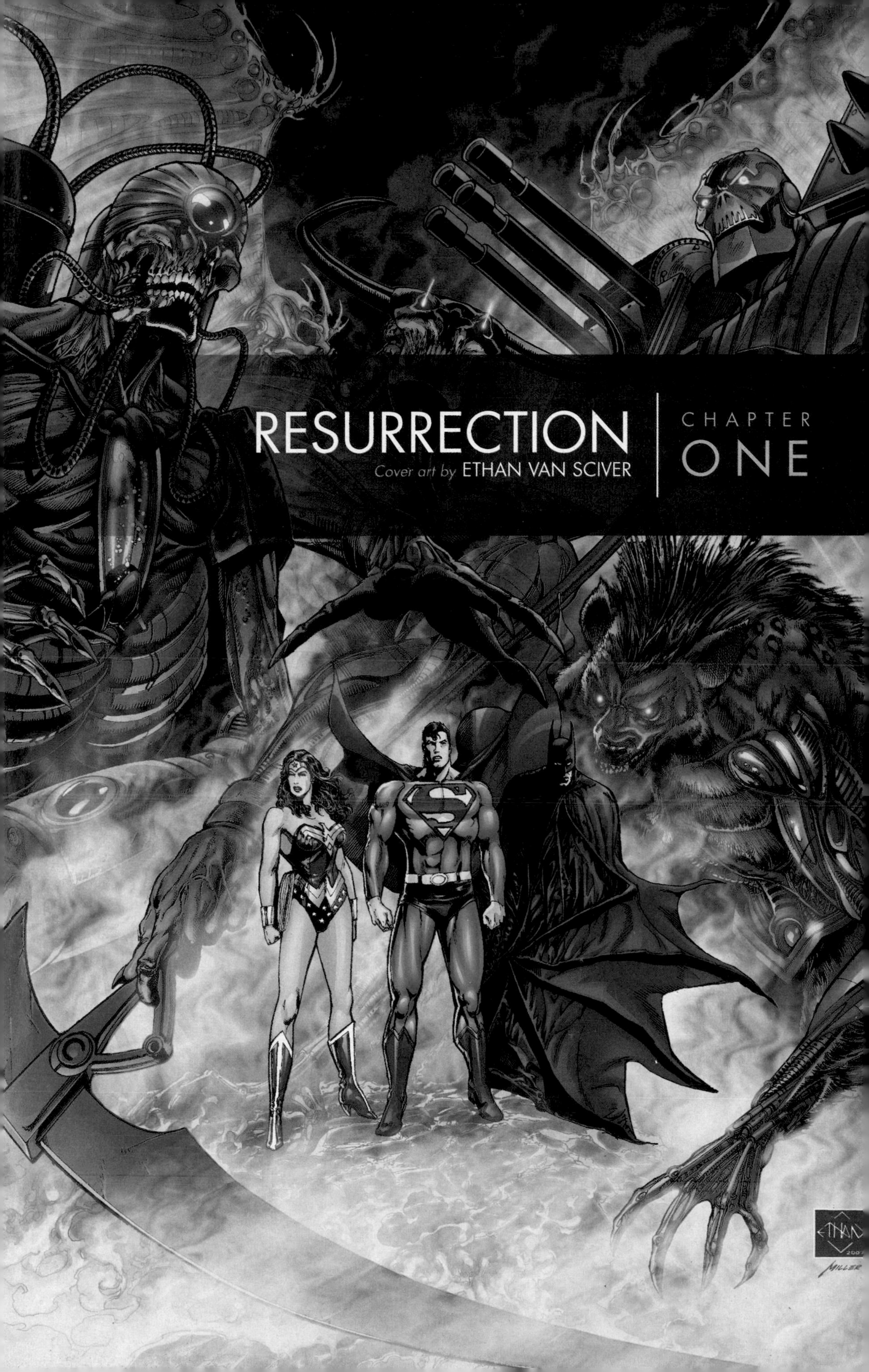

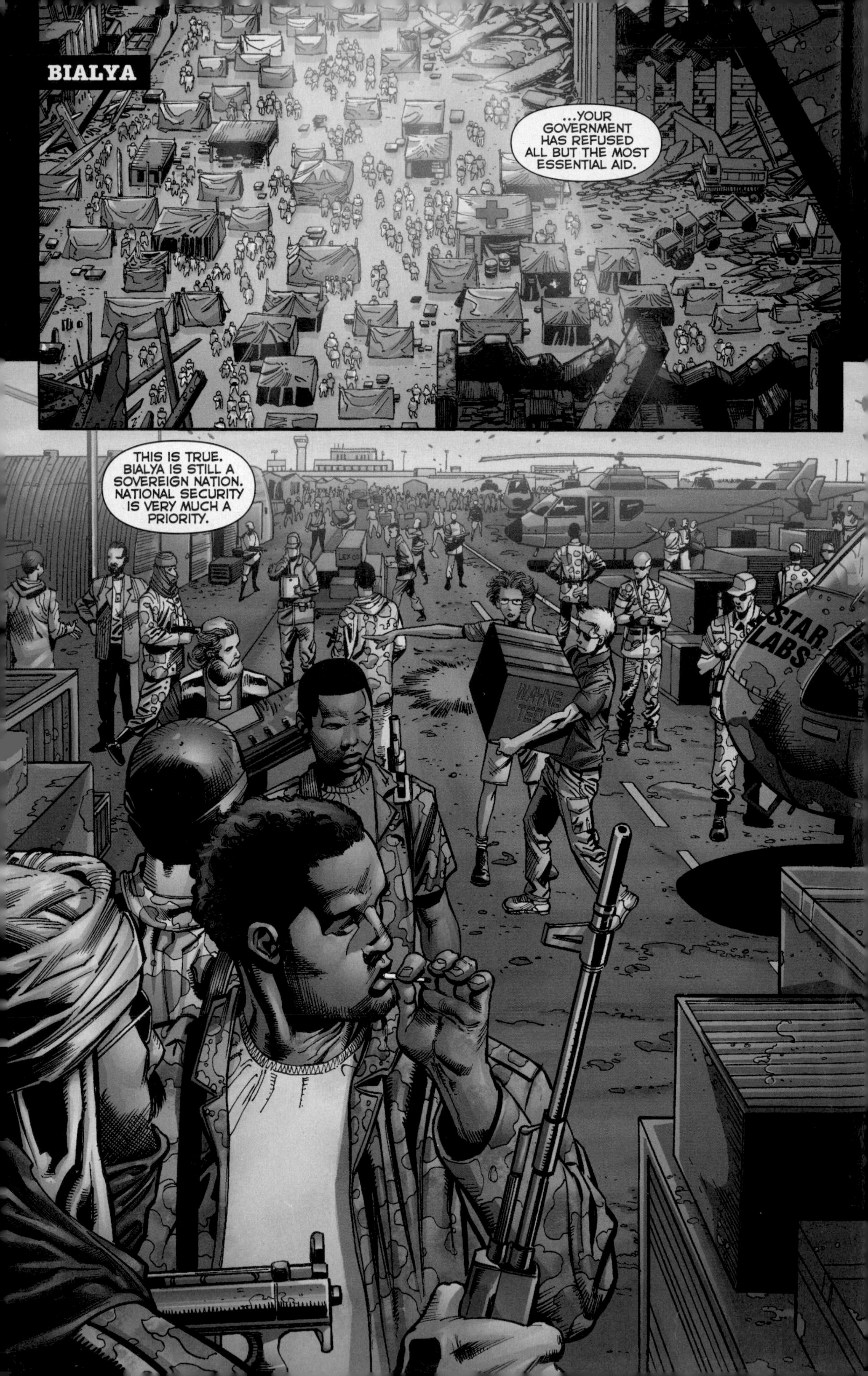
BIALYA
...YOUR GOVERNMENT HAS REFUSED ALL BUT THE MOST ESSENTIAL AID.
THIS IS TRUE. BIALYA IS STILL A SOVEREIGN NATION. NATIONAL SECURITY IS VERY MUCH A PRIORITY.
S.T.A.R. LABS

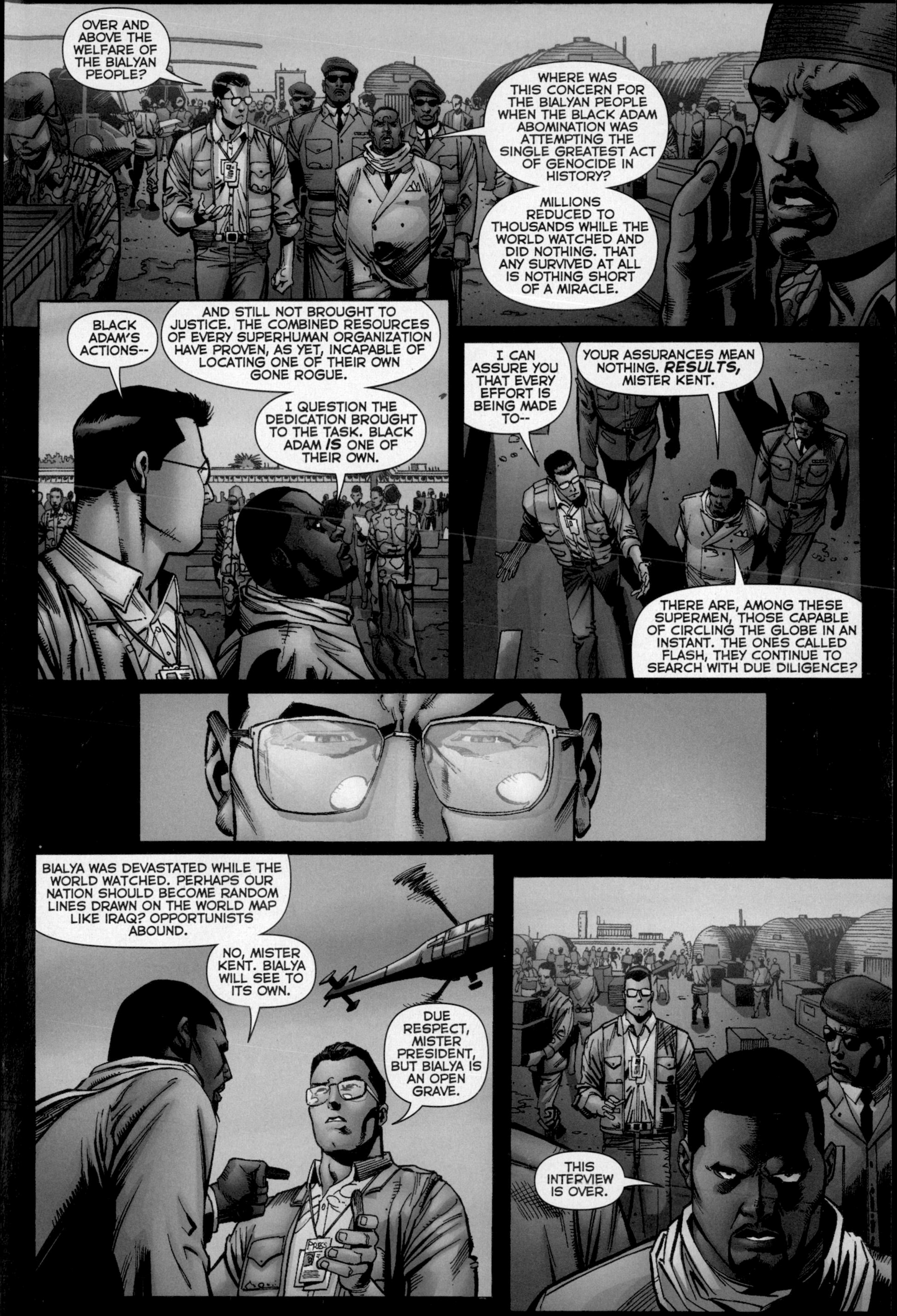

OVER AND ABOVE THE WELFARE OF THE BIALYAN PEOPLE?
WHERE WAS THIS CONCERN FOR THE BIALYAN PEOPLE WHEN THE BLACK ADAM ABOMINATION WAS ATTEMPTING THE SINGLE GREATEST ACT OF GENOCIDE IN HISTORY?
MILLIONS REDUCED TO THOUSANDS WHILE THE WORLD WATCHED AND DID NOTHING. THAT ANY SURVIVED AT ALL IS NOTHING SHORT OF A MIRACLE.
BLACK ADAM'S ACTIONS--
AND STILL NOT BROUGHT TO JUSTICE. THE COMBINED RESOURCES OF EVERY SUPERHUMAN ORGANIZATION HAVE PROVEN, AS YET, INCAPABLE OF LOCATING ONE OF THEIR OWN GONE ROGUE.
I QUESTION THE DEDICATION BROUGHT TO THE TASK. BLACK ADAM *IS* ONE OF THEIR OWN.
I CAN ASSURE YOU THAT EVERY EFFORT IS BEING MADE TO--
YOUR ASSURANCES MEAN NOTHING. ***RESULTS,*** MISTER KENT.
THERE ARE, AMONG THESE SUPERMEN, THOSE CAPABLE OF CIRCLING THE GLOBE IN AN INSTANT. THE ONES CALLED FLASH, THEY CONTINUE TO SEARCH WITH DUE DILIGENCE?
BIALYA WAS DEVASTATED WHILE THE WORLD WATCHED. PERHAPS OUR NATION SHOULD BECOME RANDOM LINES DRAWN ON THE WORLD MAP LIKE IRAQ? OPPORTUNISTS ABOUND.
NO, MISTER KENT. BIALYA WILL SEE TO ITS OWN.
DUE RESPECT, MISTER PRESIDENT, BUT BIALYA IS AN OPEN GRAVE.
THIS INTERVIEW IS OVER.

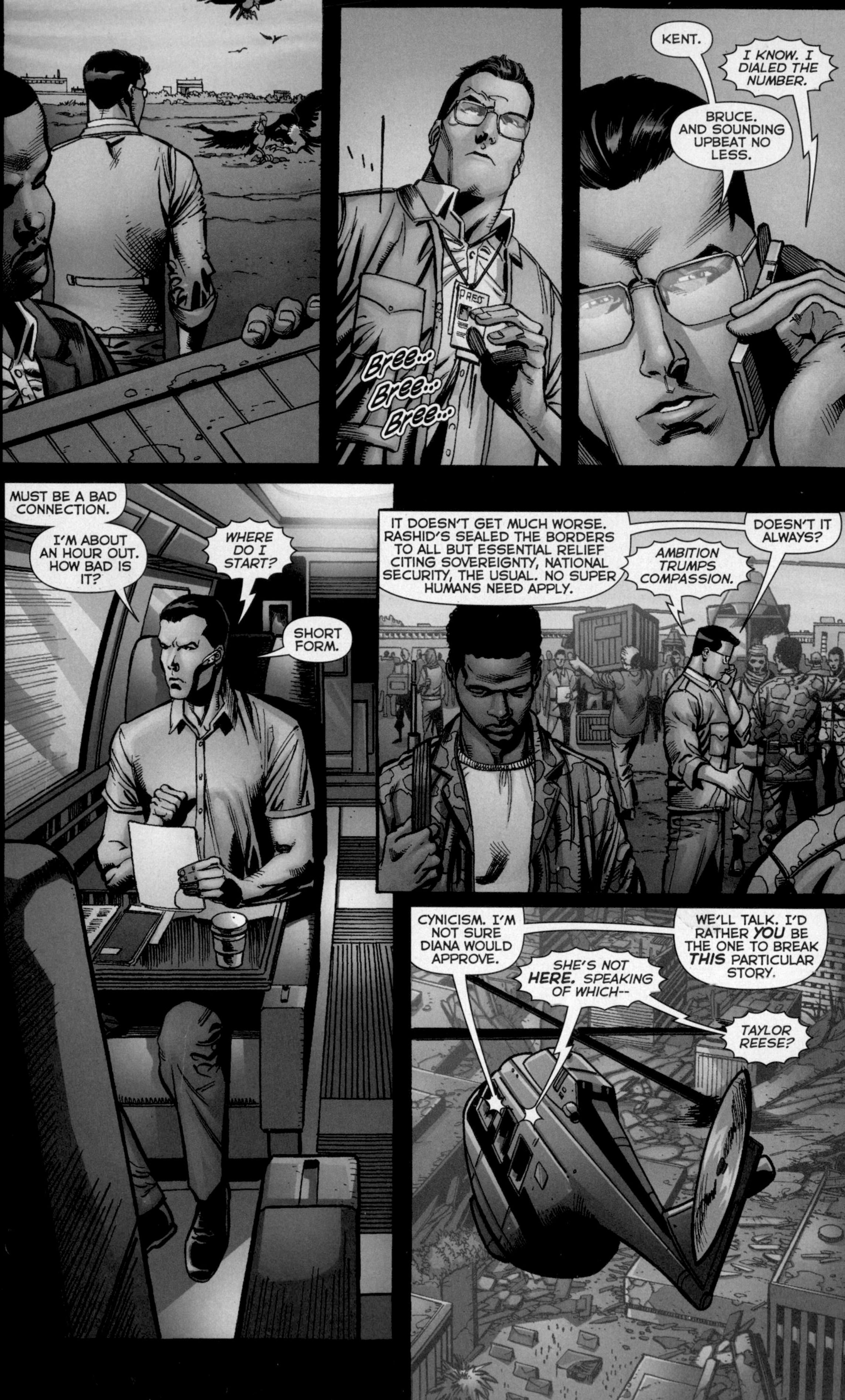
Bree...
Bree...
Bree...
KENT.
I KNOW. I DIALED THE NUMBER.
BRUCE. AND SOUNDING UPBEAT NO LESS.
MUST BE A BAD CONNECTION.
I'M ABOUT AN HOUR OUT. HOW BAD IS IT?
WHERE DO I START?
SHORT FORM.
IT DOESN'T GET MUCH WORSE. RASHID'S SEALED THE BORDERS TO ALL BUT ESSENTIAL RELIEF CITING SOVEREIGNTY, NATIONAL SECURITY, THE USUAL. NO SUPER HUMANS NEED APPLY.
DOESN'T IT ALWAYS?
AMBITION TRUMPS COMPASSION.
CYNICISM. I'M NOT SURE DIANA WOULD APPROVE.
SHE'S NOT HERE. SPEAKING OF WHICH--
WE'LL TALK. I'D RATHER YOU BE THE ONE TO BREAK THIS PARTICULAR STORY.
TAYLOR REESE?

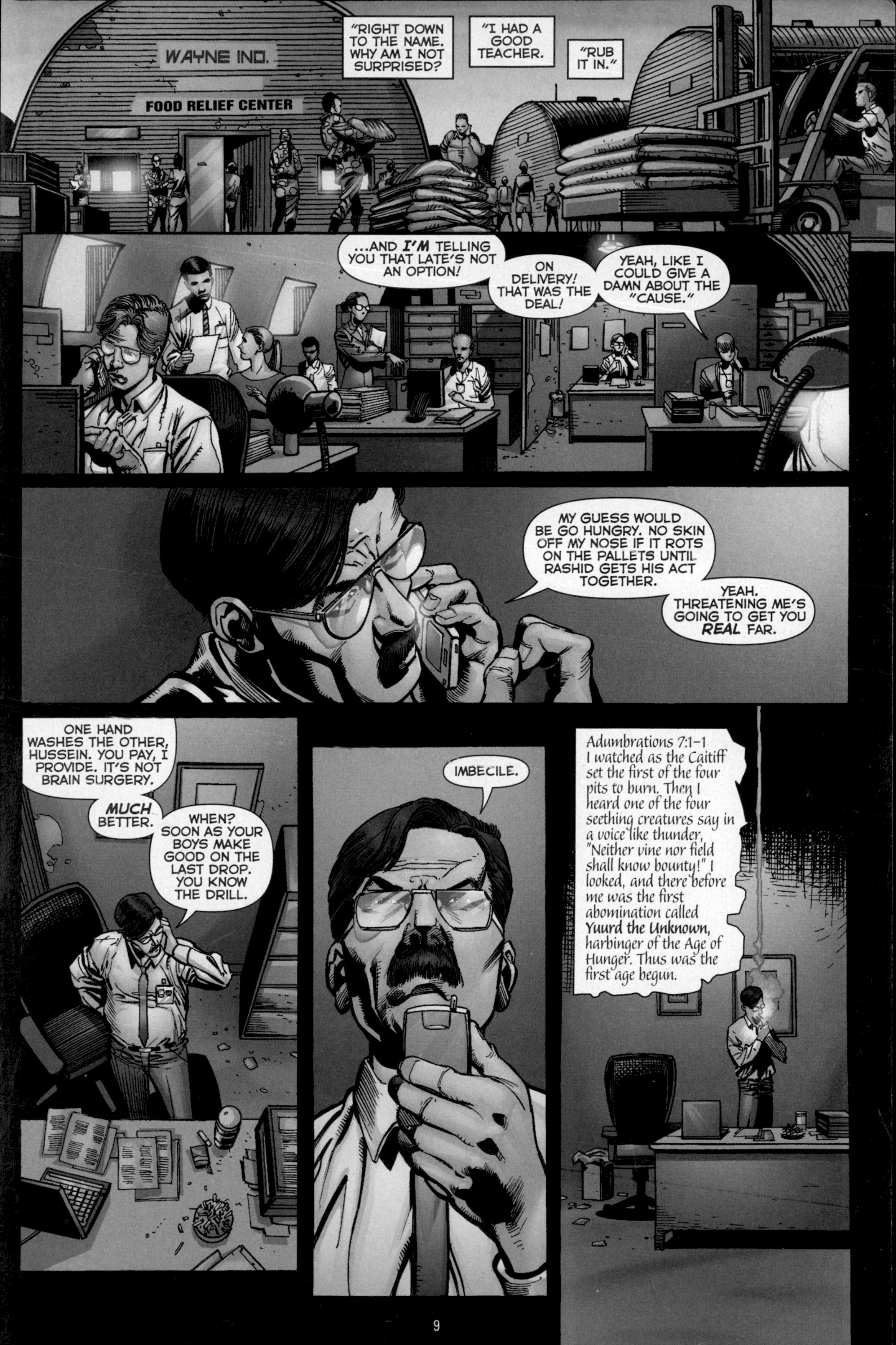
WAYNE IND.
FOOD RELIEF CENTER
"RIGHT DOWN TO THE NAME. WHY AM I NOT SURPRISED?
"I HAD A GOOD TEACHER.
"RUB IT IN."
...AND I'M TELLING YOU THAT LATE'S NOT AN OPTION!
ON DELIVERY! THAT WAS THE DEAL!
YEAH, LIKE I COULD GIVE A DAMN ABOUT THE "CAUSE."
MY GUESS WOULD BE GO HUNGRY. NO SKIN OFF MY NOSE IF IT ROTS ON THE PALLETS UNTIL RASHID GETS HIS ACT TOGETHER.
YEAH. THREATENING ME'S GOING TO GET YOU REAL FAR.
ONE HAND WASHES THE OTHER, HUSSEIN. YOU PAY, I PROVIDE. IT'S NOT BRAIN SURGERY.
MUCH BETTER.
WHEN? SOON AS YOUR BOYS MAKE GOOD ON THE LAST DROP. YOU KNOW THE DRILL.
IMBECILE.
Adumbrations 7:1–1 I watched as the Caitiff set the first of the four pits to burn. Then I heard one of the four seething creatures say in a voice like thunder, "Neither vine nor field shall know bounty!" I looked, and there before me was the first abomination called Yuurd the Unknown, harbinger of the Age of Hunger. Thus was the first age begun.

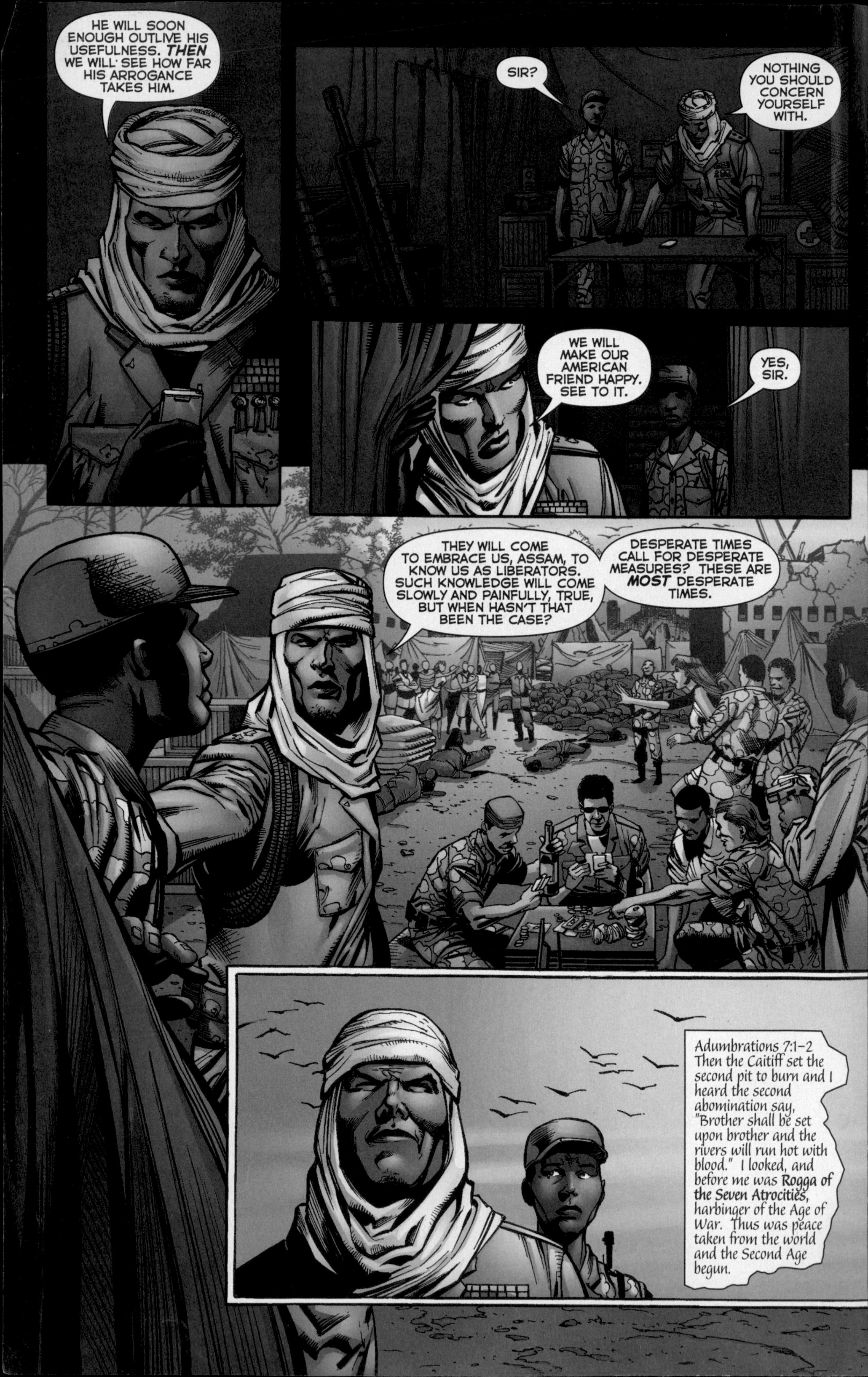
HE WILL SOON ENOUGH OUTLIVE HIS USEFULNESS. THEN WE WILL SEE HOW FAR HIS ARROGANCE TAKES HIM.
SIR?
NOTHING YOU SHOULD CONCERN YOURSELF WITH.
WE WILL MAKE OUR AMERICAN FRIEND HAPPY. SEE TO IT.
YES, SIR.
THEY WILL COME TO EMBRACE US, ASSAM, TO KNOW US AS LIBERATORS. SUCH KNOWLEDGE WILL COME SLOWLY AND PAINFULLY, TRUE, BUT WHEN HASN'T THAT BEEN THE CASE?
DESPERATE TIMES CALL FOR DESPERATE MEASURES? THESE ARE MOST DESPERATE TIMES.
Adumbrations 7:1–2 Then the Caitiff set the second pit to burn and I heard the second abomination say, "Brother shall be set upon brother and the rivers will run hot with blood." I looked, and before me was Rogga of the Seven Atrocities, harbinger of the Age of War. Thus was peace taken from the world and the Second Age begun.

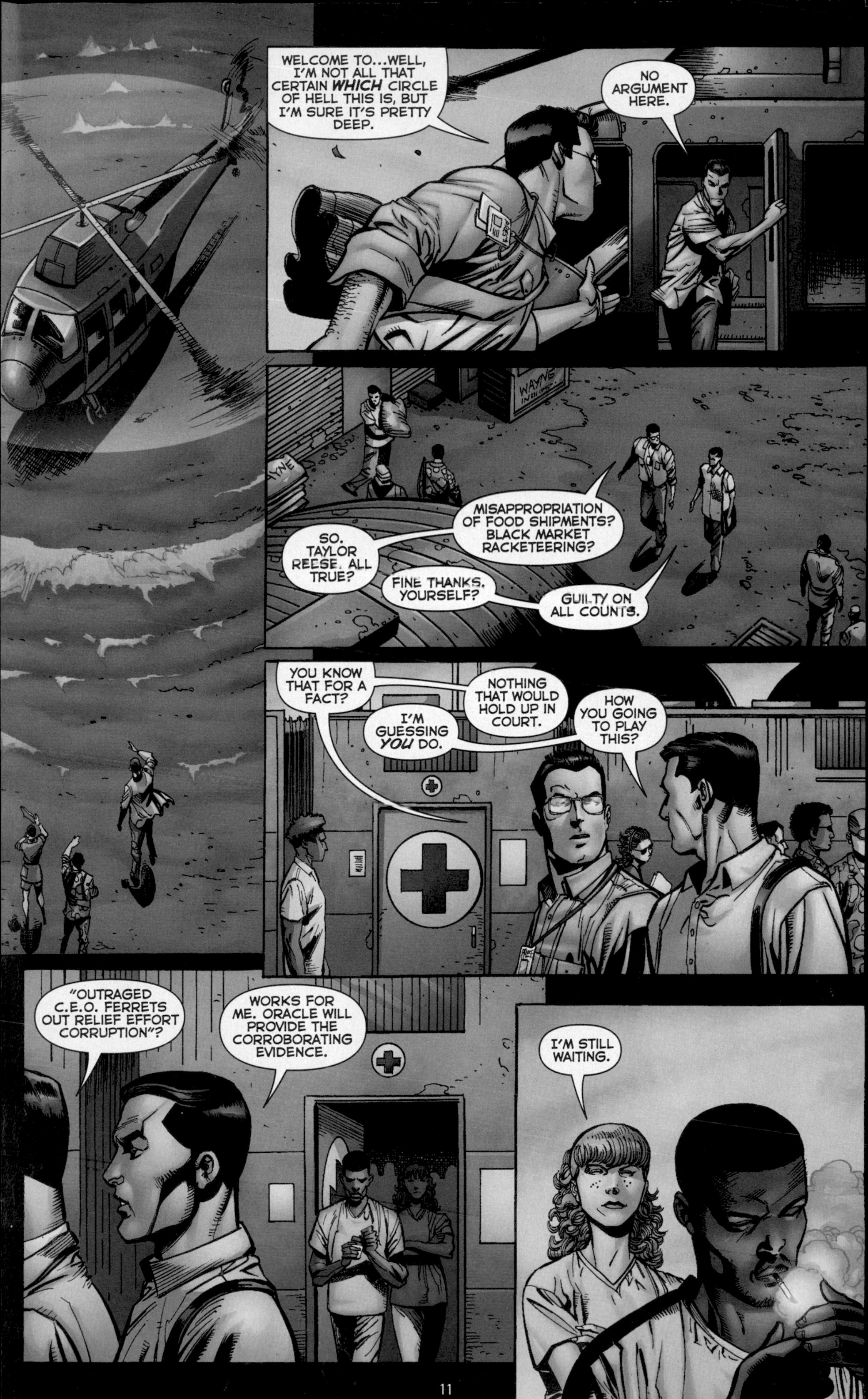
WELCOME TO...WELL, I'M NOT ALL THAT CERTAIN WHICH CIRCLE OF HELL THIS IS, BUT I'M SURE IT'S PRETTY DEEP.
NO ARGUMENT HERE.
WAYNE
SO. TAYLOR REESE. ALL TRUE?
MISAPPROPRIATION OF FOOD SHIPMENTS? BLACK MARKET RACKETEERING?
FINE THANKS. YOURSELF?
GUILTY ON ALL COUNTS.
YOU KNOW THAT FOR A FACT?
NOTHING THAT WOULD HOLD UP IN COURT.
I'M GUESSING YOU DO.
HOW YOU GOING TO PLAY THIS?
"OUTRAGED C.E.O. FERRETS OUT RELIEF EFFORT CORRUPTION"?
WORKS FOR ME. ORACLE WILL PROVIDE THE CORROBORATING EVIDENCE.
I'M STILL WAITING.

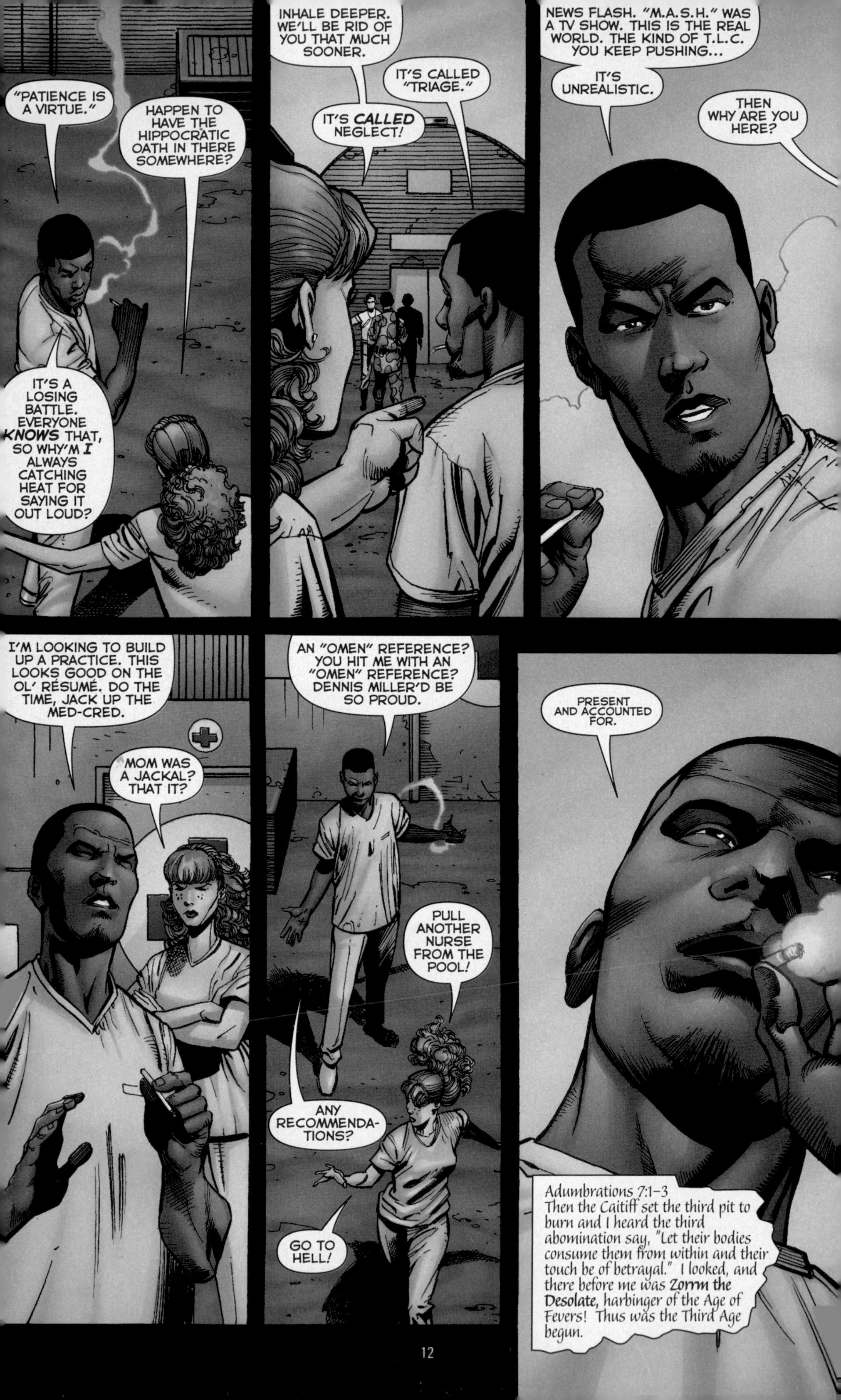
"PATIENCE IS A VIRTUE."
HAPPEN TO HAVE THE HIPPOCRATIC OATH IN THERE SOMEWHERE?
IT'S A LOSING BATTLE. EVERYONE **KNOWS** THAT, SO WHY'M ***I*** ALWAYS CATCHING HEAT FOR SAYING IT OUT LOUD?
INHALE DEEPER. WE'LL BE RID OF YOU THAT MUCH SOONER.
IT'S CALLED "TRIAGE."
IT'S ***CALLED*** NEGLECT!
NEWS FLASH. "M.A.S.H." WAS A TV SHOW. THIS IS THE REAL WORLD. THE KIND OF T.L.C. YOU KEEP PUSHING...
IT'S UNREALISTIC.
THEN WHY ARE YOU HERE?
I'M LOOKING TO BUILD UP A PRACTICE. THIS LOOKS GOOD ON THE OL' RÉSUMÉ. DO THE TIME, JACK UP THE MED-CRED.
MOM WAS A JACKAL? THAT IT?
AN "OMEN" REFERENCE? YOU HIT ME WITH AN "OMEN" REFERENCE? DENNIS MILLER'D BE SO PROUD.
PULL ANOTHER NURSE FROM THE POOL!
ANY RECOMMENDA-TIONS?
GO TO HELL!
PRESENT AND ACCOUNTED FOR.
Adumbrations 7:1–3
Then the Caitiff set the third pit to burn and I heard the third abomination say, "Let their bodies consume them from within and their touch be of betrayal." I looked, and there before me was **Zorrm the Desolate**, harbinger of the Age of Fevers! Thus was the Third Age begun.

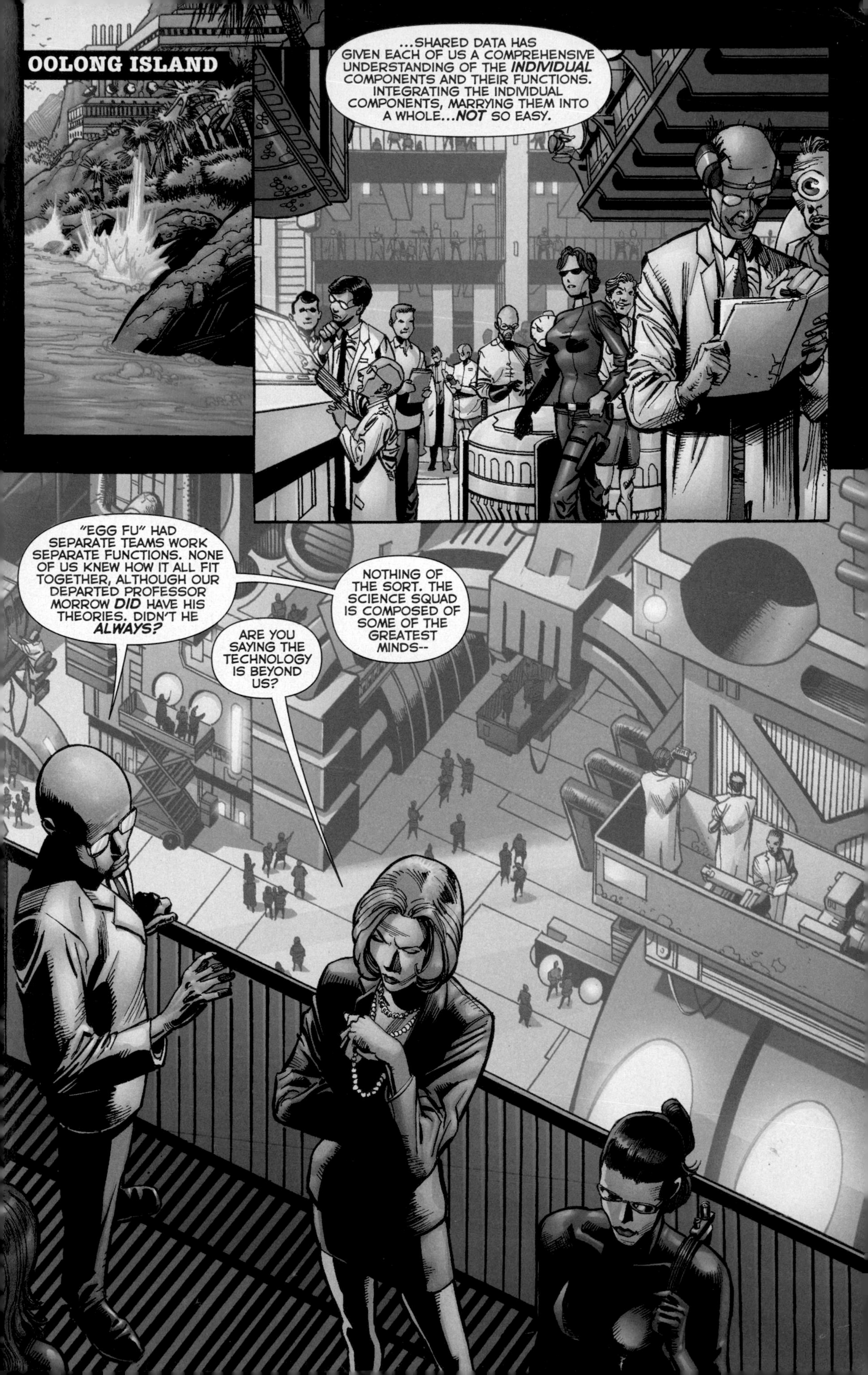
OOLONG ISLAND
...SHARED DATA HAS GIVEN EACH OF US A COMPREHENSIVE UNDERSTANDING OF THE INDIVIDUAL COMPONENTS AND THEIR FUNCTIONS. INTEGRATING THE INDIVIDUAL COMPONENTS, MARRYING THEM INTO A WHOLE...NOT SO EASY.
"EGG FU" HAD SEPARATE TEAMS WORK SEPARATE FUNCTIONS. NONE OF US KNEW HOW IT ALL FIT TOGETHER, ALTHOUGH OUR DEPARTED PROFESSOR MORROW DID HAVE HIS THEORIES. DIDN'T HE ALWAYS?
ARE YOU SAYING THE TECHNOLOGY IS BEYOND US?
NOTHING OF THE SORT. THE SCIENCE SQUAD IS COMPOSED OF SOME OF THE GREATEST MINDS--

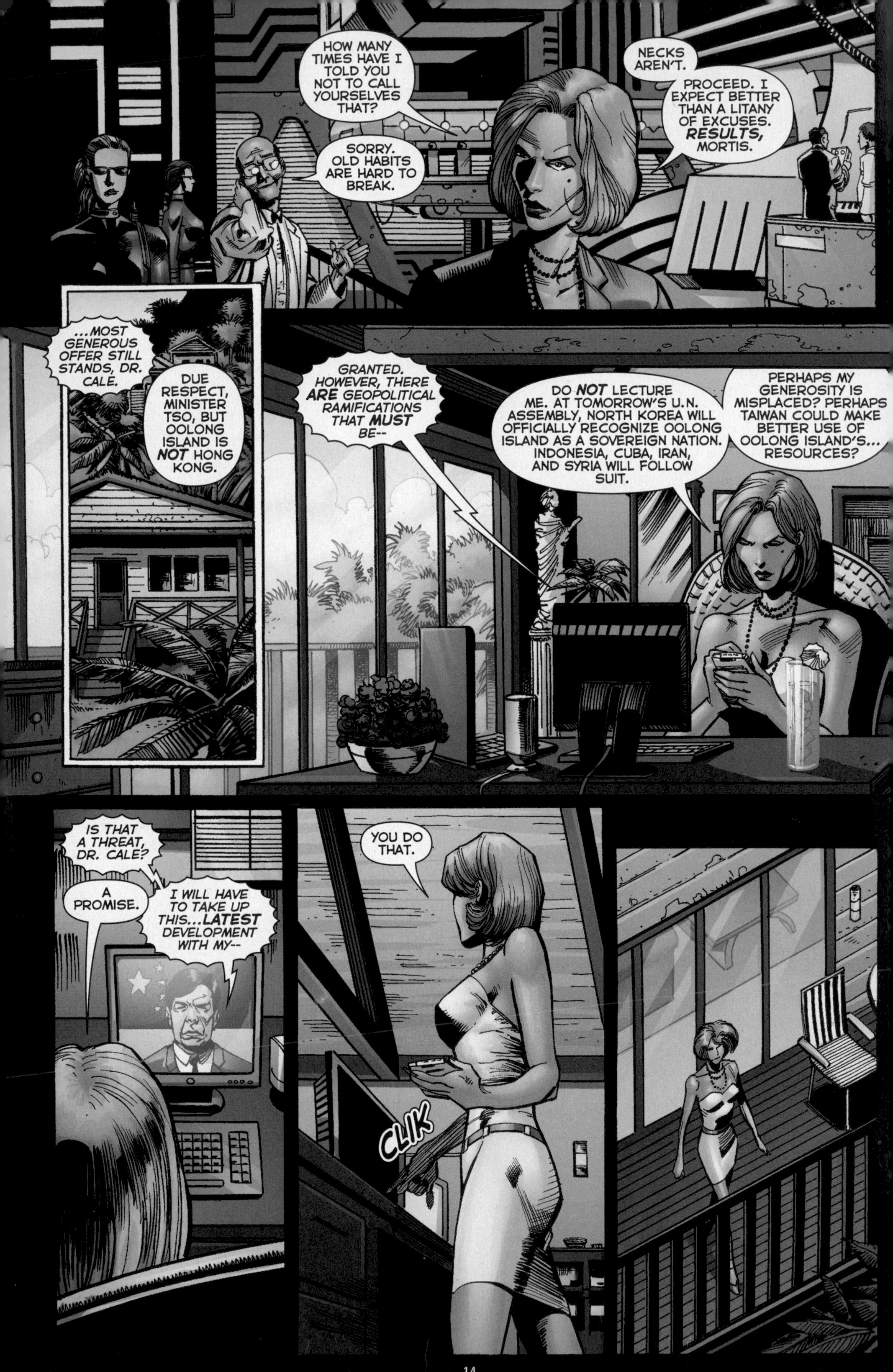
HOW MANY TIMES HAVE I TOLD YOU NOT TO CALL YOURSELVES THAT?
SORRY. OLD HABITS ARE HARD TO BREAK.
NECKS AREN'T.
PROCEED. I EXPECT BETTER THAN A LITANY OF EXCUSES. RESULTS, MORTIS.
...MOST GENEROUS OFFER STILL STANDS, DR. CALE.
DUE RESPECT, MINISTER TSO, BUT OOLONG ISLAND IS NOT HONG KONG.
GRANTED. HOWEVER, THERE ARE GEOPOLITICAL RAMIFICATIONS THAT MUST BE--
DO NOT LECTURE ME. AT TOMORROW'S U.N. ASSEMBLY, NORTH KOREA WILL OFFICIALLY RECOGNIZE OOLONG ISLAND AS A SOVEREIGN NATION. INDONESIA, CUBA, IRAN, AND SYRIA WILL FOLLOW SUIT.
PERHAPS MY GENEROSITY IS MISPLACED? PERHAPS TAIWAN COULD MAKE BETTER USE OF OOLONG ISLAND'S... RESOURCES?
IS THAT A THREAT, DR. CALE?
A PROMISE.
I WILL HAVE TO TAKE UP THIS...LATEST DEVELOPMENT WITH MY--
YOU DO THAT.
CLIK

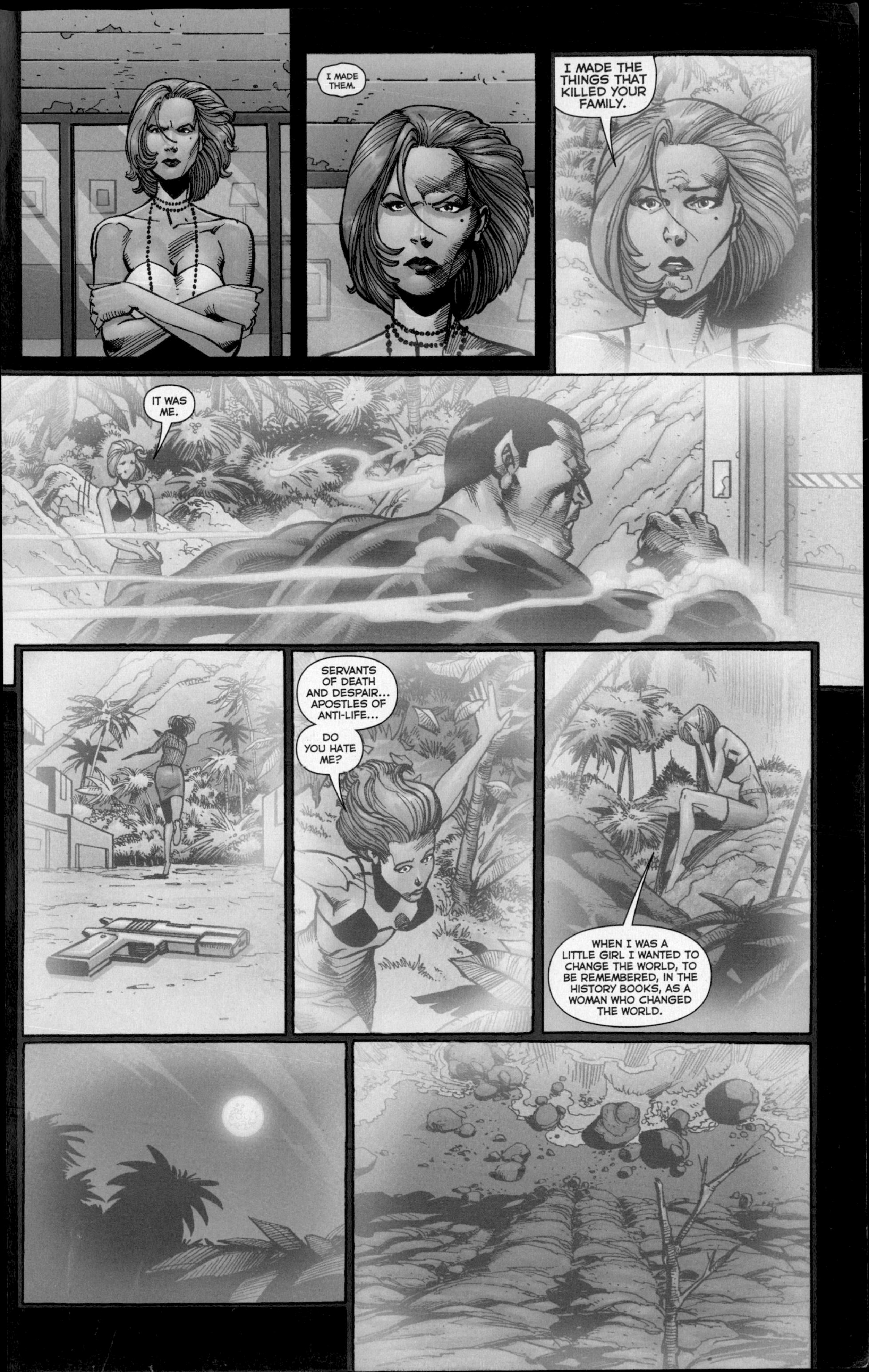
I MADE THEM.
I MADE THE THINGS THAT KILLED YOUR FAMILY.
IT WAS ME.
SERVANTS OF DEATH AND DESPAIR... APOSTLES OF ANTI-LIFE...
DO YOU HATE ME?
WHEN I WAS A LITTLE GIRL I WANTED TO CHANGE THE WORLD, TO BE REMEMBERED, IN THE HISTORY BOOKS, AS A WOMAN WHO CHANGED THE WORLD.

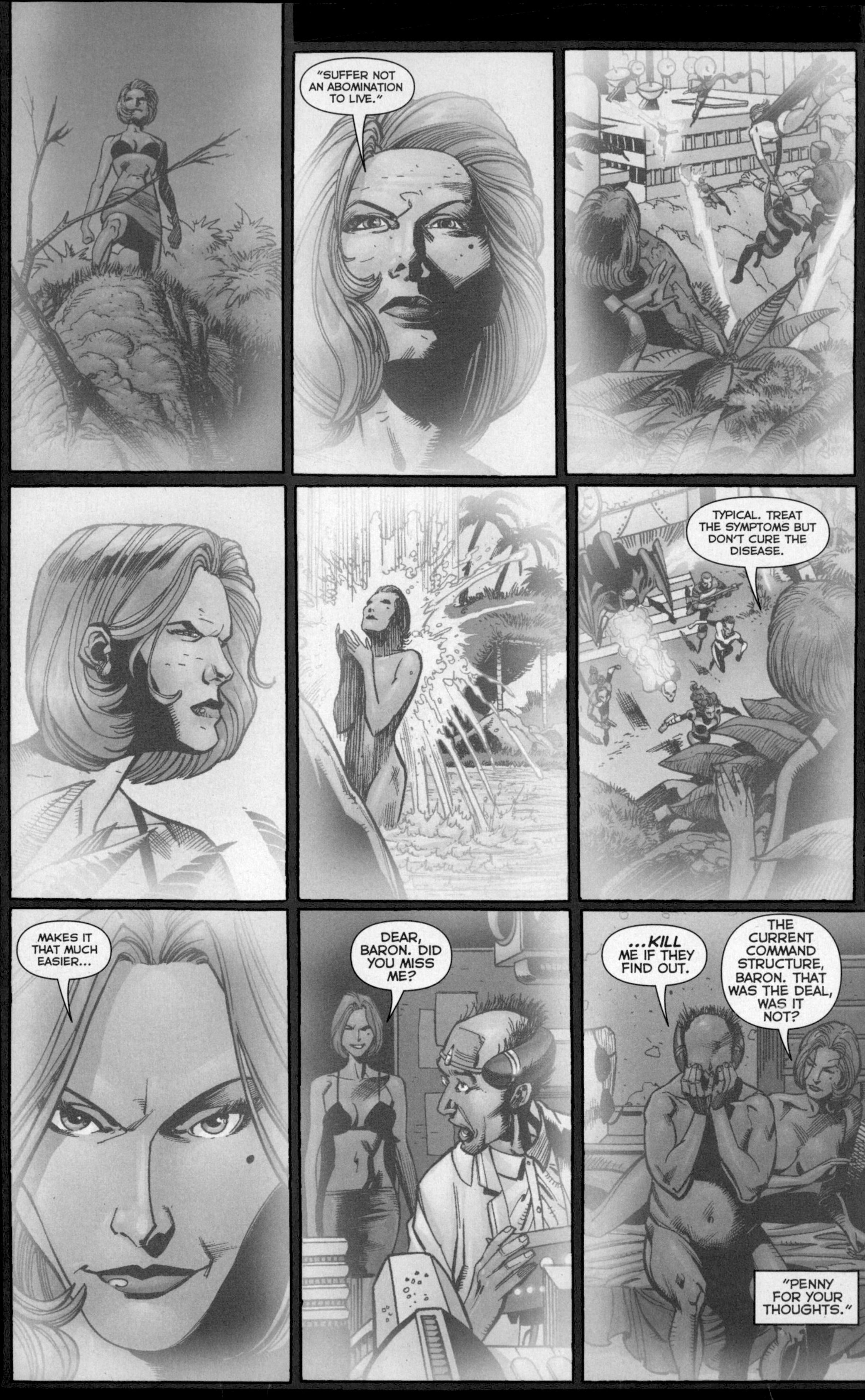
"SUFFER NOT AN ABOMINATION TO LIVE."
TYPICAL. TREAT THE SYMPTOMS BUT DON'T CURE THE DISEASE.
MAKES IT THAT MUCH EASIER...
DEAR, BARON. DID YOU MISS ME?
...KILL ME IF THEY FIND OUT.
THE CURRENT COMMAND STRUCTURE, BARON. THAT WAS THE DEAL, WAS IT NOT?
"PENNY FOR YOUR THOUGHTS."

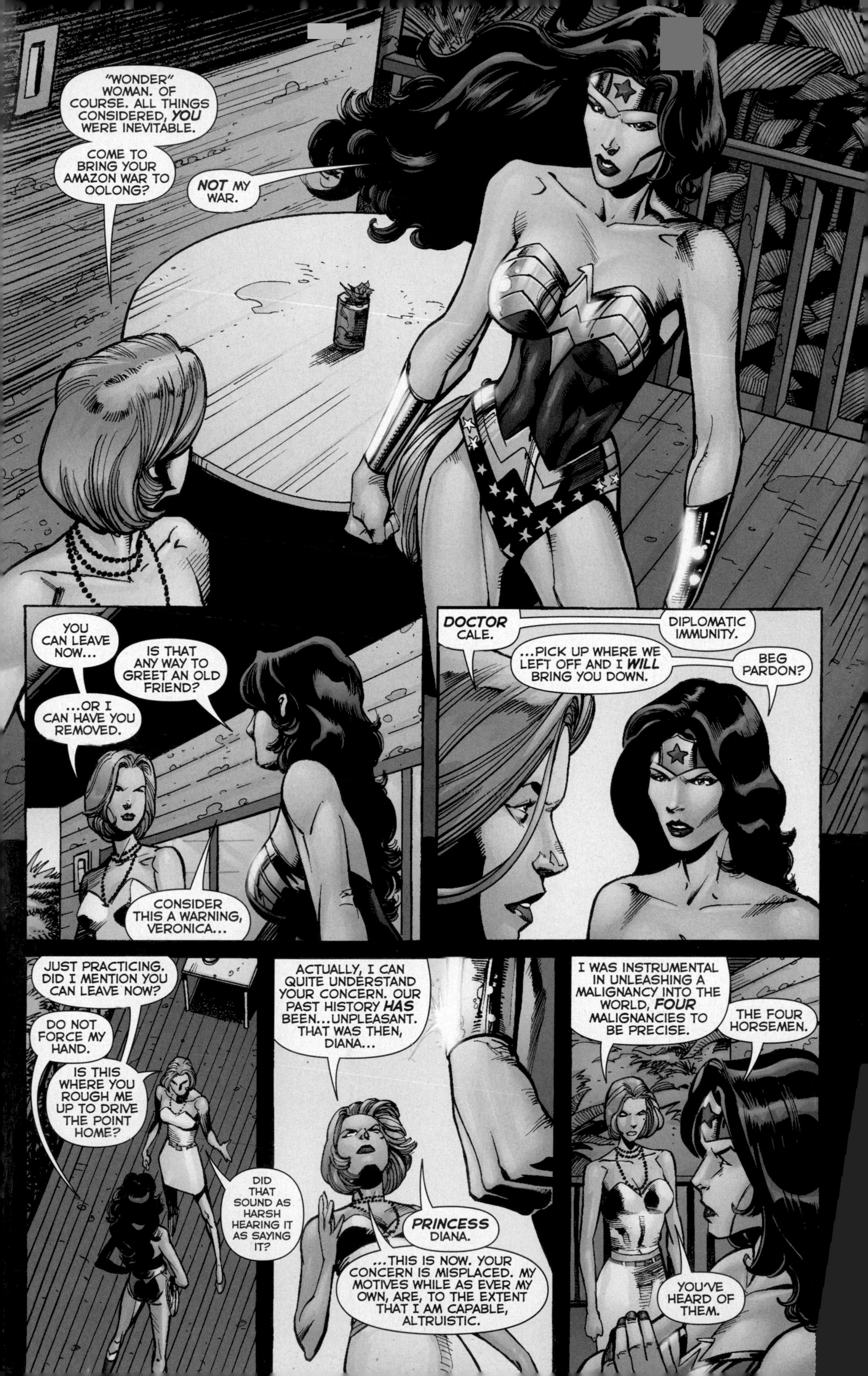
"WONDER" WOMAN. OF COURSE. ALL THINGS CONSIDERED, YOU WERE INEVITABLE.
COME TO BRING YOUR AMAZON WAR TO OOLONG?
NOT MY WAR.
YOU CAN LEAVE NOW...
IS THAT ANY WAY TO GREET AN OLD FRIEND?
...OR I CAN HAVE YOU REMOVED.
CONSIDER THIS A WARNING, VERONICA...
DOCTOR CALE.
DIPLOMATIC IMMUNITY.
...PICK UP WHERE WE LEFT OFF AND I WILL BRING YOU DOWN.
BEG PARDON?
JUST PRACTICING. DID I MENTION YOU CAN LEAVE NOW?
DO NOT FORCE MY HAND.
IS THIS WHERE YOU ROUGH ME UP TO DRIVE THE POINT HOME?
DID THAT SOUND AS HARSH HEARING IT AS SAYING IT?
ACTUALLY, I CAN QUITE UNDERSTAND YOUR CONCERN. OUR PAST HISTORY HAS BEEN...UNPLEASANT. THAT WAS THEN, DIANA...
PRINCESS DIANA.
...THIS IS NOW. YOUR CONCERN IS MISPLACED. MY MOTIVES WHILE AS EVER MY OWN, ARE, TO THE EXTENT THAT I AM CAPABLE, ALTRUISTIC.
I WAS INSTRUMENTAL IN UNLEASHING A MALIGNANCY INTO THE WORLD, FOUR MALIGNANCIES TO BE PRECISE.
THE FOUR HORSEMEN.
YOU'VE HEARD OF THEM.

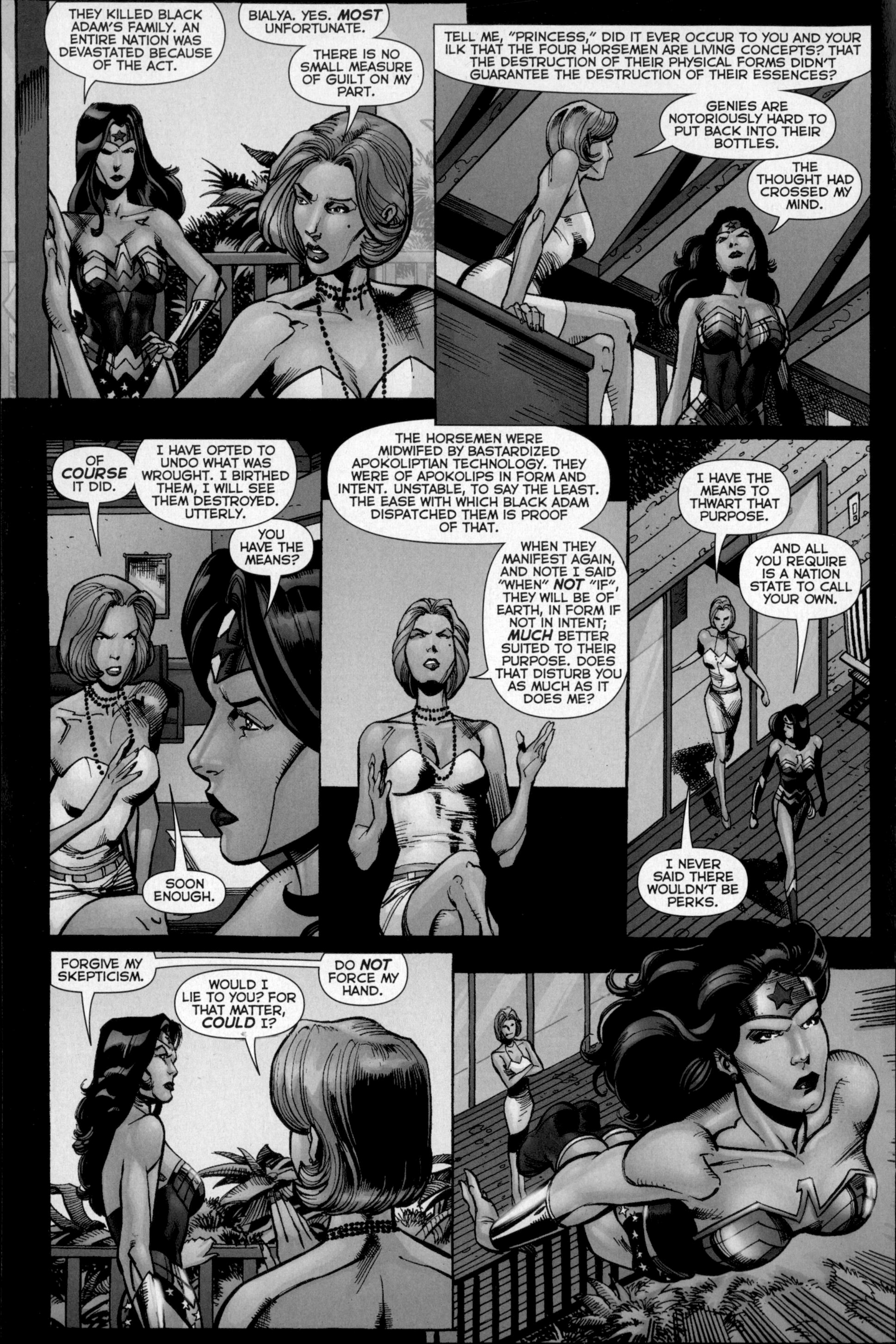
THEY KILLED BLACK ADAM'S FAMILY. AN ENTIRE NATION WAS DEVASTATED BECAUSE OF THE ACT.
BIALYA. YES. MOST UNFORTUNATE.
THERE IS NO SMALL MEASURE OF GUILT ON MY PART.
TELL ME, "PRINCESS," DID IT EVER OCCUR TO YOU AND YOUR ILK THAT THE FOUR HORSEMEN ARE LIVING CONCEPTS? THAT THE DESTRUCTION OF THEIR PHYSICAL FORMS DIDN'T GUARANTEE THE DESTRUCTION OF THEIR ESSENCES?
GENIES ARE NOTORIOUSLY HARD TO PUT BACK INTO THEIR BOTTLES.
THE THOUGHT HAD CROSSED MY MIND.
OF COURSE IT DID.
I HAVE OPTED TO UNDO WHAT WAS WROUGHT. I BIRTHED THEM, I WILL SEE THEM DESTROYED. UTTERLY.
YOU HAVE THE MEANS?
SOON ENOUGH.
THE HORSEMEN WERE MIDWIFED BY BASTARDIZED APOKOLIPTIAN TECHNOLOGY. THEY WERE OF APOKOLIPS IN FORM AND INTENT. UNSTABLE, TO SAY THE LEAST. THE EASE WITH WHICH BLACK ADAM DISPATCHED THEM IS PROOF OF THAT.
WHEN THEY MANIFEST AGAIN, AND NOTE I SAID "WHEN" NOT "IF", THEY WILL BE OF EARTH, IN FORM IF NOT IN INTENT; MUCH BETTER SUITED TO THEIR PURPOSE. DOES THAT DISTURB YOU AS MUCH AS IT DOES ME?
I HAVE THE MEANS TO THWART THAT PURPOSE.
AND ALL YOU REQUIRE IS A NATION STATE TO CALL YOUR OWN.
I NEVER SAID THERE WOULDN'T BE PERKS.
FORGIVE MY SKEPTICISM.
WOULD I LIE TO YOU? FOR THAT MATTER, COULD I?
DO NOT FORCE MY HAND.

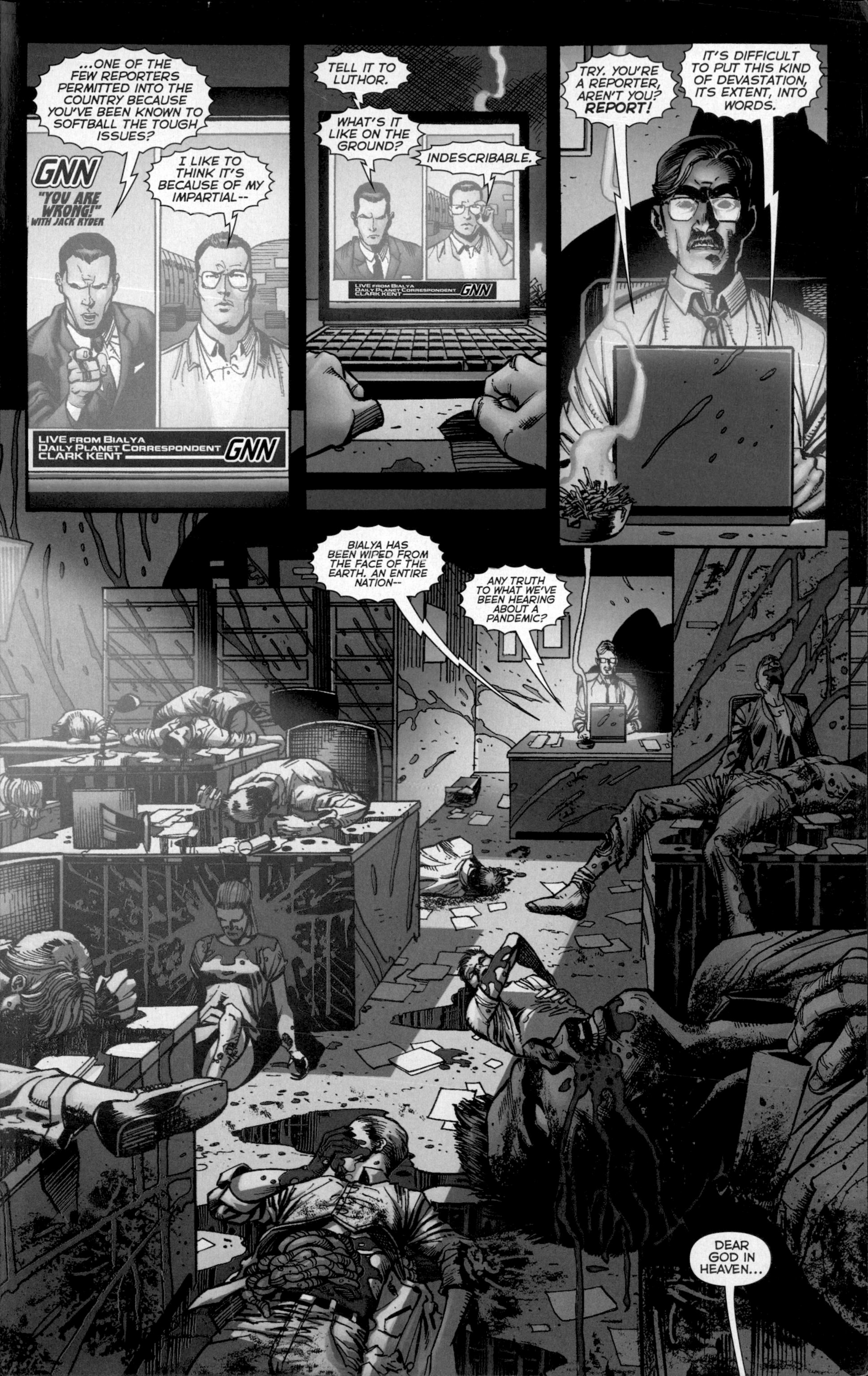
...ONE OF THE FEW REPORTERS PERMITTED INTO THE COUNTRY BECAUSE YOU'VE BEEN KNOWN TO SOFTBALL THE TOUGH ISSUES?
GNN
"YOU ARE WRONG!" WITH JACK RYDER
I LIKE TO THINK IT'S BECAUSE OF MY IMPARTIAL--
LIVE FROM BIALYA
DAILY PLANET CORRESPONDENT
CLARK KENT
GNN
TELL IT TO LUTHOR.
WHAT'S IT LIKE ON THE GROUND?
INDESCRIBABLE.
LIVE FROM BIALYA
DAILY PLANET CORRESPONDENT
CLARK KENT
GNN
TRY. YOU'RE A REPORTER, AREN'T YOU? REPORT!
IT'S DIFFICULT TO PUT THIS KIND OF DEVASTATION, ITS EXTENT, INTO WORDS.
BIALYA HAS BEEN WIPED FROM THE FACE OF THE EARTH. AN ENTIRE NATION--
ANY TRUTH TO WHAT WE'VE BEEN HEARING ABOUT A PANDEMIC?
DEAR GOD IN HEAVEN...

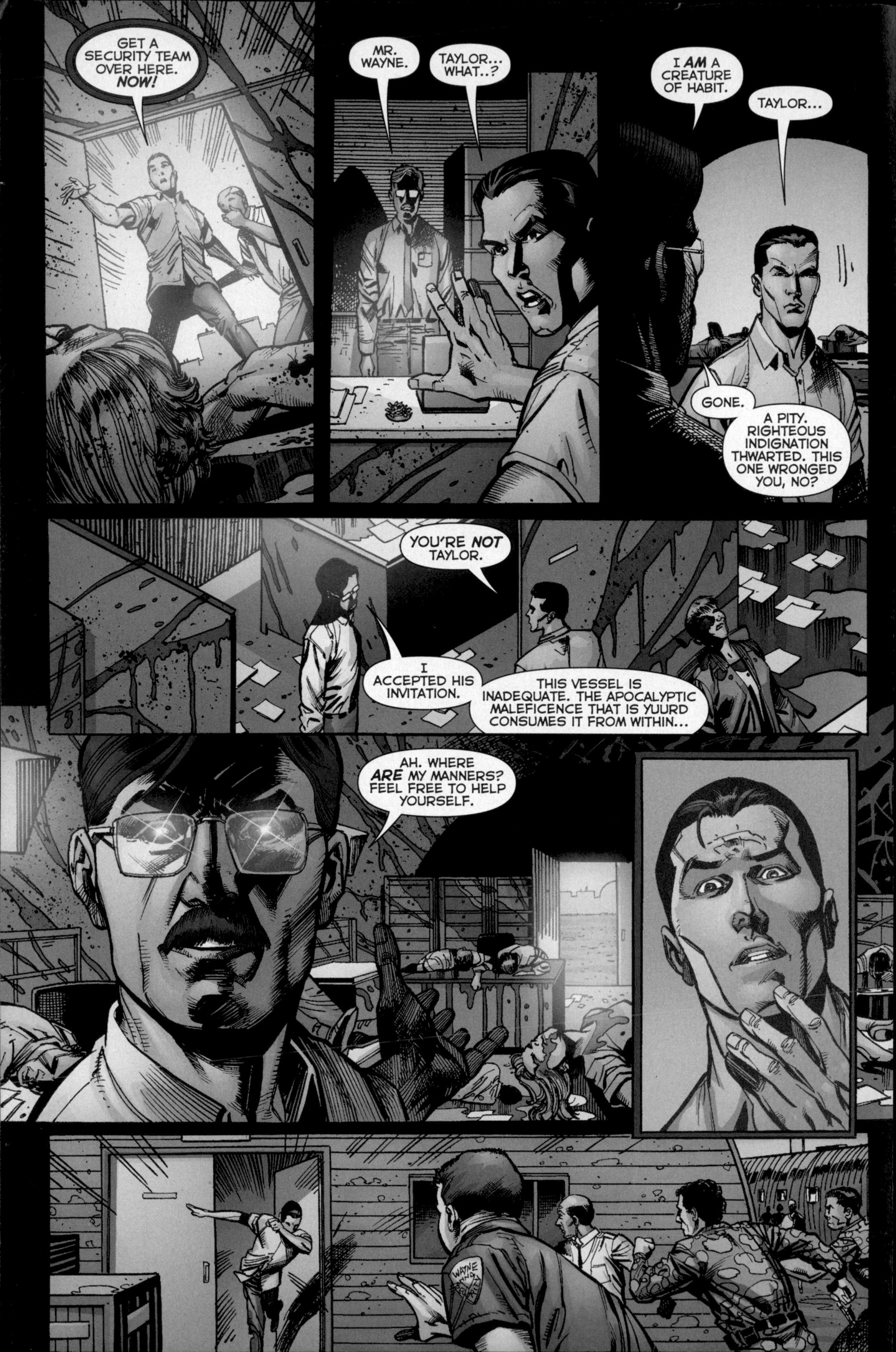
GET A SECURITY TEAM OVER HERE. NOW!
MR. WAYNE.
TAYLOR... WHAT..?
I AM A CREATURE OF HABIT.
TAYLOR...
GONE.
A PITY. RIGHTEOUS INDIGNATION THWARTED. THIS ONE WRONGED YOU, NO?
YOU'RE NOT TAYLOR.
I ACCEPTED HIS INVITATION.
THIS VESSEL IS INADEQUATE. THE APOCALYPTIC MALEFICENCE THAT IS YUURD CONSUMES IT FROM WITHIN...
AH. WHERE ARE MY MANNERS? FEEL FREE TO HELP YOURSELF.

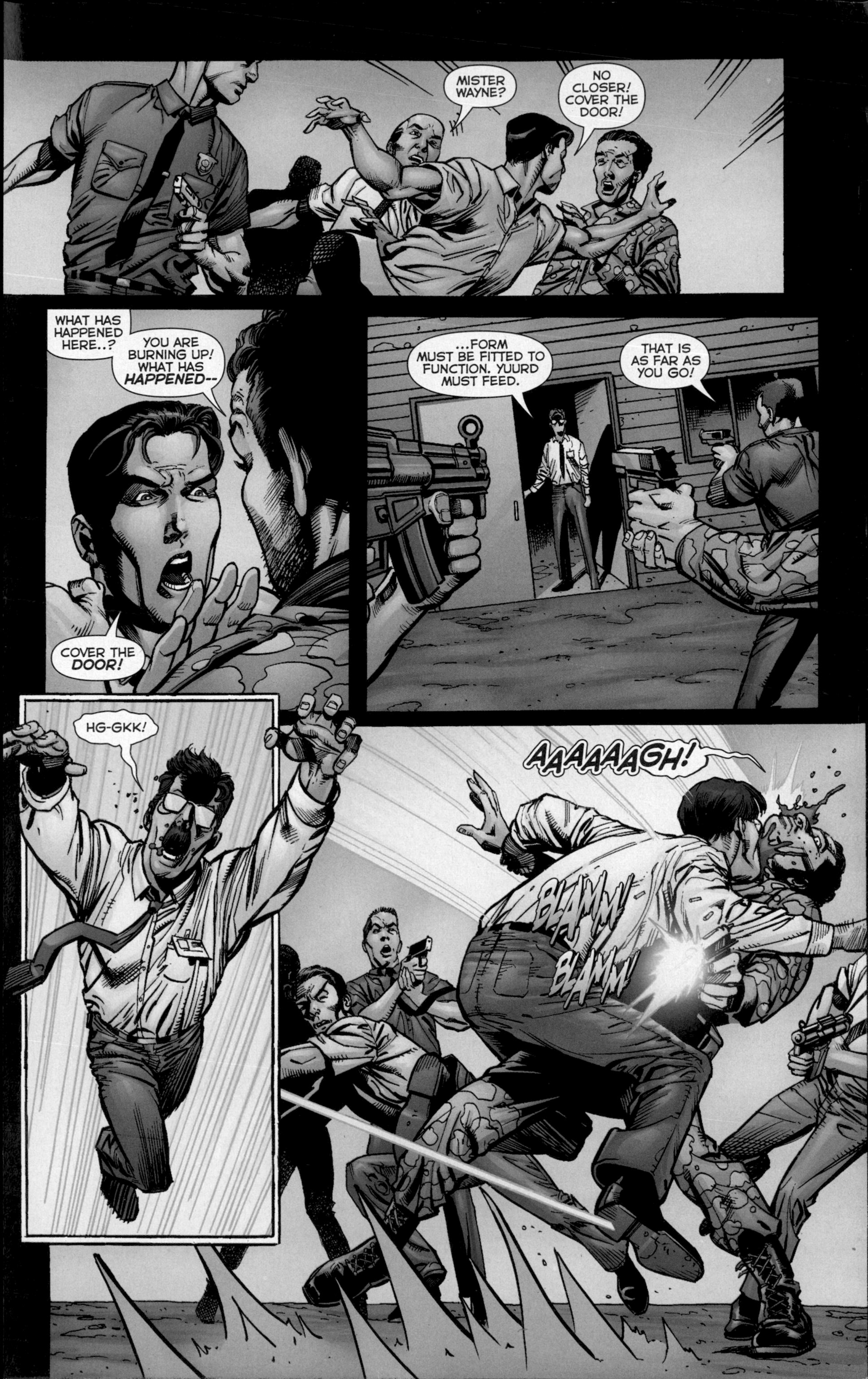
MISTER WAYNE?
NO CLOSER! COVER THE DOOR!
WHAT HAS HAPPENED HERE..?
YOU ARE BURNING UP! WHAT HAS HAPPENED--
COVER THE DOOR!
...FORM MUST BE FITTED TO FUNCTION. YUURD MUST FEED.
THAT IS AS FAR AS YOU GO!
HG-GKK!
AAAAAAGH!
BLAMM!
BLAMM!

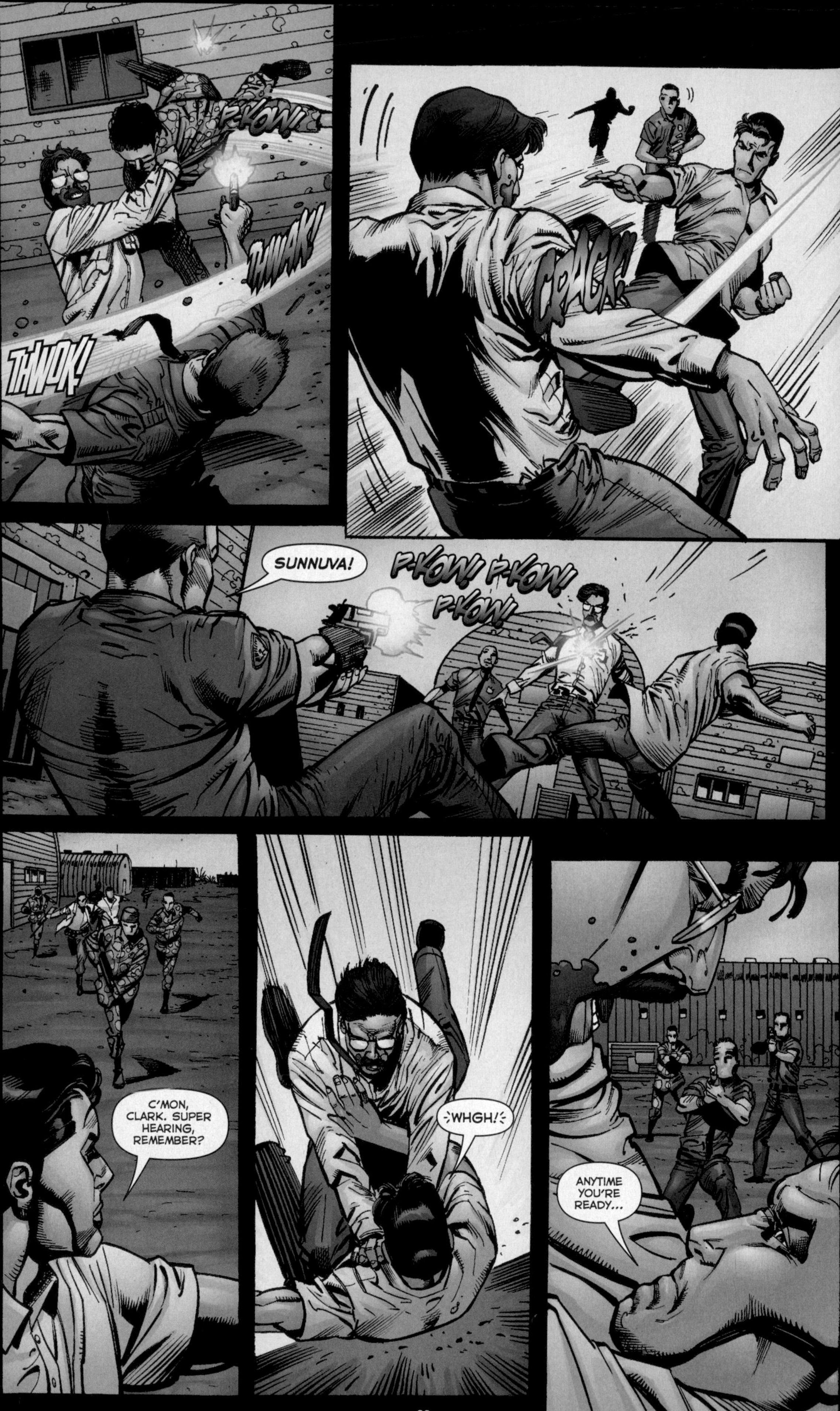

P-KOW!
THWAK!
THWOK!
CRACK!
SUNNUVA!
P-KOW! P-KOW!
P-KOW!
C'MON, CLARK. SUPER HEARING, REMEMBER?
WHGH!
ANYTIME YOU'RE READY...

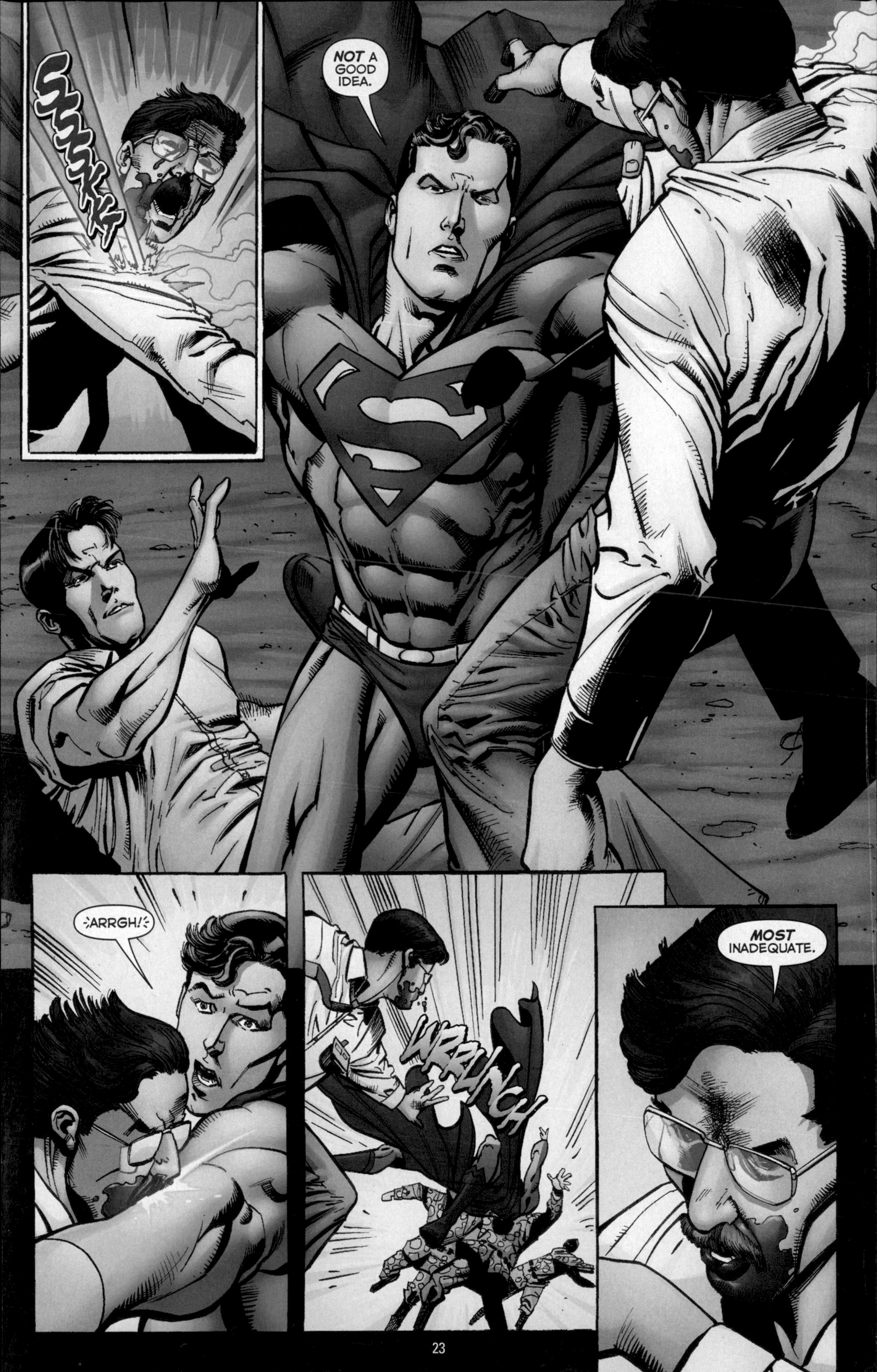
SSSKKT
NOT A GOOD IDEA.
ARRGH!
WRUNCH
MOST INADEQUATE.

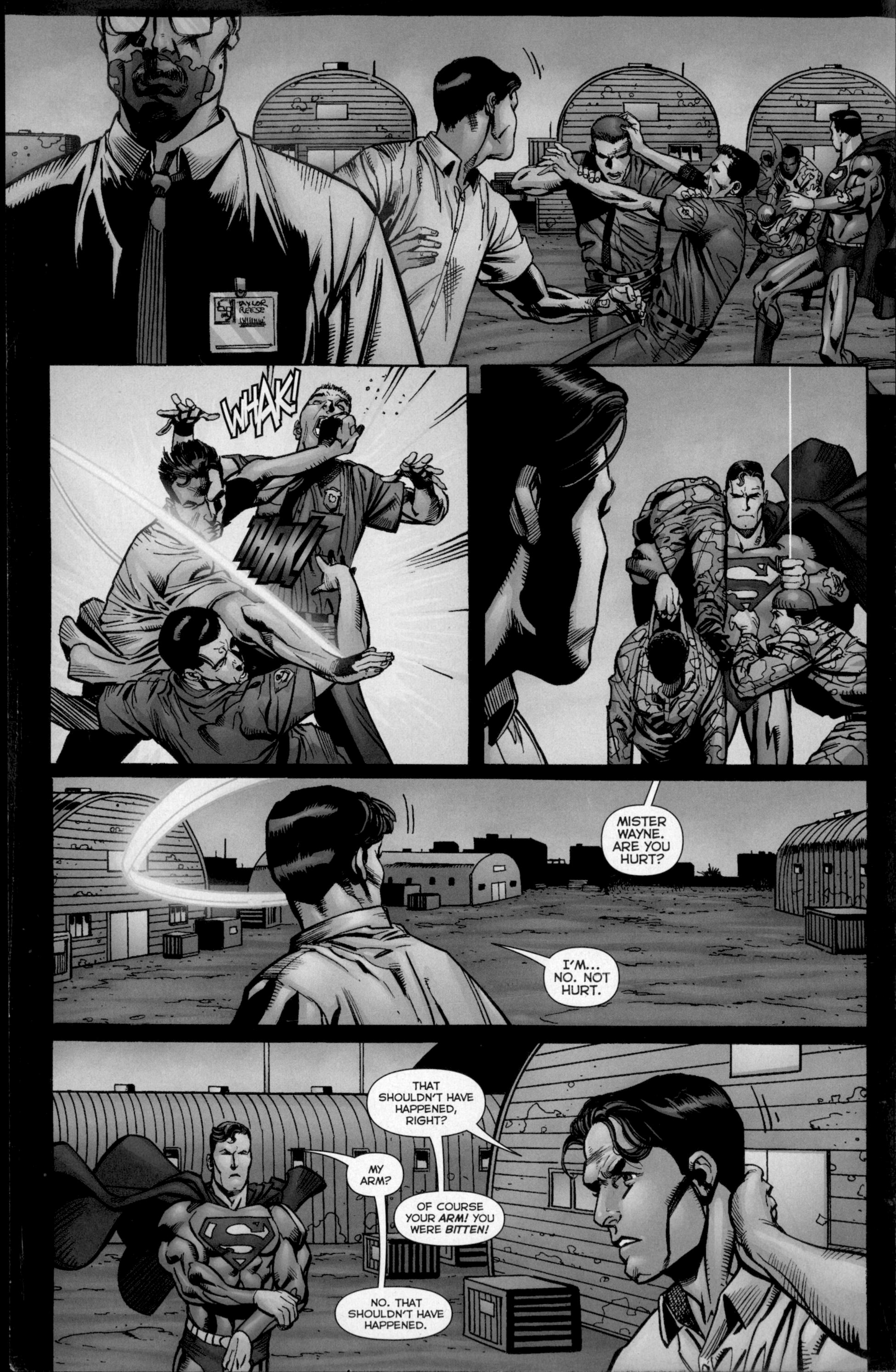
TAYLOR REESE
WHAK!
THAK!
MISTER WAYNE. ARE YOU HURT?
I'M... NO. NOT HURT.
THAT SHOULDN'T HAVE HAPPENED, RIGHT?
MY ARM?
OF COURSE YOUR *ARM!* YOU WERE *BITTEN!*
NO. THAT SHOULDN'T HAVE HAPPENED.

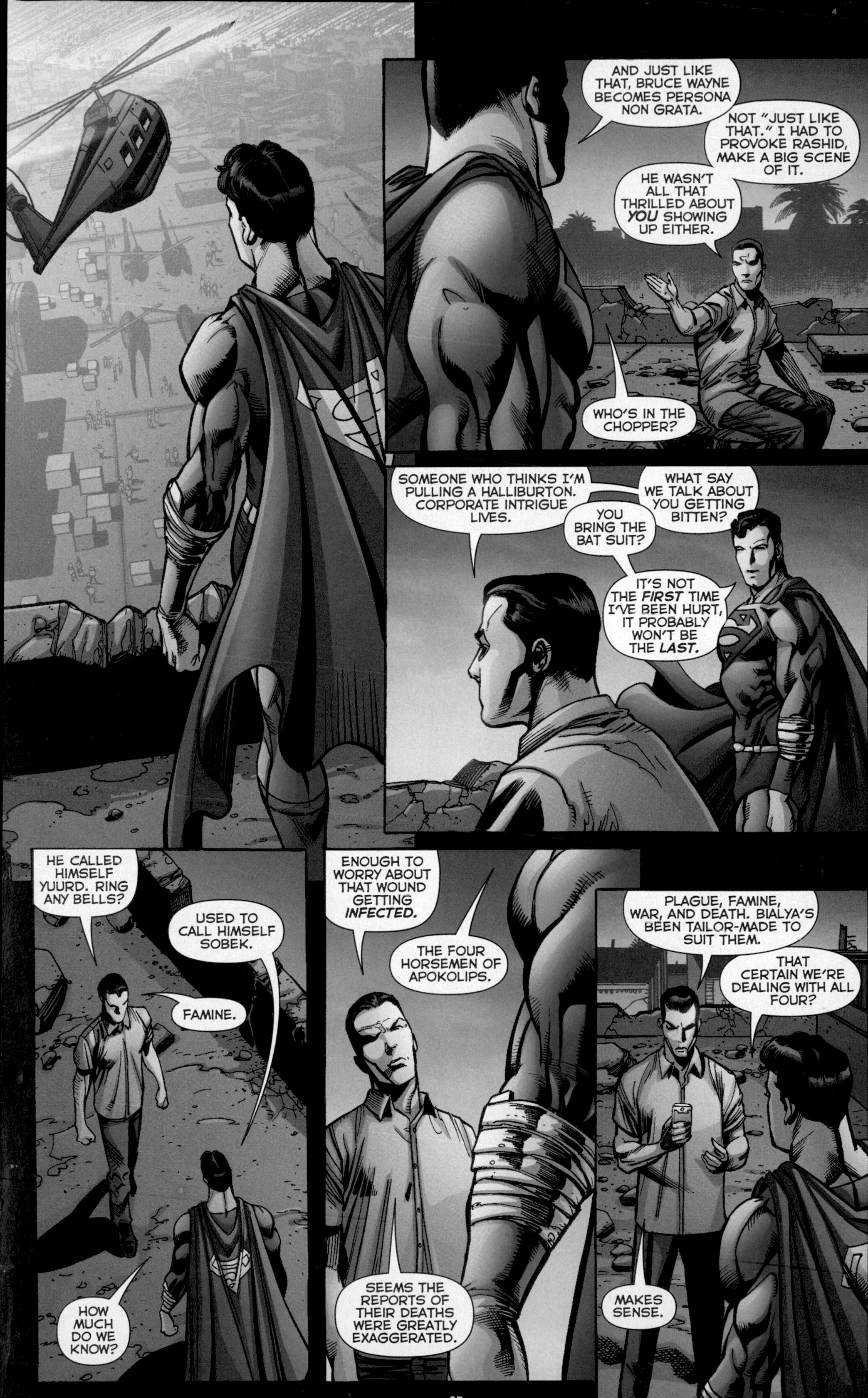
AND JUST LIKE THAT, BRUCE WAYNE BECOMES PERSONA NON GRATA.
NOT "JUST LIKE THAT." I HAD TO PROVOKE RASHID, MAKE A BIG SCENE OF IT.
HE WASN'T ALL THAT THRILLED ABOUT YOU SHOWING UP EITHER.
WHO'S IN THE CHOPPER?
SOMEONE WHO THINKS I'M PULLING A HALLIBURTON. CORPORATE INTRIGUE LIVES.
WHAT SAY WE TALK ABOUT YOU GETTING BITTEN?
YOU BRING THE BAT SUIT?
IT'S NOT THE FIRST TIME I'VE BEEN HURT, IT PROBABLY WON'T BE THE LAST.
HE CALLED HIMSELF YUURD. RING ANY BELLS?
USED TO CALL HIMSELF SOBEK.
FAMINE.
HOW MUCH DO WE KNOW?
ENOUGH TO WORRY ABOUT THAT WOUND GETTING INFECTED.
THE FOUR HORSEMEN OF APOKOLIPS.
SEEMS THE REPORTS OF THEIR DEATHS WERE GREATLY EXAGGERATED.
PLAGUE, FAMINE, WAR, AND DEATH. BIALYA'S BEEN TAILOR-MADE TO SUIT THEM.
THAT CERTAIN WE'RE DEALING WITH ALL FOUR?
MAKES SENSE.

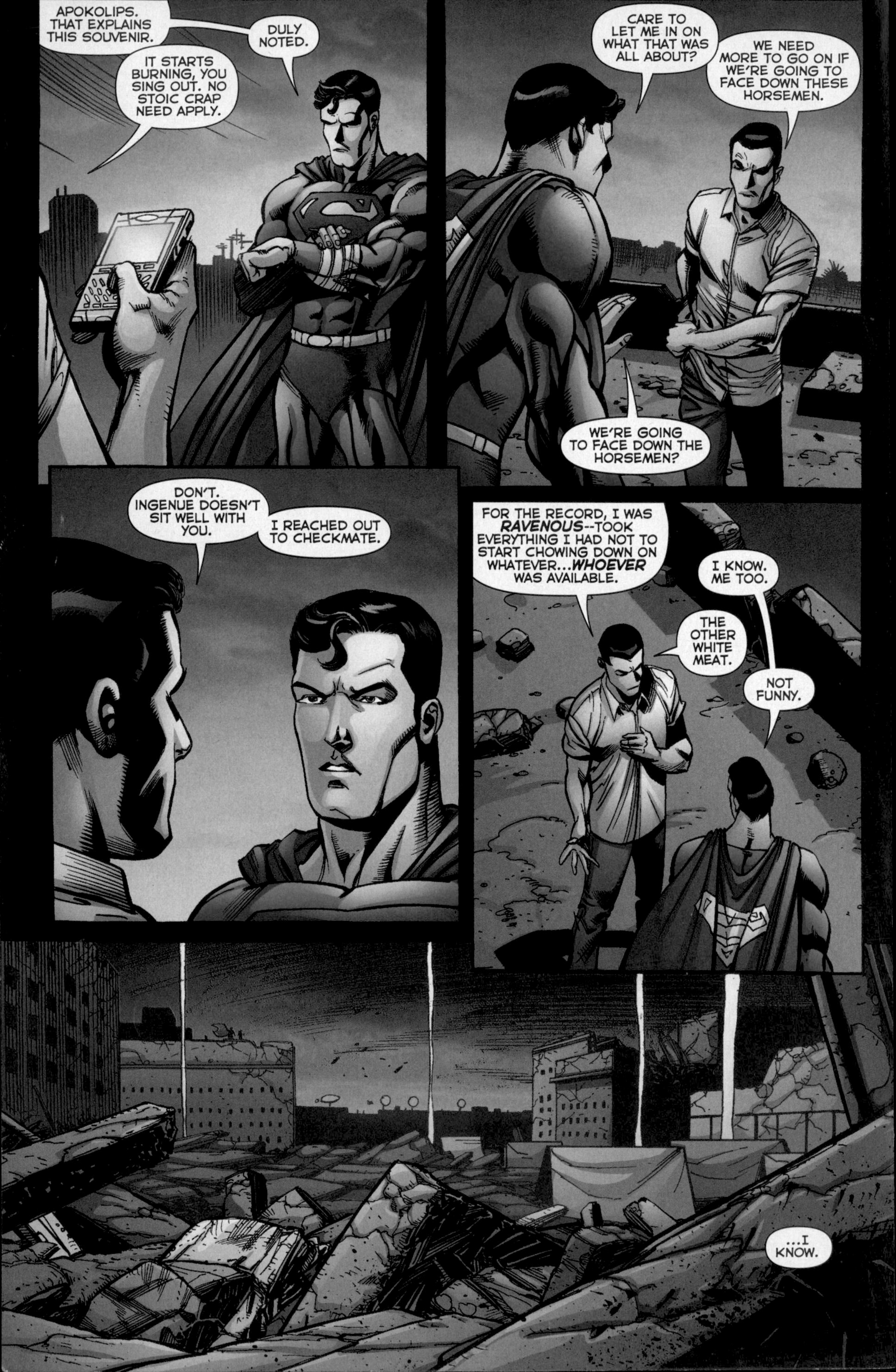

APOKOLIPS. THAT EXPLAINS THIS SOUVENIR.
DULY NOTED.
IT STARTS BURNING, YOU SING OUT. NO STOIC CRAP NEED APPLY.
CARE TO LET ME IN ON WHAT THAT WAS ALL ABOUT?
WE NEED MORE TO GO ON IF WE'RE GOING TO FACE DOWN THESE HORSEMEN.
WE'RE GOING TO FACE DOWN THE HORSEMEN?
DON'T. INGENUE DOESN'T SIT WELL WITH YOU.
I REACHED OUT TO CHECKMATE.
FOR THE RECORD, I WAS RAVENOUS--TOOK EVERYTHING I HAD NOT TO START CHOWING DOWN ON WHATEVER...WHOEVER WAS AVAILABLE.
I KNOW. ME TOO.
THE OTHER WHITE MEAT.
NOT FUNNY.
...I KNOW.

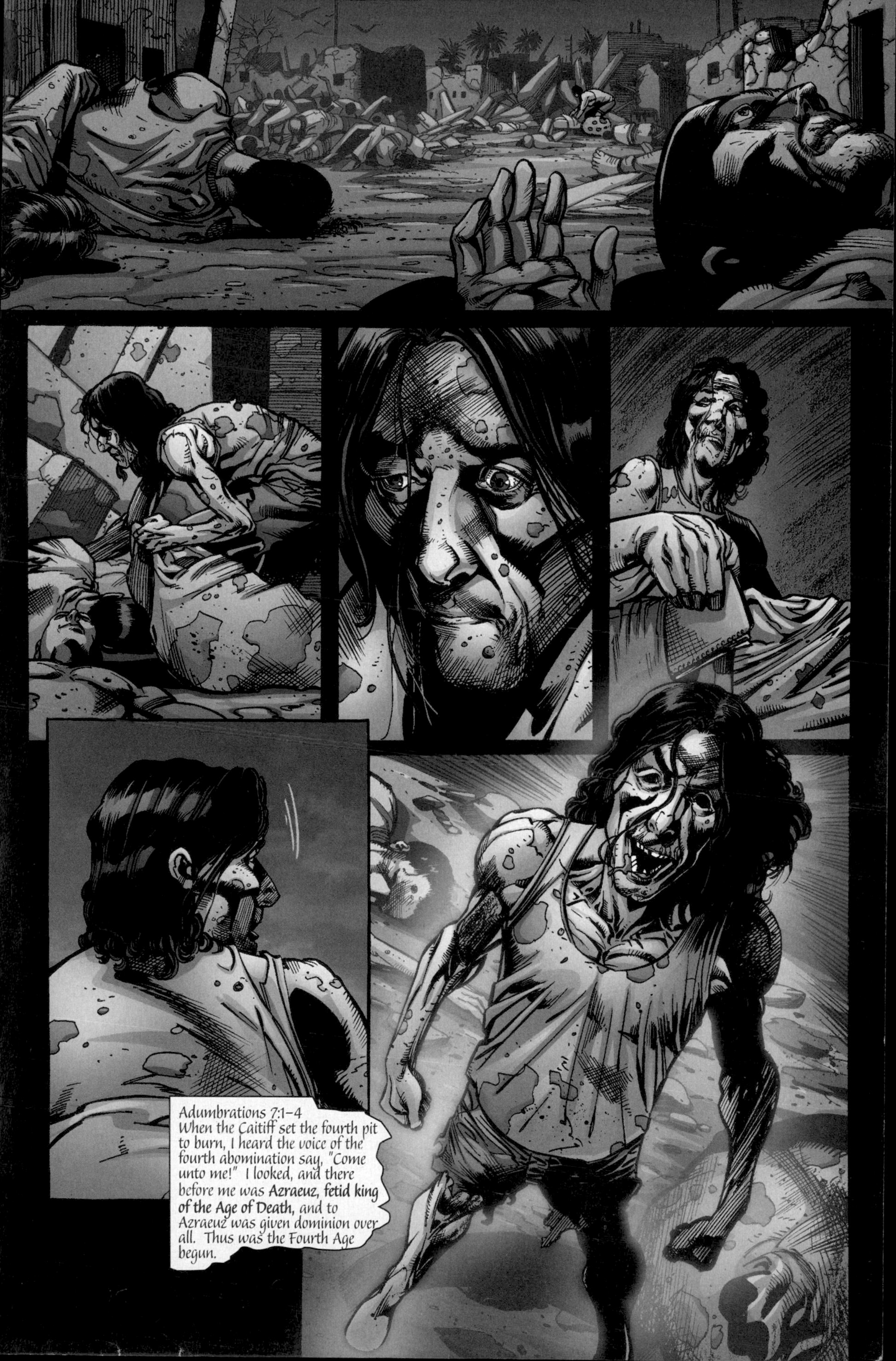
Adumbrations 7:1–4
When the Caitiff set the fourth pit to burn, I heard the voice of the fourth abomination say, "Come unto me!" I looked, and there before me was **Azraeuz, fetid king of the Age of Death,** and to Azraeuz was given dominion over all. Thus was the Fourth Age begun.

CHAPTER TWO

DEATH MARCH

Cover art by ETHAN VAN SCIVER

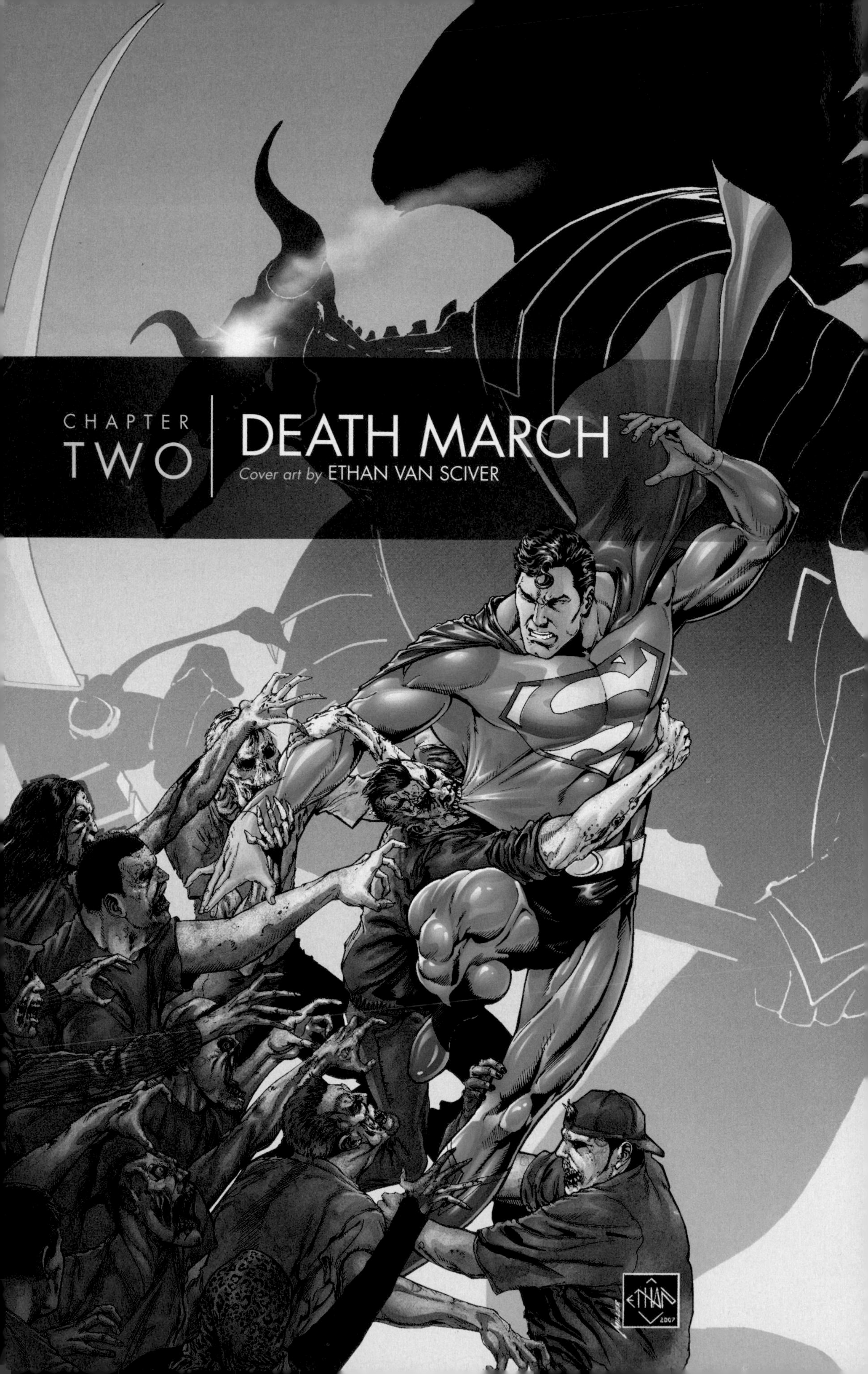

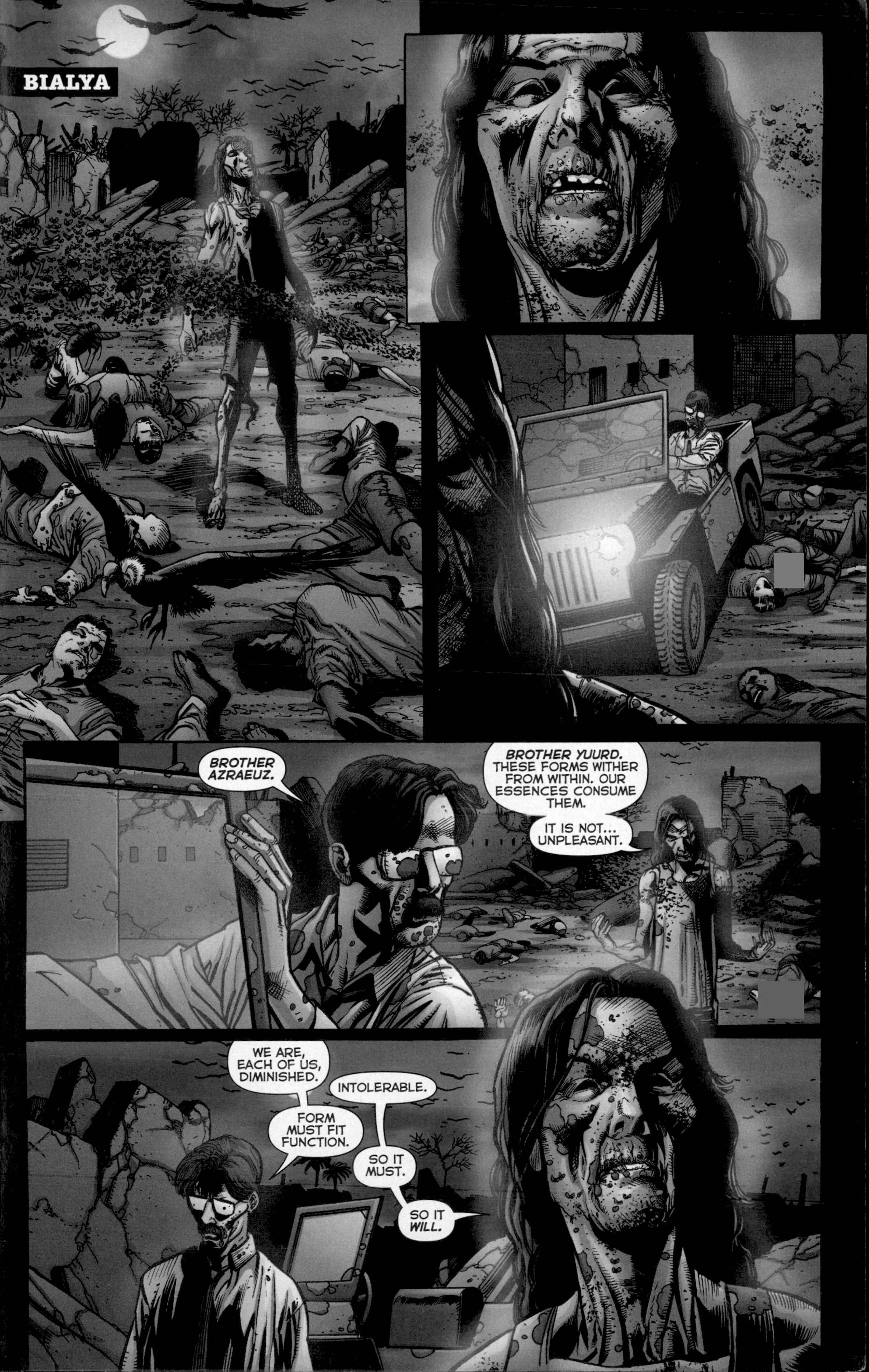
BIALYA
BROTHER AZRAEUZ.
BROTHER YUURD. THESE FORMS WITHER FROM WITHIN. OUR ESSENCES CONSUME THEM.
IT IS NOT... UNPLEASANT.
WE ARE, EACH OF US, DIMINISHED.
INTOLERABLE.
FORM MUST FIT FUNCTION.
SO IT MUST.
SO IT WILL.

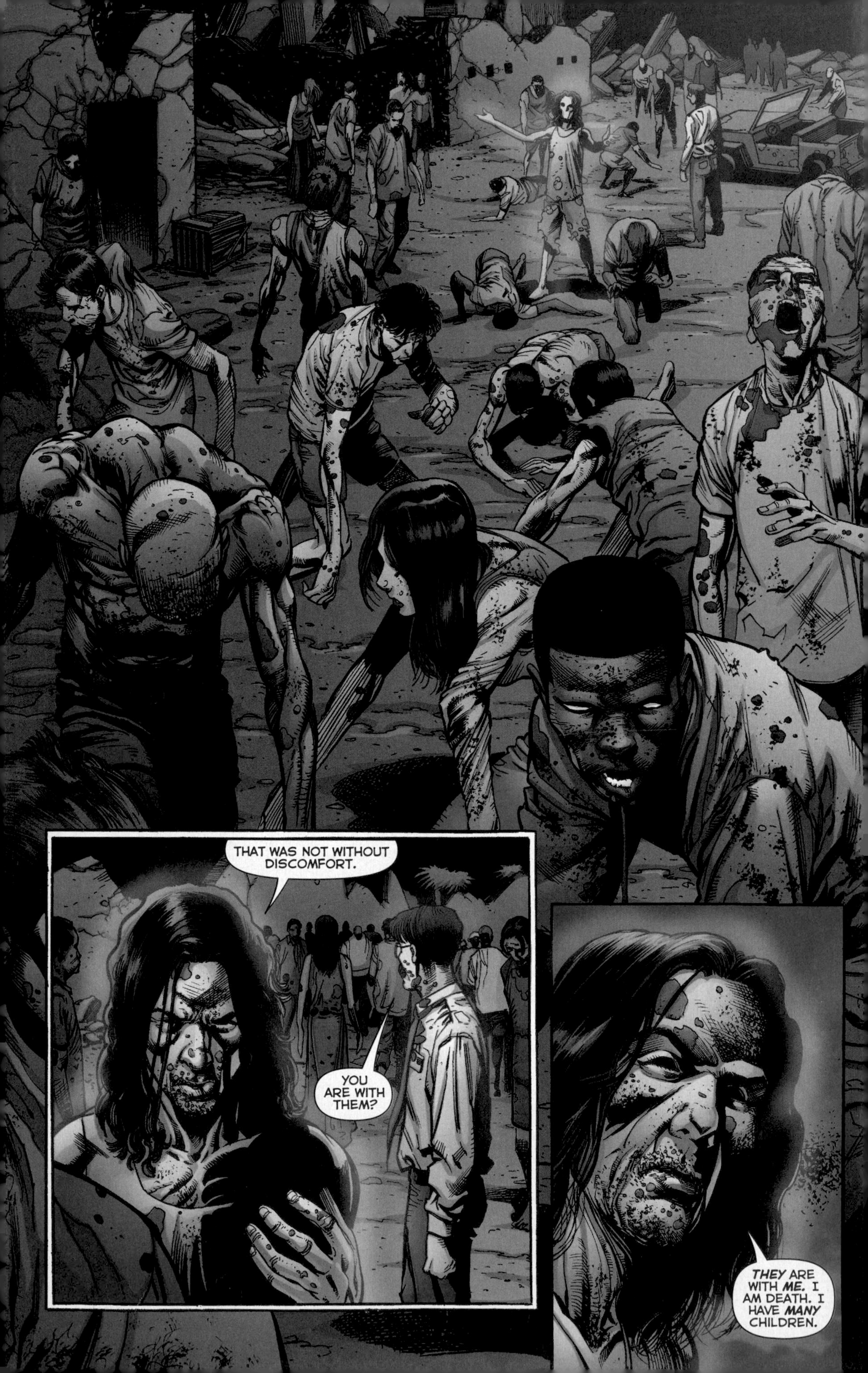
THAT WAS NOT WITHOUT DISCOMFORT.
YOU ARE WITH THEM?
THEY ARE WITH ME. I AM DEATH. I HAVE MANY CHILDREN.

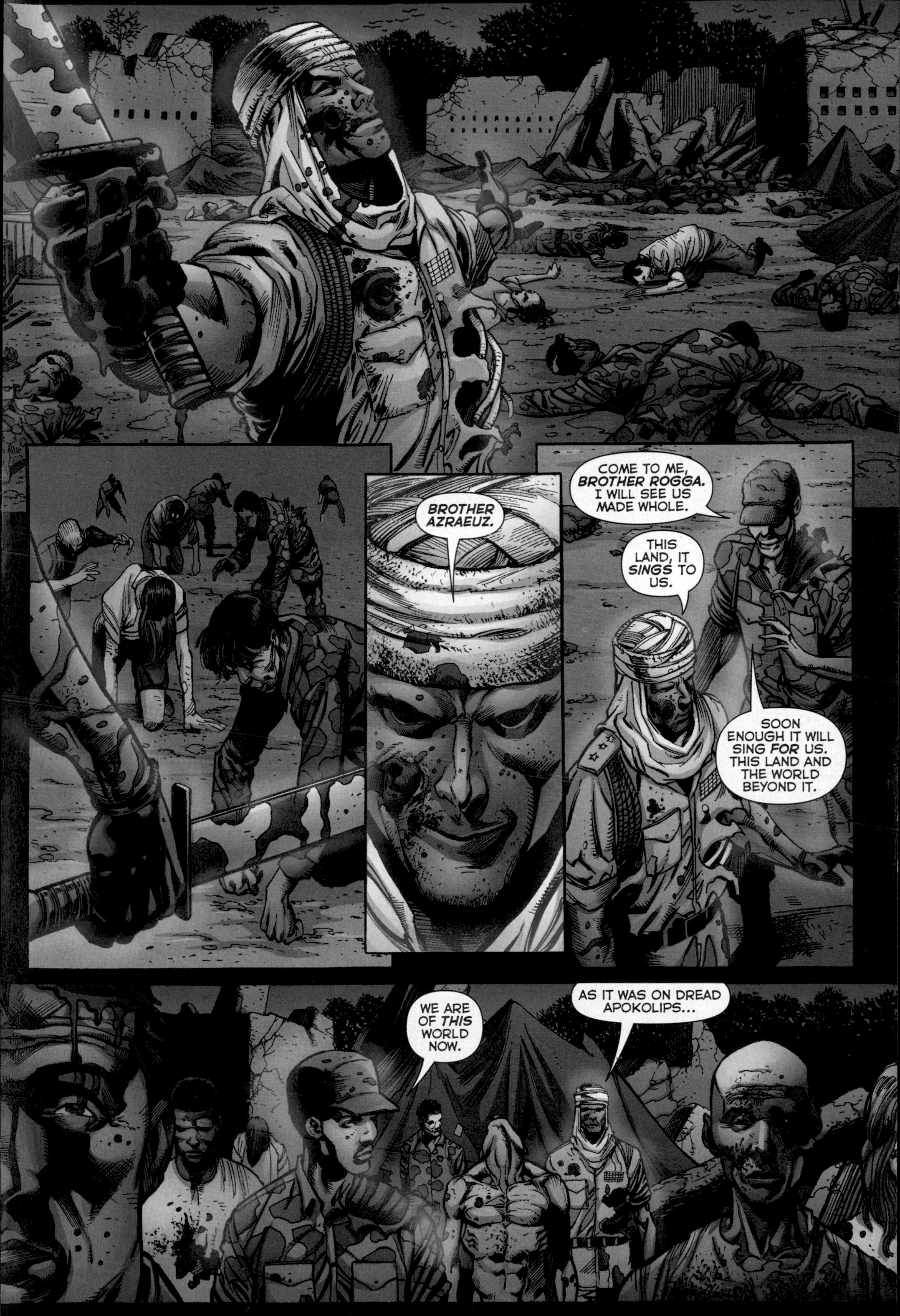
BROTHER AZRAEUZ.
COME TO ME, BROTHER ROGGA. I WILL SEE US MADE WHOLE.
THIS LAND, IT SINGS TO US.
SOON ENOUGH IT WILL SING FOR US. THIS LAND AND THE WORLD BEYOND IT.
WE ARE OF THIS WORLD NOW.
AS IT WAS ON DREAD APOKOLIPS...

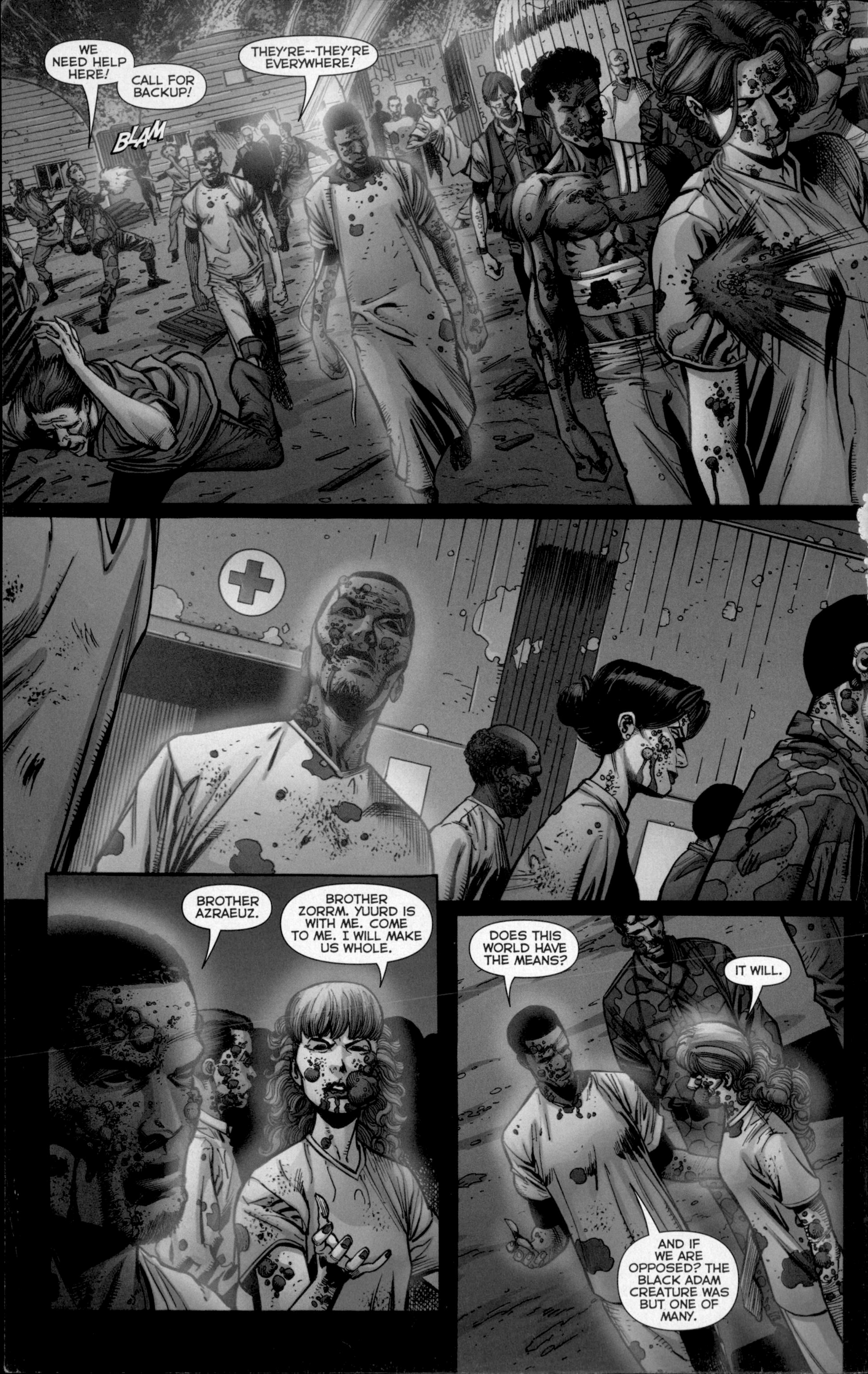
WE NEED HELP HERE!
CALL FOR BACKUP!
BLAM
THEY'RE--THEY'RE EVERYWHERE!
BROTHER AZRAEUZ.
BROTHER ZORRM. YUURD IS WITH ME. COME TO ME. I WILL MAKE US WHOLE.
DOES THIS WORLD HAVE THE MEANS?
IT WILL.
AND IF WE ARE OPPOSED? THE BLACK ADAM CREATURE WAS BUT ONE OF MANY.

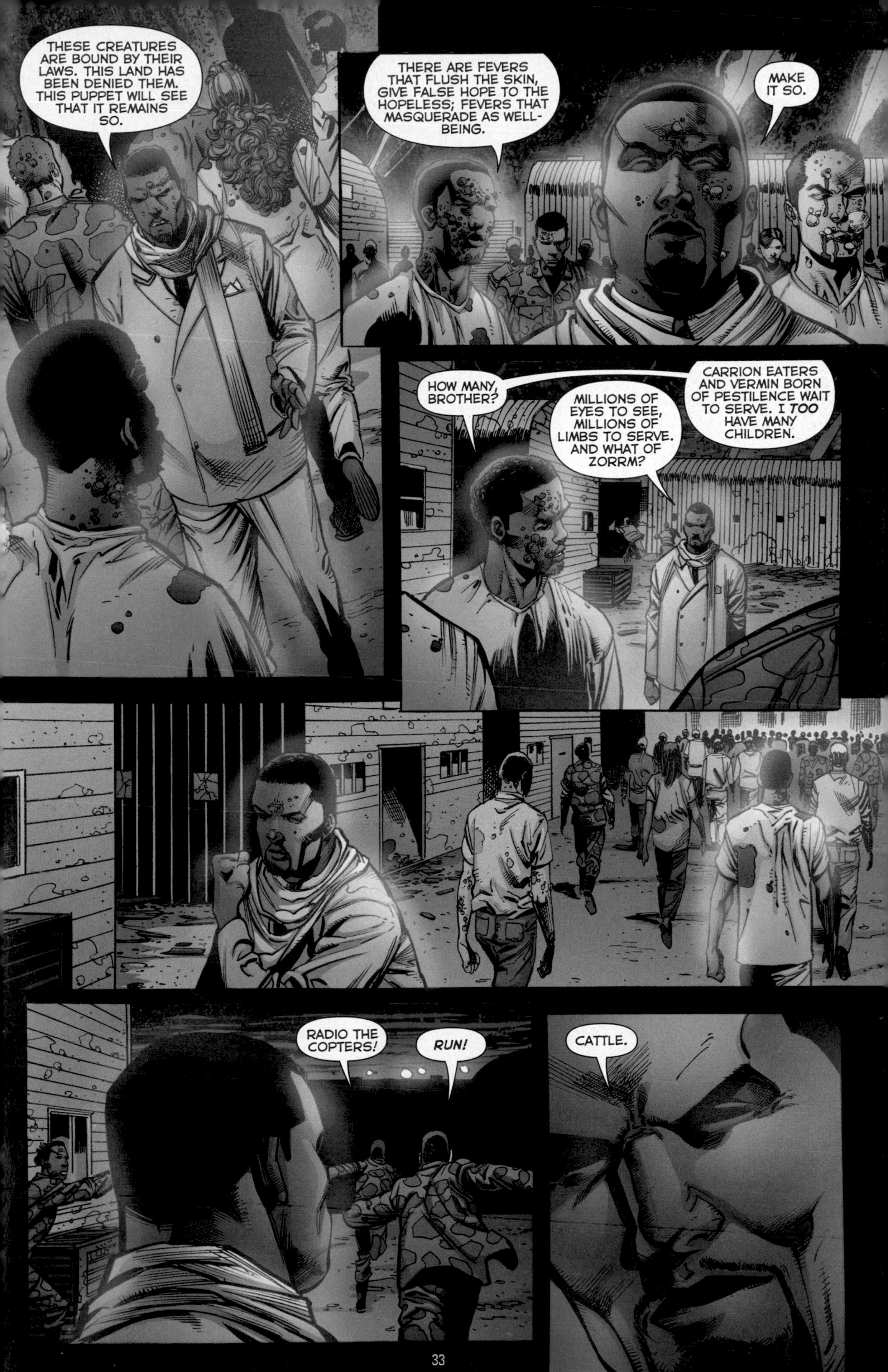
THESE CREATURES ARE BOUND BY THEIR LAWS. THIS LAND HAS BEEN DENIED THEM. THIS PUPPET WILL SEE THAT IT REMAINS SO.
THERE ARE FEVERS THAT FLUSH THE SKIN, GIVE FALSE HOPE TO THE HOPELESS; FEVERS THAT MASQUERADE AS WELL-BEING.
MAKE IT SO.
HOW MANY, BROTHER?
CARRION EATERS AND VERMIN BORN OF PESTILENCE WAIT TO SERVE. I *TOO* HAVE MANY CHILDREN.
MILLIONS OF EYES TO SEE, MILLIONS OF LIMBS TO SERVE. AND WHAT OF ZORRM?
RADIO THE COPTERS!
RUN!
CATTLE.

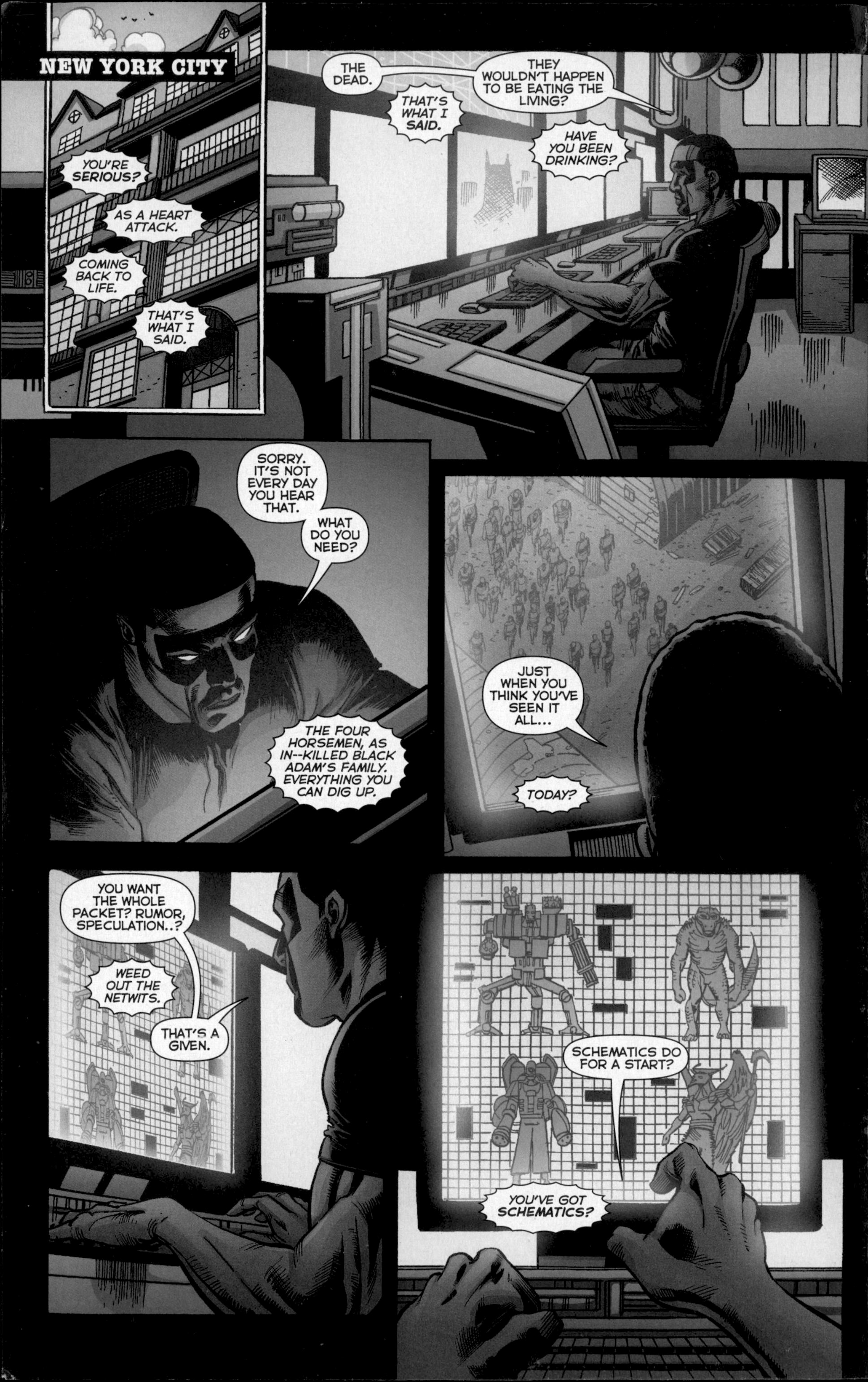
NEW YORK CITY
YOU'RE SERIOUS?
AS A HEART ATTACK.
COMING BACK TO LIFE.
THAT'S WHAT I SAID.
THE DEAD.
THEY WOULDN'T HAPPEN TO BE EATING THE LIVING?
THAT'S WHAT I SAID.
HAVE YOU BEEN DRINKING?
SORRY. IT'S NOT EVERY DAY YOU HEAR THAT.
WHAT DO YOU NEED?
THE FOUR HORSEMEN, AS IN--KILLED BLACK ADAM'S FAMILY. EVERYTHING YOU CAN DIG UP.
JUST WHEN YOU THINK YOU'VE SEEN IT ALL...
TODAY?
YOU WANT THE WHOLE PACKET? RUMOR, SPECULATION..?
WEED OUT THE NETWITS.
THAT'S A GIVEN.
SCHEMATICS DO FOR A START?
YOU'VE GOT SCHEMATICS?

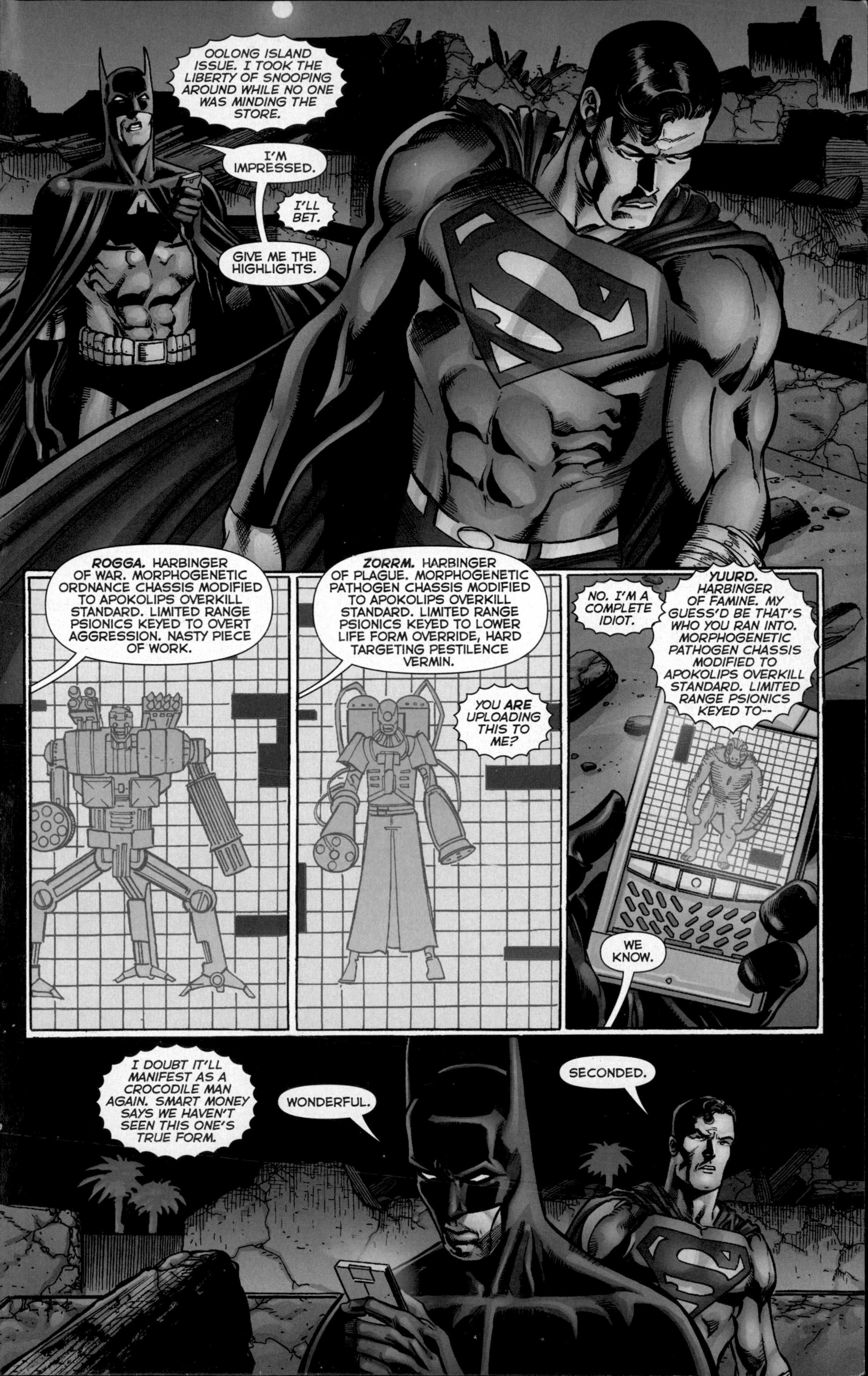
OOLONG ISLAND ISSUE. I TOOK THE LIBERTY OF SNOOPING AROUND WHILE NO ONE WAS MINDING THE STORE.
I'M IMPRESSED.
I'LL BET.
GIVE ME THE HIGHLIGHTS.
ROGGA. HARBINGER OF WAR. MORPHOGENETIC ORDNANCE CHASSIS MODIFIED TO APOKOLIPS OVERKILL STANDARD. LIMITED RANGE PSIONICS KEYED TO OVERT AGGRESSION. NASTY PIECE OF WORK.
ZORRM. HARBINGER OF PLAGUE. MORPHOGENETIC PATHOGEN CHASSIS MODIFIED TO APOKOLIPS OVERKILL STANDARD. LIMITED RANGE PSIONICS KEYED TO LOWER LIFE FORM OVERRIDE, HARD TARGETING PESTILENCE VERMIN.
YOU ARE UPLOADING THIS TO ME?
NO. I'M A COMPLETE IDIOT.
YUURD. HARBINGER OF FAMINE. MY GUESS'D BE THAT'S WHO YOU RAN INTO. MORPHOGENETIC PATHOGEN CHASSIS MODIFIED TO APOKOLIPS OVERKILL STANDARD. LIMITED RANGE PSIONICS KEYED TO--
WE KNOW.
I DOUBT IT'LL MANIFEST AS A CROCODILE MAN AGAIN. SMART MONEY SAYS WE HAVEN'T SEEN THIS ONE'S TRUE FORM.
WONDERFUL.
SECONDED.

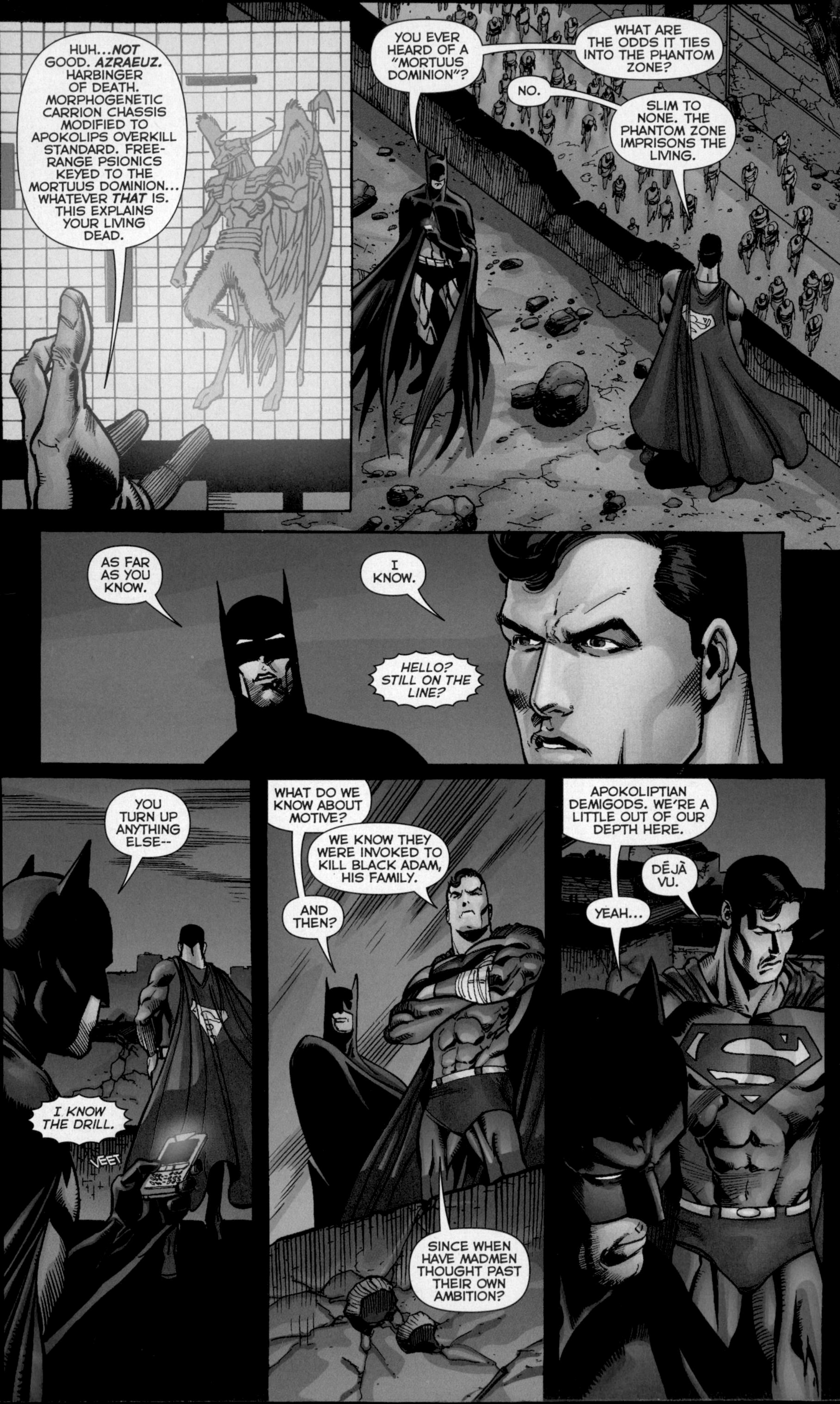

HUH...NOT GOOD. AZRAEUZ. HARBINGER OF DEATH. MORPHOGENETIC CARRION CHASSIS MODIFIED TO APOKOLIPS OVERKILL STANDARD. FREE-RANGE PSIONICS KEYED TO THE MORTUUS DOMINION... WHATEVER THAT IS. THIS EXPLAINS YOUR LIVING DEAD.
YOU EVER HEARD OF A "MORTUUS DOMINION"?
WHAT ARE THE ODDS IT TIES INTO THE PHANTOM ZONE?
NO.
SLIM TO NONE. THE PHANTOM ZONE IMPRISONS THE LIVING.
AS FAR AS YOU KNOW.
I KNOW.
HELLO? STILL ON THE LINE?
YOU TURN UP ANYTHING ELSE--
I KNOW THE DRILL.
VEET
WHAT DO WE KNOW ABOUT MOTIVE?
WE KNOW THEY WERE INVOKED TO KILL BLACK ADAM, HIS FAMILY.
AND THEN?
SINCE WHEN HAVE MADMEN THOUGHT PAST THEIR OWN AMBITION?
APOKOLIPTIAN DEMIGODS. WE'RE A LITTLE OUT OF OUR DEPTH HERE.
DÉJÀ VU.
YEAH...

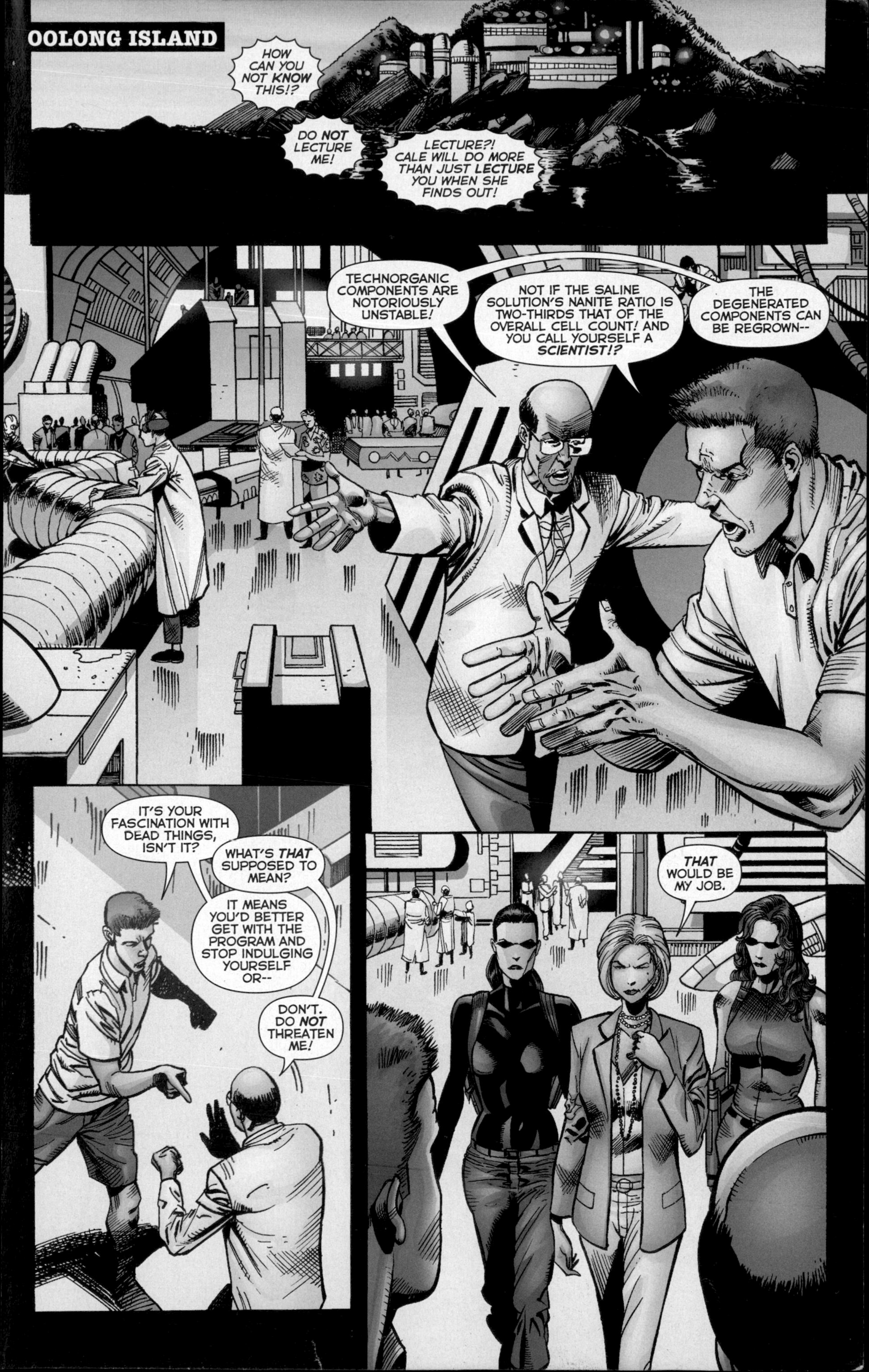
OOLONG ISLAND
HOW CAN YOU NOT KNOW THIS!?
DO NOT LECTURE ME!
LECTURE?! CALE WILL DO MORE THAN JUST LECTURE YOU WHEN SHE FINDS OUT!
TECHNORGANIC COMPONENTS ARE NOTORIOUSLY UNSTABLE!
NOT IF THE SALINE SOLUTION'S NANITE RATIO IS TWO-THIRDS THAT OF THE OVERALL CELL COUNT! AND YOU CALL YOURSELF A SCIENTIST!?
THE DEGENERATED COMPONENTS CAN BE REGROWN--
IT'S YOUR FASCINATION WITH DEAD THINGS, ISN'T IT?
WHAT'S THAT SUPPOSED TO MEAN?
IT MEANS YOU'D BETTER GET WITH THE PROGRAM AND STOP INDULGING YOURSELF OR--
DON'T. DO NOT THREATEN ME!
THAT WOULD BE MY JOB.

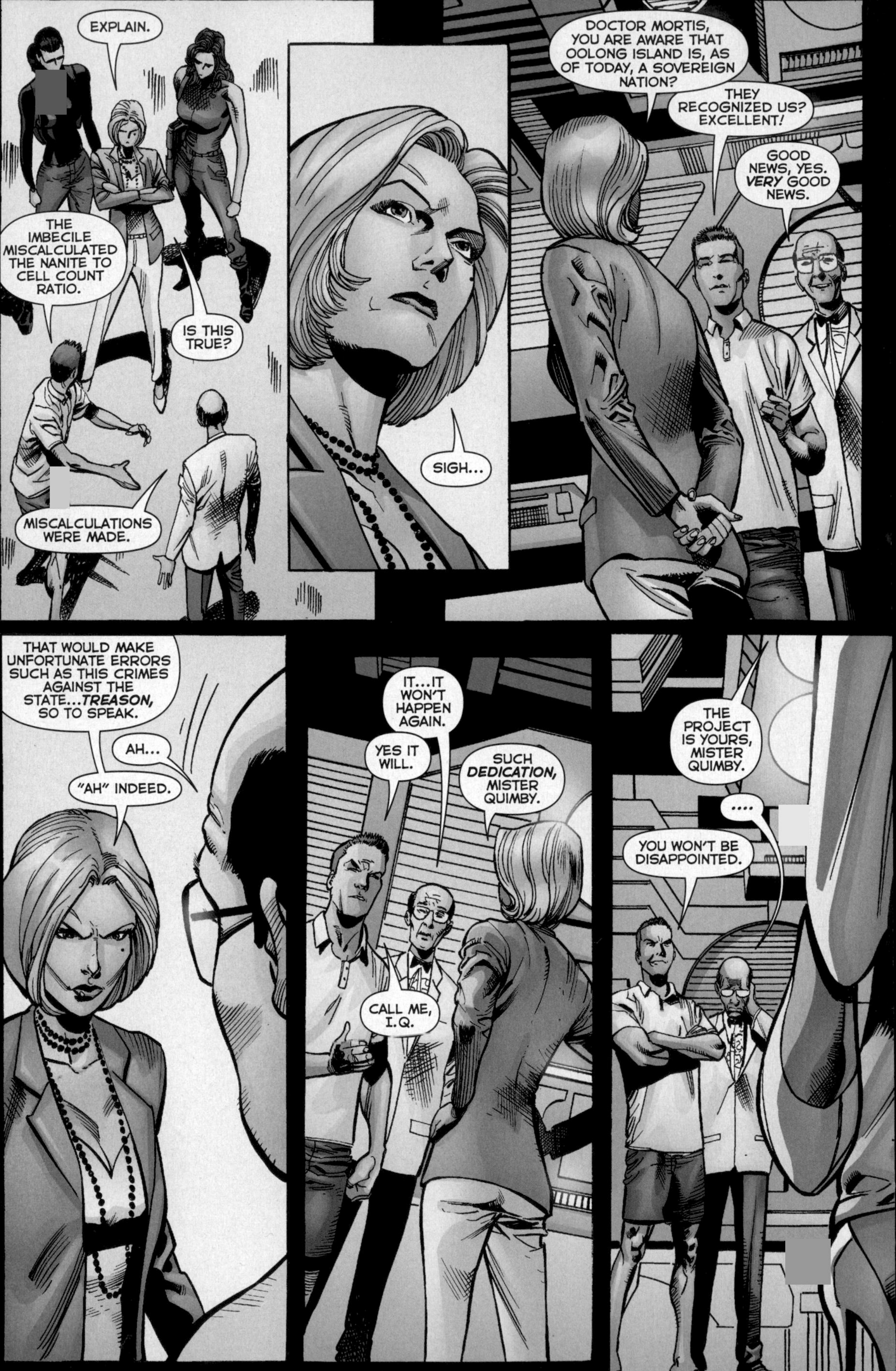
EXPLAIN.
THE IMBECILE MISCALCULATED THE NANITE TO CELL COUNT RATIO.
IS THIS TRUE?
MISCALCULATIONS WERE MADE.
SIGH...
DOCTOR MORTIS, YOU ARE AWARE THAT OOLONG ISLAND IS, AS OF TODAY, A SOVEREIGN NATION?
THEY RECOGNIZED US? EXCELLENT!
GOOD NEWS, YES. VERY GOOD NEWS.
THAT WOULD MAKE UNFORTUNATE ERRORS SUCH AS THIS CRIMES AGAINST THE STATE...TREASON, SO TO SPEAK.
AH...
"AH" INDEED.
IT...IT WON'T HAPPEN AGAIN.
YES IT WILL.
SUCH DEDICATION, MISTER QUIMBY.
CALL ME, I.Q.
THE PROJECT IS YOURS, MISTER QUIMBY.
....
YOU WON'T BE DISAPPOINTED.

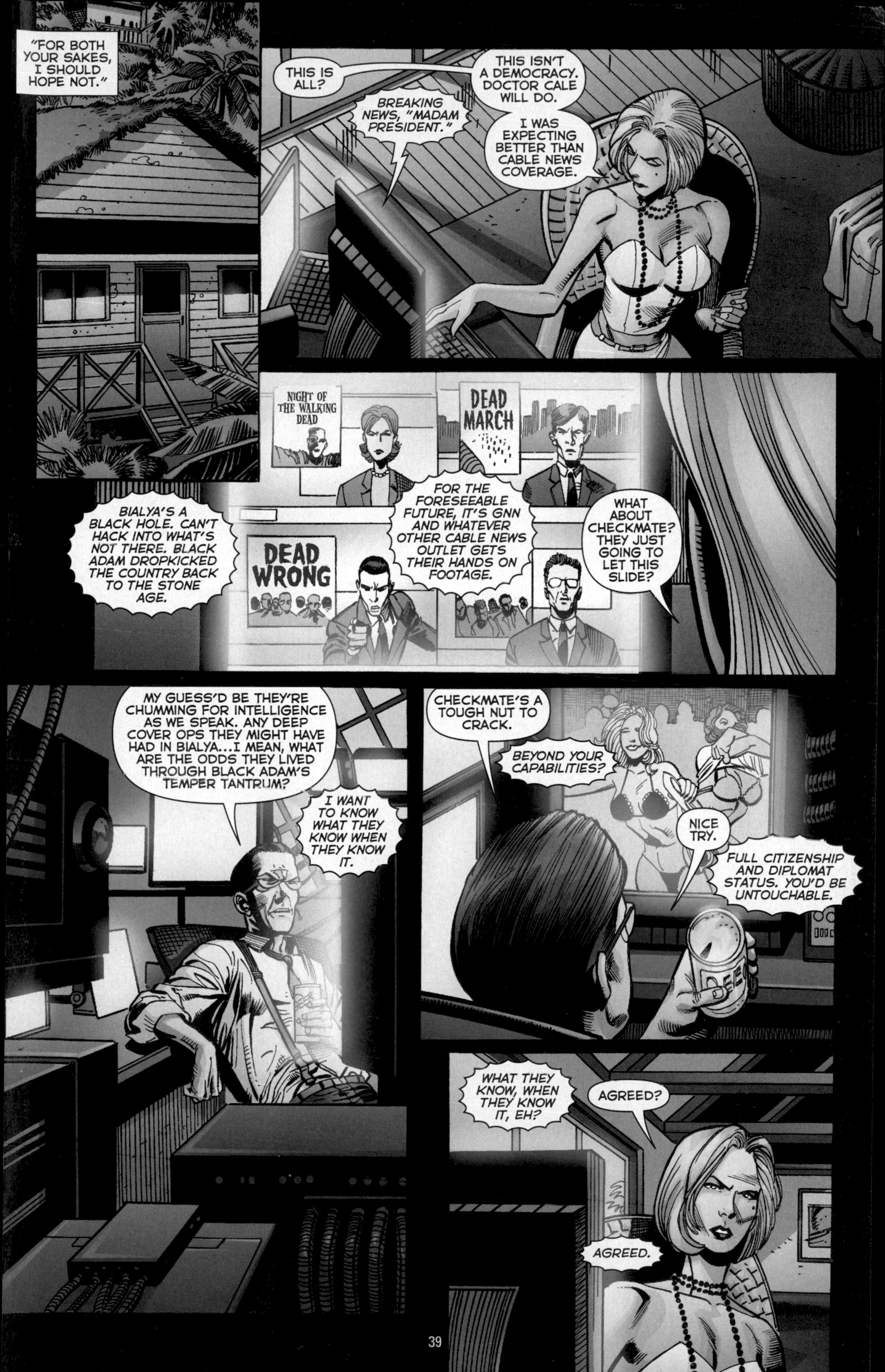
"FOR BOTH YOUR SAKES, I SHOULD HOPE NOT."
THIS IS ALL?
THIS ISN'T A DEMOCRACY. DOCTOR CALE WILL DO.
BREAKING NEWS, "MADAM PRESIDENT."
I WAS EXPECTING BETTER THAN CABLE NEWS COVERAGE.
NIGHT OF THE WALKING DEAD
DEAD MARCH
BIALYA'S A BLACK HOLE. CAN'T HACK INTO WHAT'S NOT THERE. BLACK ADAM DROPKICKED THE COUNTRY BACK TO THE STONE AGE.
FOR THE FORESEEABLE FUTURE, IT'S GNN AND WHATEVER OTHER CABLE NEWS OUTLET GETS THEIR HANDS ON FOOTAGE.
WHAT ABOUT CHECKMATE? THEY JUST GOING TO LET THIS SLIDE?
DEAD WRONG
MY GUESS'D BE THEY'RE CHUMMING FOR INTELLIGENCE AS WE SPEAK. ANY DEEP COVER OPS THEY MIGHT HAVE HAD IN BIALYA...I MEAN, WHAT ARE THE ODDS THEY LIVED THROUGH BLACK ADAM'S TEMPER TANTRUM?
I WANT TO KNOW WHAT THEY KNOW WHEN THEY KNOW IT.
CHECKMATE'S A TOUGH NUT TO CRACK.
BEYOND YOUR CAPABILITIES?
NICE TRY.
FULL CITIZENSHIP AND DIPLOMAT STATUS. YOU'D BE UNTOUCHABLE.
WHAT THEY KNOW, WHEN THEY KNOW IT, EH?
AGREED?
AGREED.

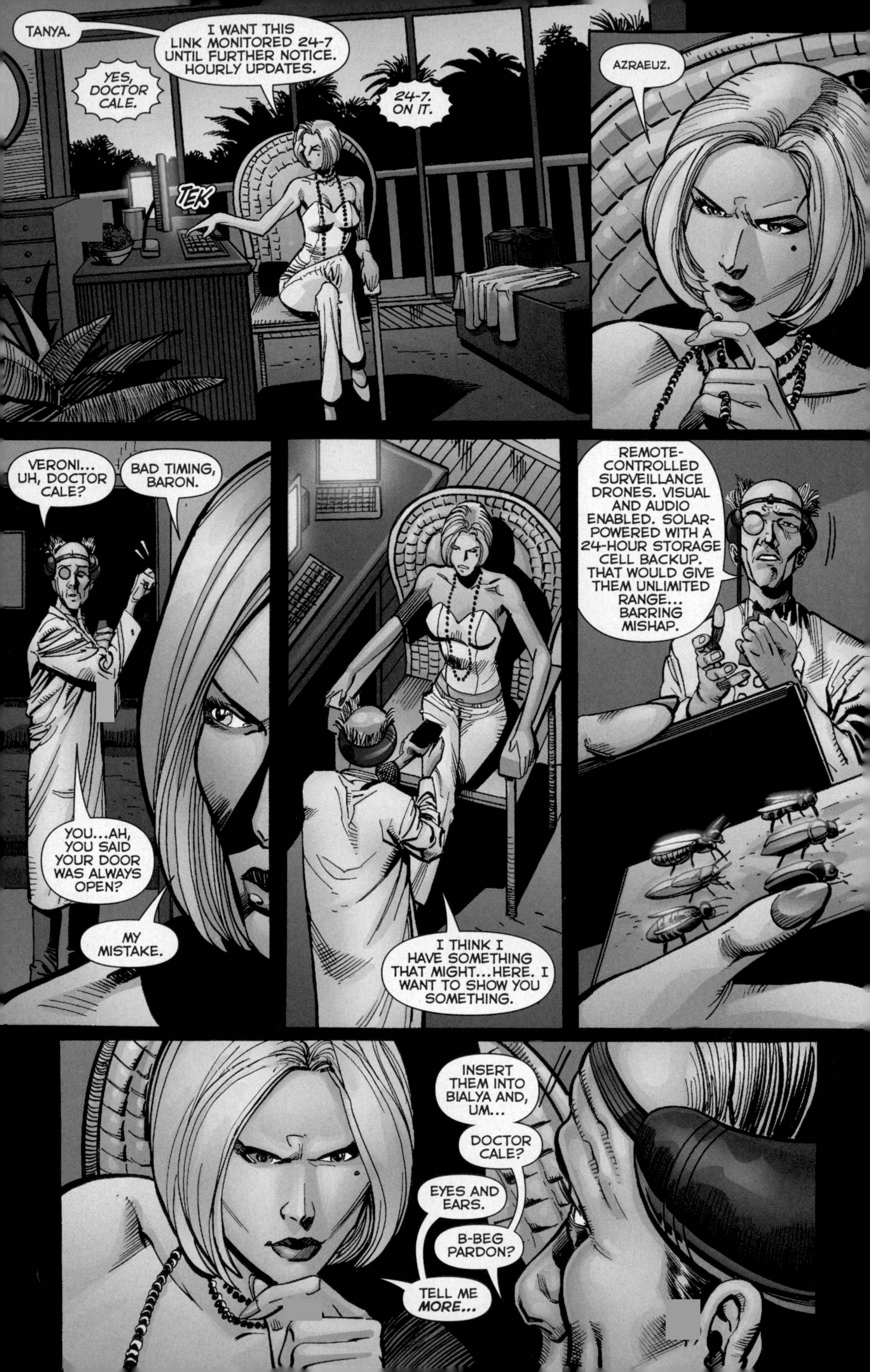
TANYA.
I WANT THIS LINK MONITORED 24-7 UNTIL FURTHER NOTICE. HOURLY UPDATES.
YES, DOCTOR CALE.
24-7. ON IT.
TEK
AZRAEUZ.
VERONI... UH, DOCTOR CALE?
BAD TIMING, BARON.
YOU...AH, YOU SAID YOUR DOOR WAS ALWAYS OPEN?
MY MISTAKE.
I THINK I HAVE SOMETHING THAT MIGHT...HERE. I WANT TO SHOW YOU SOMETHING.
REMOTE-CONTROLLED SURVEILLANCE DRONES. VISUAL AND AUDIO ENABLED. SOLAR-POWERED WITH A 24-HOUR STORAGE CELL BACKUP. THAT WOULD GIVE THEM UNLIMITED RANGE... BARRING MISHAP.
INSERT THEM INTO BIALYA AND, UM...
DOCTOR CALE?
EYES AND EARS.
B-BEG PARDON?
TELL ME MORE...

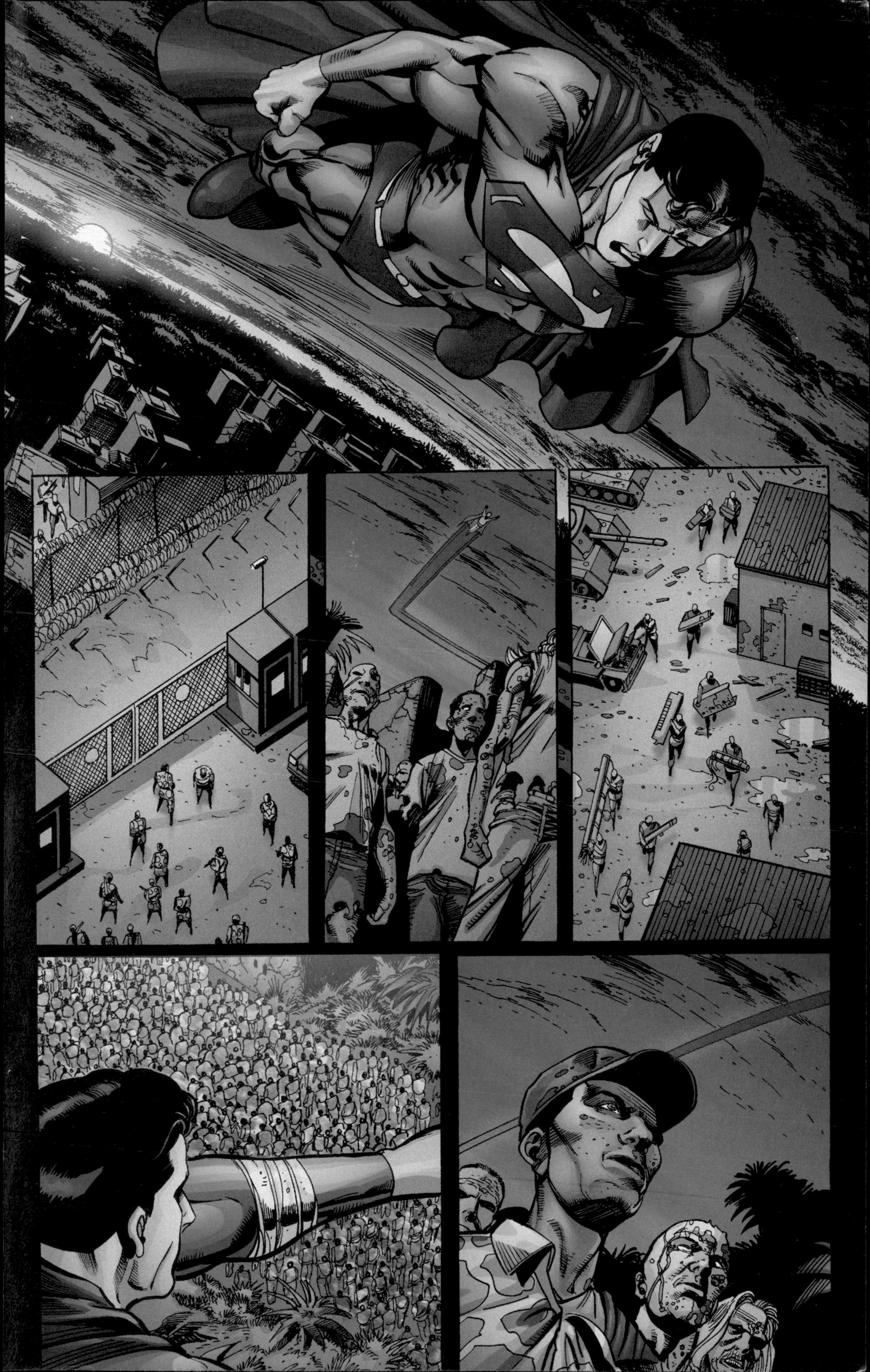

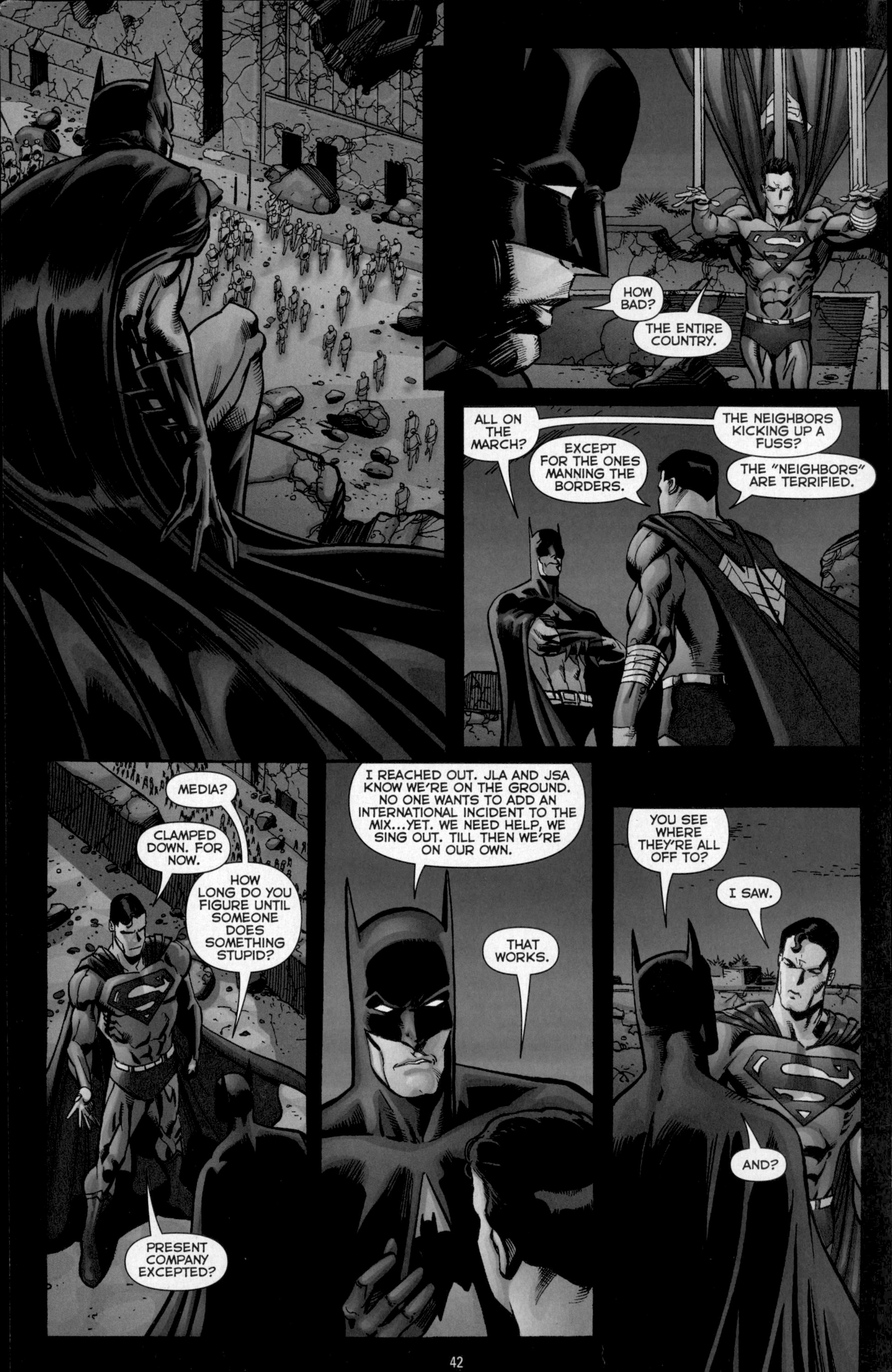
HOW BAD?
THE ENTIRE COUNTRY.
ALL ON THE MARCH?
EXCEPT FOR THE ONES MANNING THE BORDERS.
THE NEIGHBORS KICKING UP A FUSS?
THE "NEIGHBORS" ARE TERRIFIED.
MEDIA?
CLAMPED DOWN. FOR NOW.
HOW LONG DO YOU FIGURE UNTIL SOMEONE DOES SOMETHING STUPID?
PRESENT COMPANY EXCEPTED?
I REACHED OUT. JLA AND JSA KNOW WE'RE ON THE GROUND. NO ONE WANTS TO ADD AN INTERNATIONAL INCIDENT TO THE MIX...YET. WE NEED HELP, WE SING OUT. TILL THEN WE'RE ON OUR OWN.
THAT WORKS.
YOU SEE WHERE THEY'RE ALL OFF TO?
I SAW.
AND?

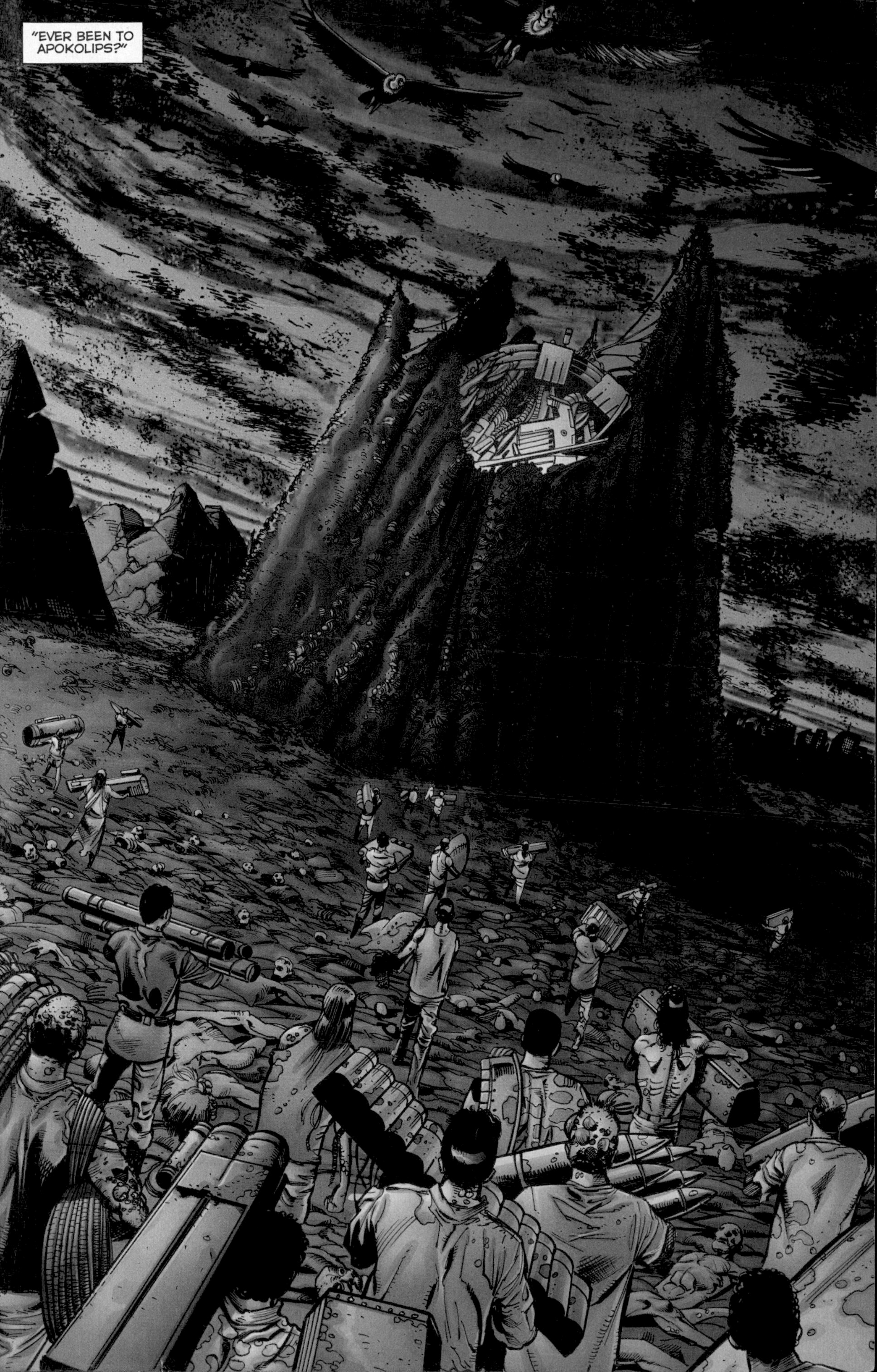
"EVER BEEN TO APOKOLIPS?"

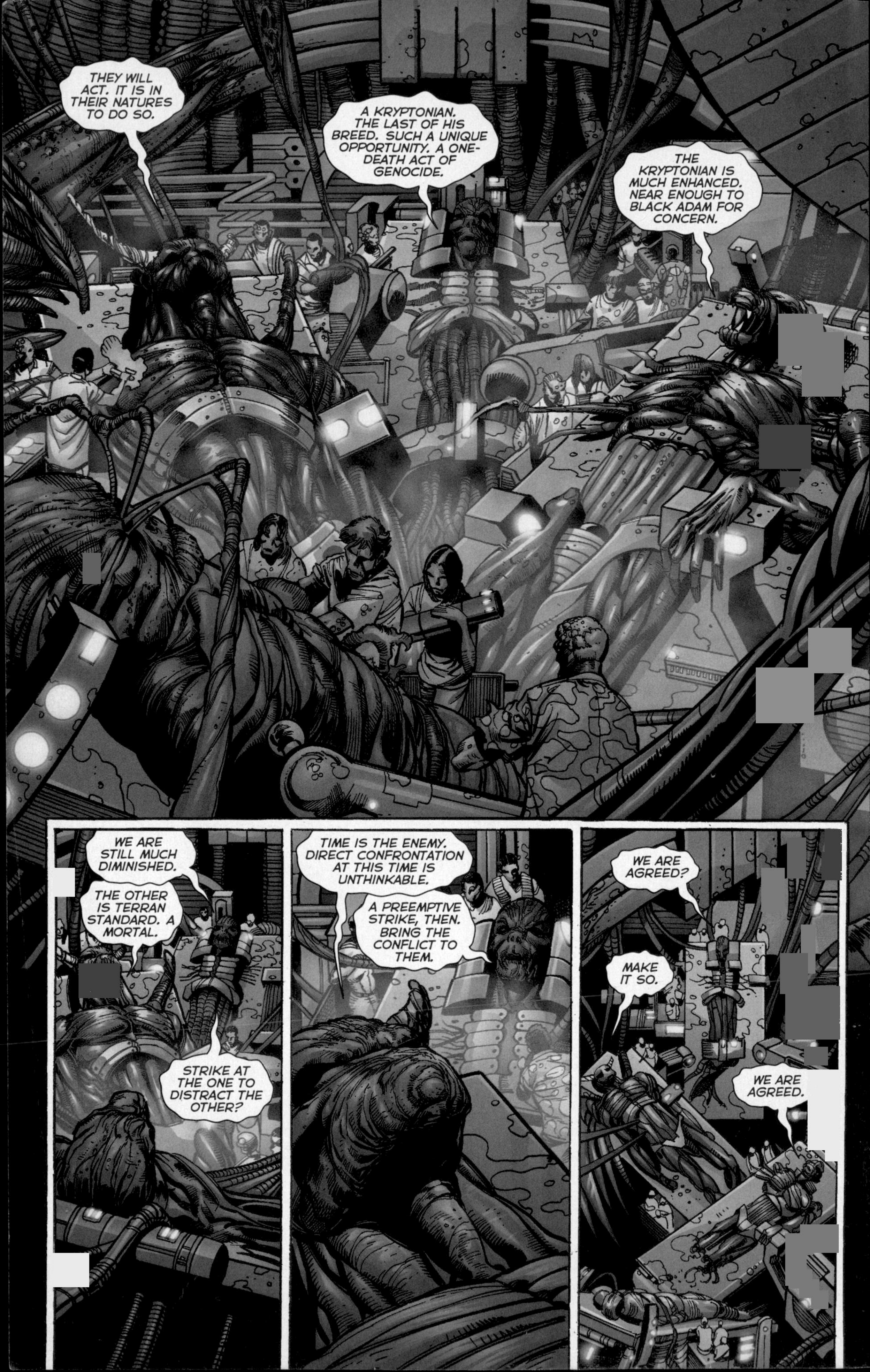
THEY WILL ACT. IT IS IN THEIR NATURES TO DO SO.
A KRYPTONIAN. THE LAST OF HIS BREED. SUCH A UNIQUE OPPORTUNITY. A ONE-DEATH ACT OF GENOCIDE.
THE KRYPTONIAN IS MUCH ENHANCED. NEAR ENOUGH TO BLACK ADAM FOR CONCERN.
WE ARE STILL MUCH DIMINISHED.
THE OTHER IS TERRAN STANDARD. A MORTAL.
STRIKE AT THE ONE TO DISTRACT THE OTHER?
TIME IS THE ENEMY. DIRECT CONFRONTATION AT THIS TIME IS UNTHINKABLE.
A PREEMPTIVE STRIKE, THEN. BRING THE CONFLICT TO THEM.
WE ARE AGREED?
MAKE IT SO.
WE ARE AGREED.

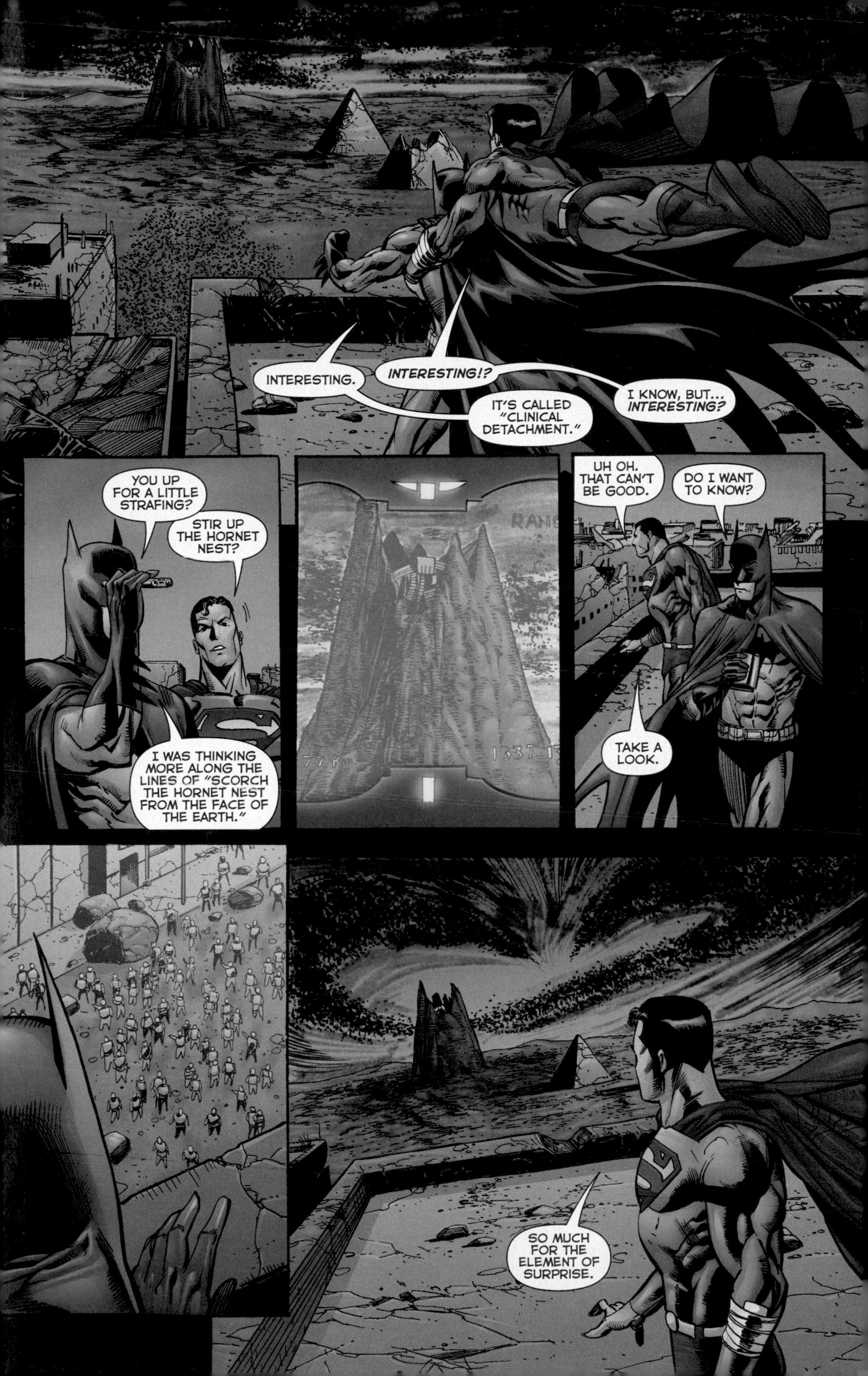
INTERESTING.
INTERESTING!?
IT'S CALLED "CLINICAL DETACHMENT."
I KNOW, BUT... INTERESTING?
YOU UP FOR A LITTLE STRAFING?
STIR UP THE HORNET NEST?
I WAS THINKING MORE ALONG THE LINES OF "SCORCH THE HORNET NEST FROM THE FACE OF THE EARTH."
UH OH. THAT CAN'T BE GOOD.
DO I WANT TO KNOW?
TAKE A LOOK.
SO MUCH FOR THE ELEMENT OF SURPRISE.

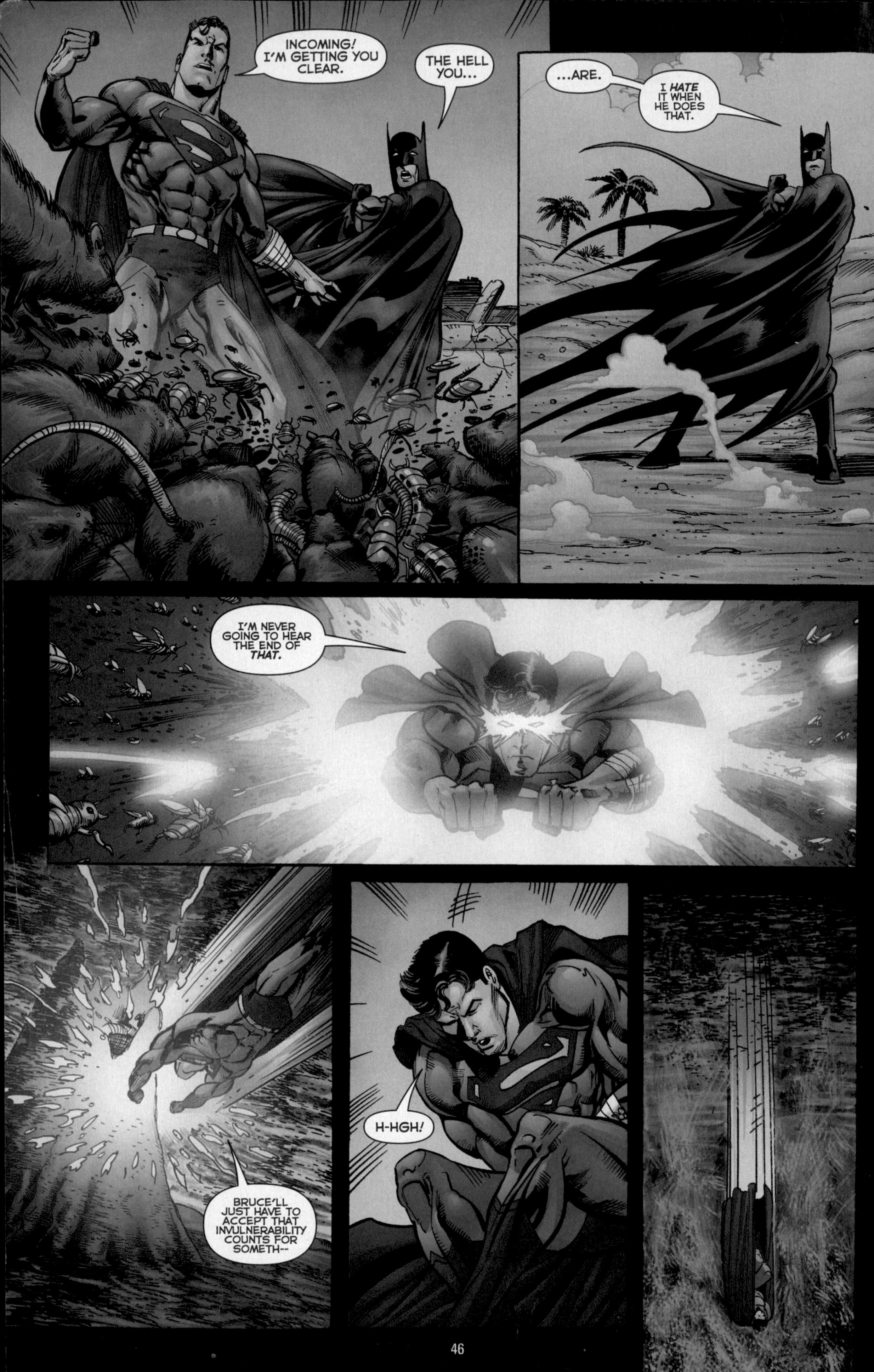
INCOMING! I'M GETTING YOU CLEAR.
THE HELL YOU...
...ARE.
I HATE IT WHEN HE DOES THAT.
I'M NEVER GOING TO HEAR THE END OF THAT.
BRUCE'LL JUST HAVE TO ACCEPT THAT INVULNERABILITY COUNTS FOR SOMETH--
H-HGH!

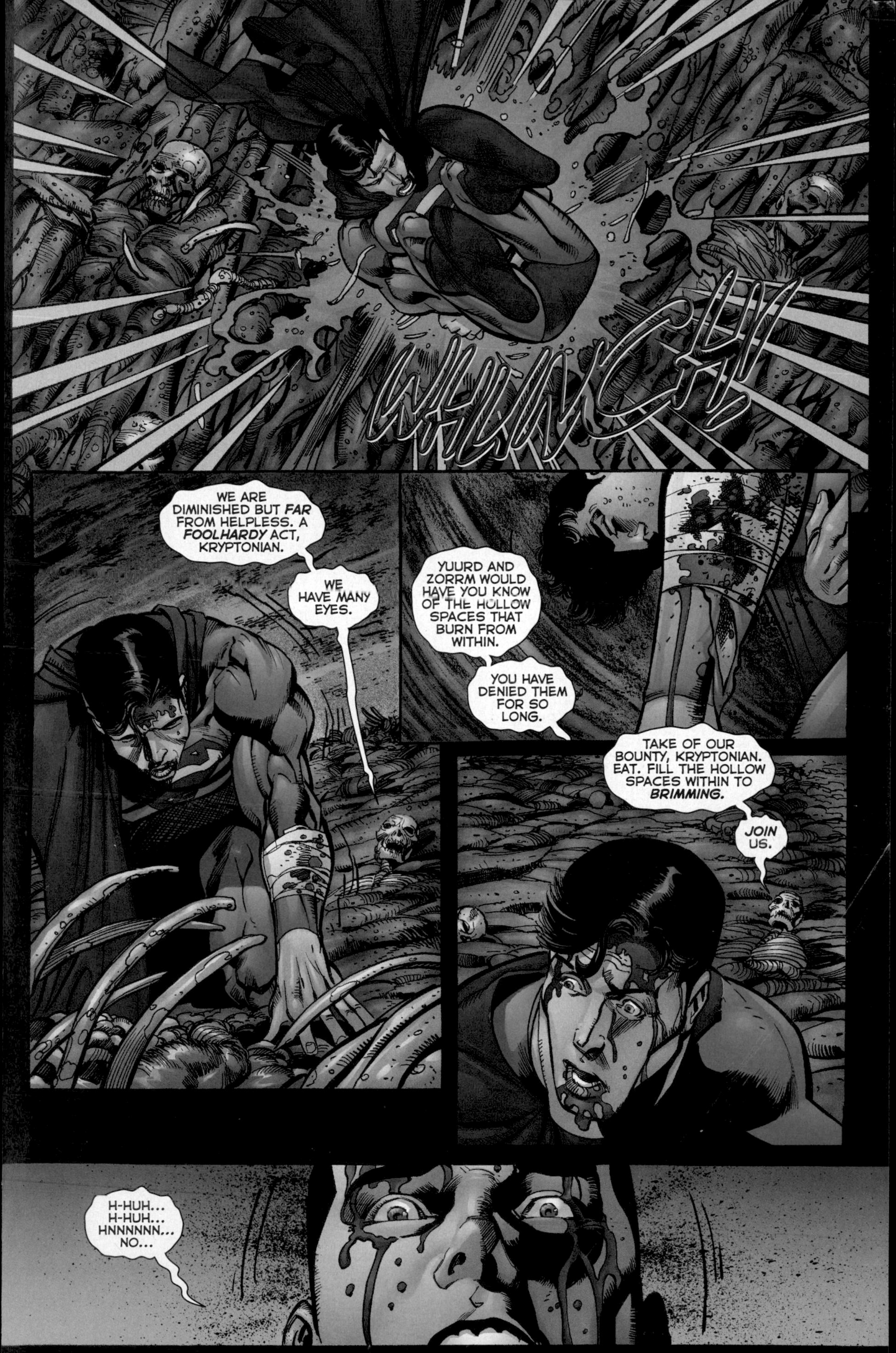
WHUNCH
WE ARE DIMINISHED BUT FAR FROM HELPLESS. A FOOLHARDY ACT, KRYPTONIAN.
WE HAVE MANY EYES.
YUURD AND ZORRM WOULD HAVE YOU KNOW OF THE HOLLOW SPACES THAT BURN FROM WITHIN.
YOU HAVE DENIED THEM FOR SO LONG.
TAKE OF OUR BOUNTY, KRYPTONIAN. EAT. FILL THE HOLLOW SPACES WITHIN TO BRIMMING.
JOIN US.
H-HUH... H-HUH... HNNNNNN... NO...

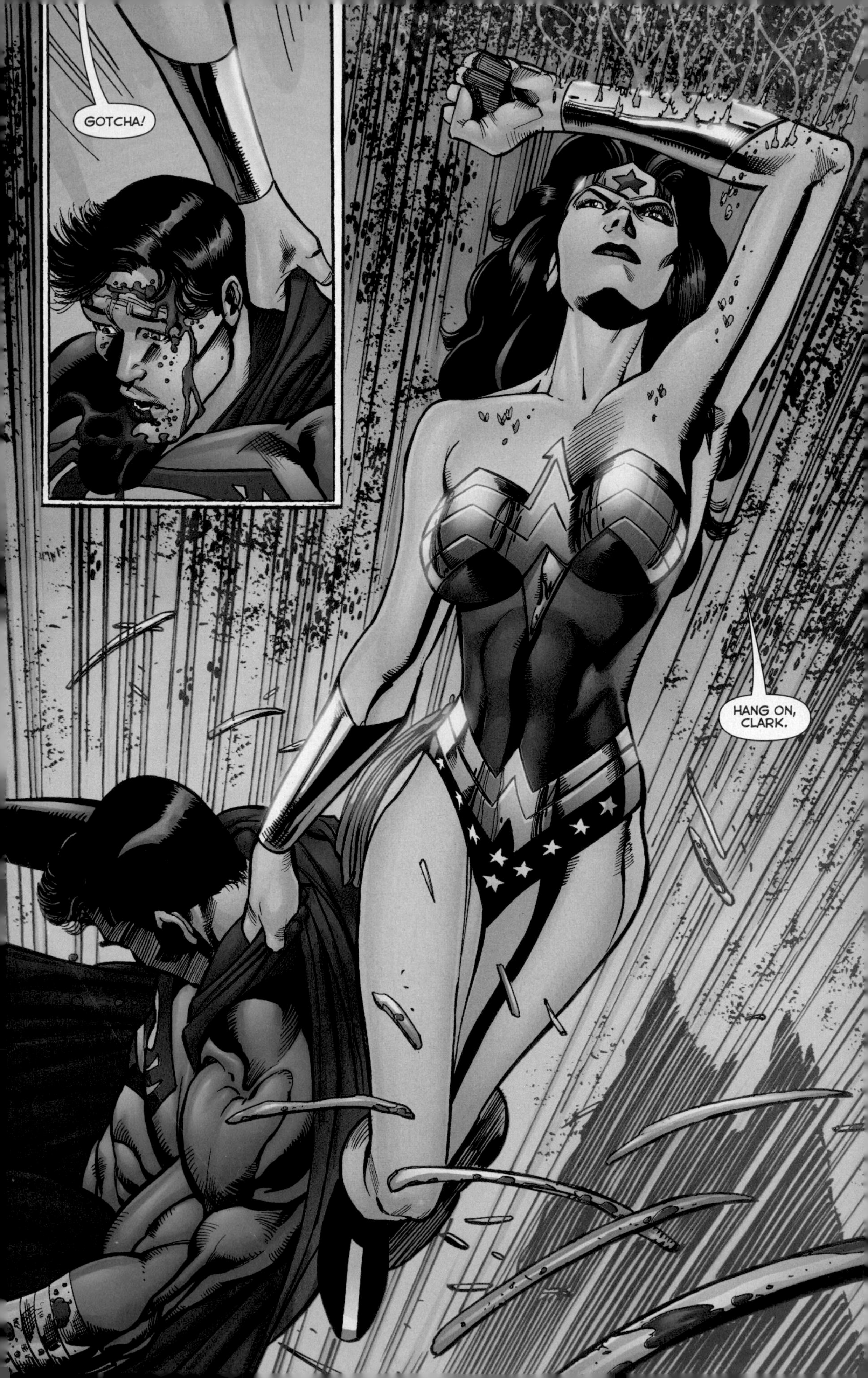
GOTCHA!
HANG ON, CLARK.

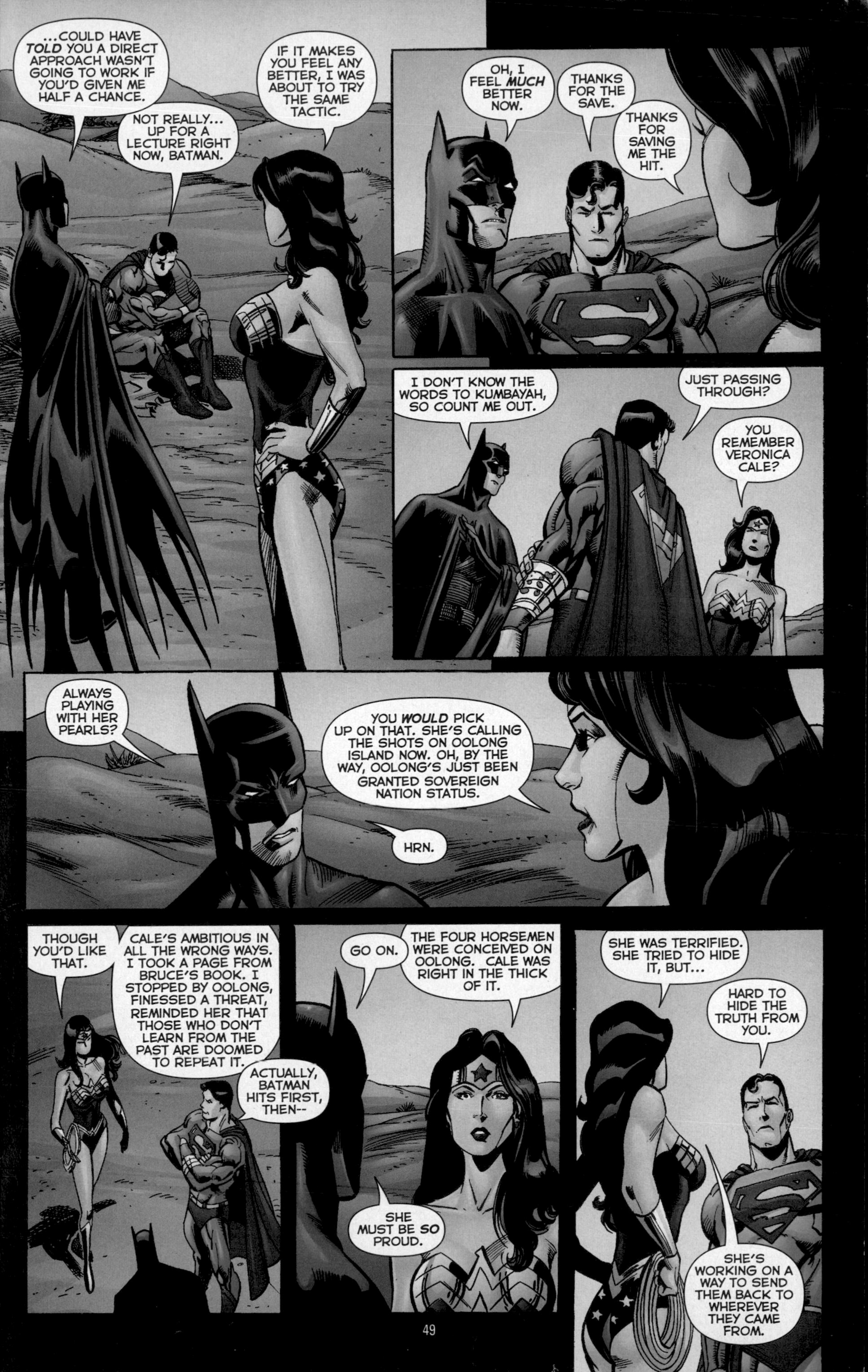
...COULD HAVE TOLD YOU A DIRECT APPROACH WASN'T GOING TO WORK IF YOU'D GIVEN ME HALF A CHANCE.
NOT REALLY... UP FOR A LECTURE RIGHT NOW, BATMAN.
IF IT MAKES YOU FEEL ANY BETTER, I WAS ABOUT TO TRY THE SAME TACTIC.
OH, I FEEL MUCH BETTER NOW.
THANKS FOR THE SAVE.
THANKS FOR SAVING ME THE HIT.
I DON'T KNOW THE WORDS TO KUMBAYAH, SO COUNT ME OUT.
JUST PASSING THROUGH?
YOU REMEMBER VERONICA CALE?
ALWAYS PLAYING WITH HER PEARLS?
YOU WOULD PICK UP ON THAT. SHE'S CALLING THE SHOTS ON OOLONG ISLAND NOW. OH, BY THE WAY, OOLONG'S JUST BEEN GRANTED SOVEREIGN NATION STATUS.
HRN.
THOUGH YOU'D LIKE THAT.
CALE'S AMBITIOUS IN ALL THE WRONG WAYS. I TOOK A PAGE FROM BRUCE'S BOOK. I STOPPED BY OOLONG, FINESSED A THREAT, REMINDED HER THAT THOSE WHO DON'T LEARN FROM THE PAST ARE DOOMED TO REPEAT IT.
ACTUALLY, BATMAN HITS FIRST, THEN--
GO ON.
THE FOUR HORSEMEN WERE CONCEIVED ON OOLONG. CALE WAS RIGHT IN THE THICK OF IT.
SHE MUST BE SO PROUD.
SHE WAS TERRIFIED. SHE TRIED TO HIDE IT, BUT...
HARD TO HIDE THE TRUTH FROM YOU.
SHE'S WORKING ON A WAY TO SEND THEM BACK TO WHEREVER THEY CAME FROM.

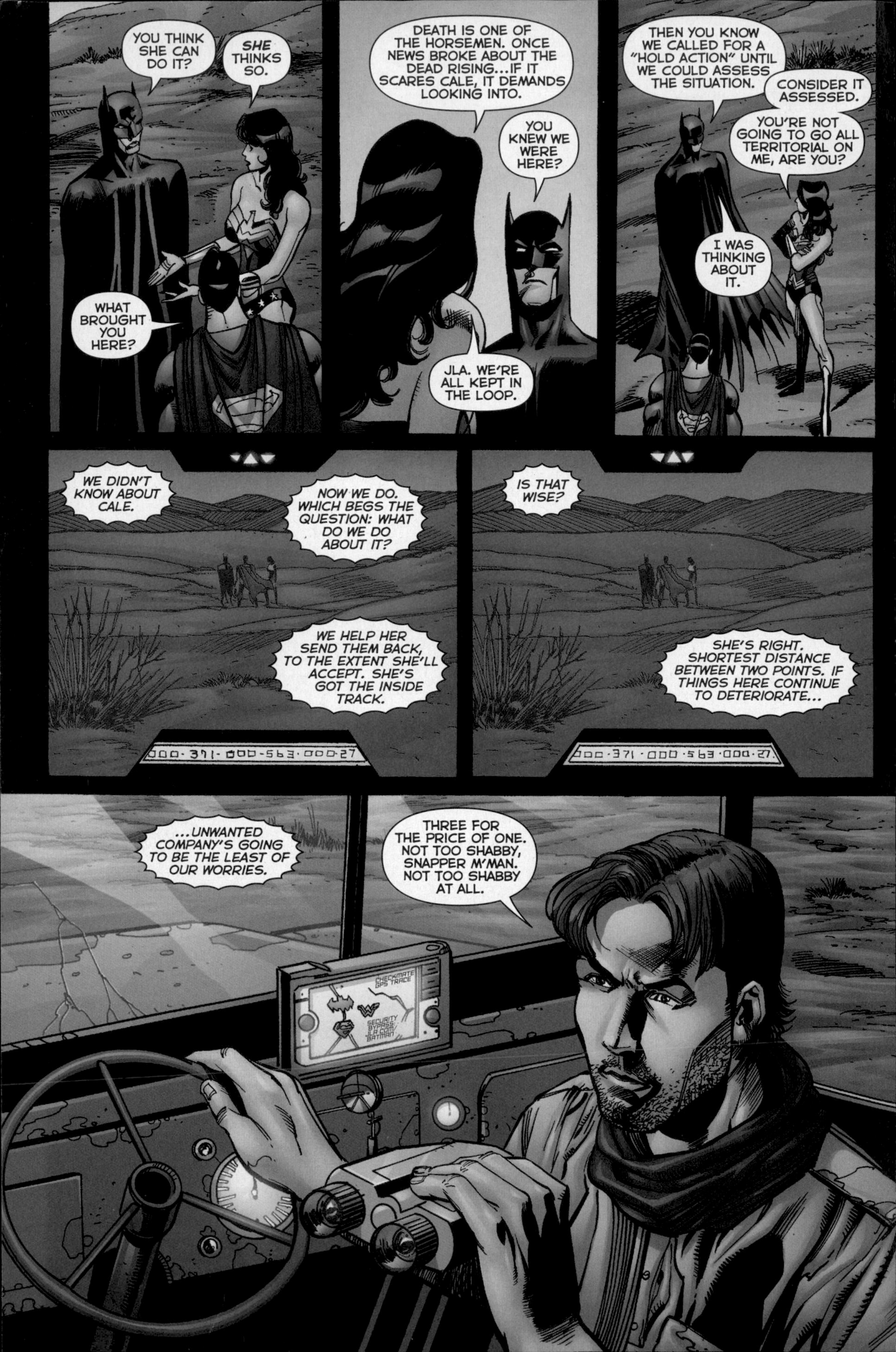
YOU THINK SHE CAN DO IT?
SHE THINKS SO.
WHAT BROUGHT YOU HERE?
DEATH IS ONE OF THE HORSEMEN. ONCE NEWS BROKE ABOUT THE DEAD RISING...IF IT SCARES CALE, IT DEMANDS LOOKING INTO.
YOU KNEW WE WERE HERE?
JLA. WE'RE ALL KEPT IN THE LOOP.
THEN YOU KNOW WE CALLED FOR A "HOLD ACTION" UNTIL WE COULD ASSESS THE SITUATION.
CONSIDER IT ASSESSED.
YOU'RE NOT GOING TO GO ALL TERRITORIAL ON ME, ARE YOU?
I WAS THINKING ABOUT IT.
WE DIDN'T KNOW ABOUT CALE.
NOW WE DO. WHICH BEGS THE QUESTION: WHAT DO WE DO ABOUT IT?
WE HELP HER SEND THEM BACK, TO THE EXTENT SHE'LL ACCEPT. SHE'S GOT THE INSIDE TRACK.
000-371-000-563-000-27
IS THAT WISE?
SHE'S RIGHT. SHORTEST DISTANCE BETWEEN TWO POINTS. IF THINGS HERE CONTINUE TO DETERIORATE...
000-371-000-563-000-27
...UNWANTED COMPANY'S GOING TO BE THE LEAST OF OUR WORRIES.
THREE FOR THE PRICE OF ONE. NOT TOO SHABBY, SNAPPER M'MAN. NOT TOO SHABBY AT ALL.
CHECKMATE GPS TRACE
SECURITY BYPASS: JLA COM/ BATMAN

SECOND COMING

Cover art by ETHAN VAN SCIVER

CHAPTER THREE

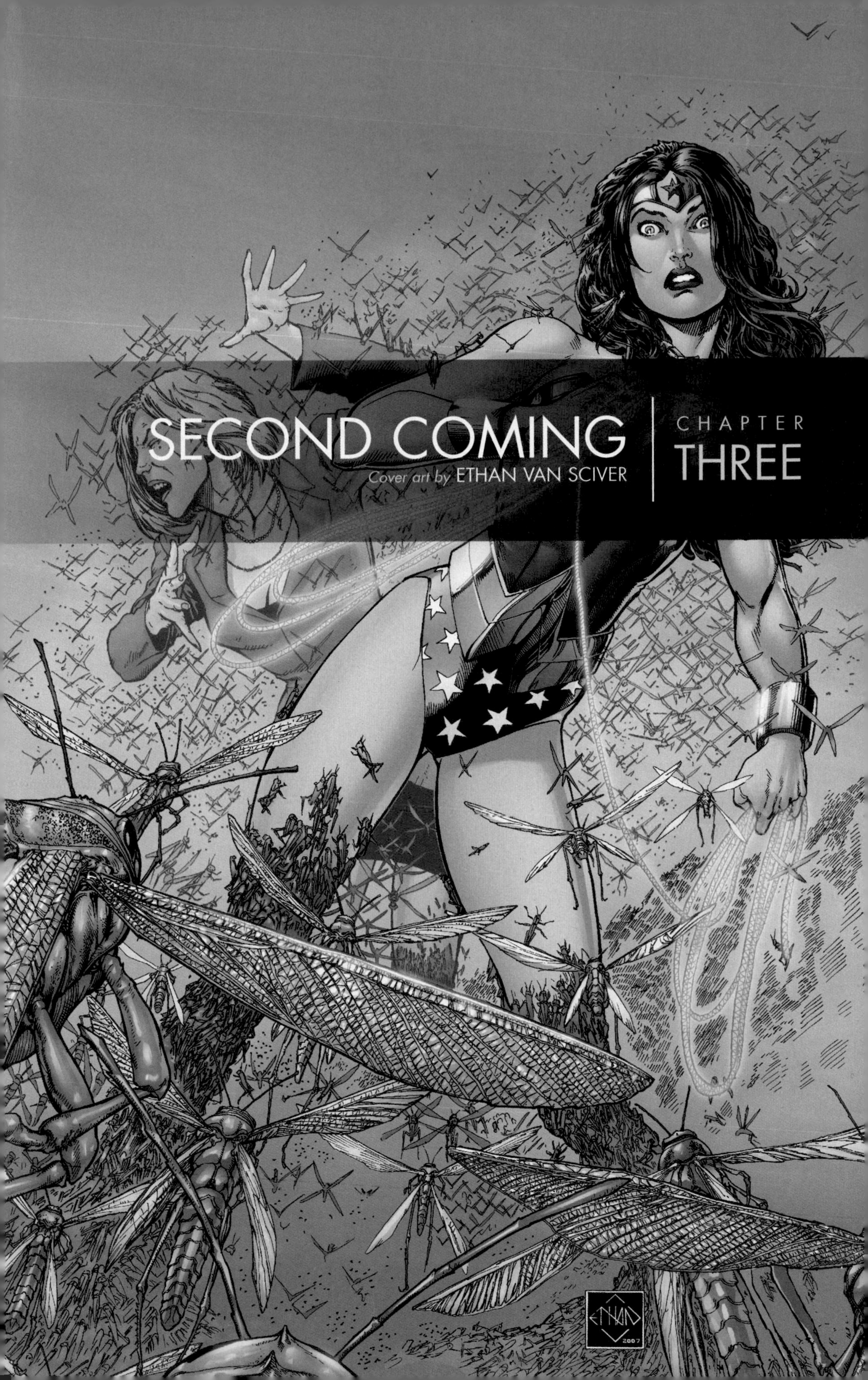

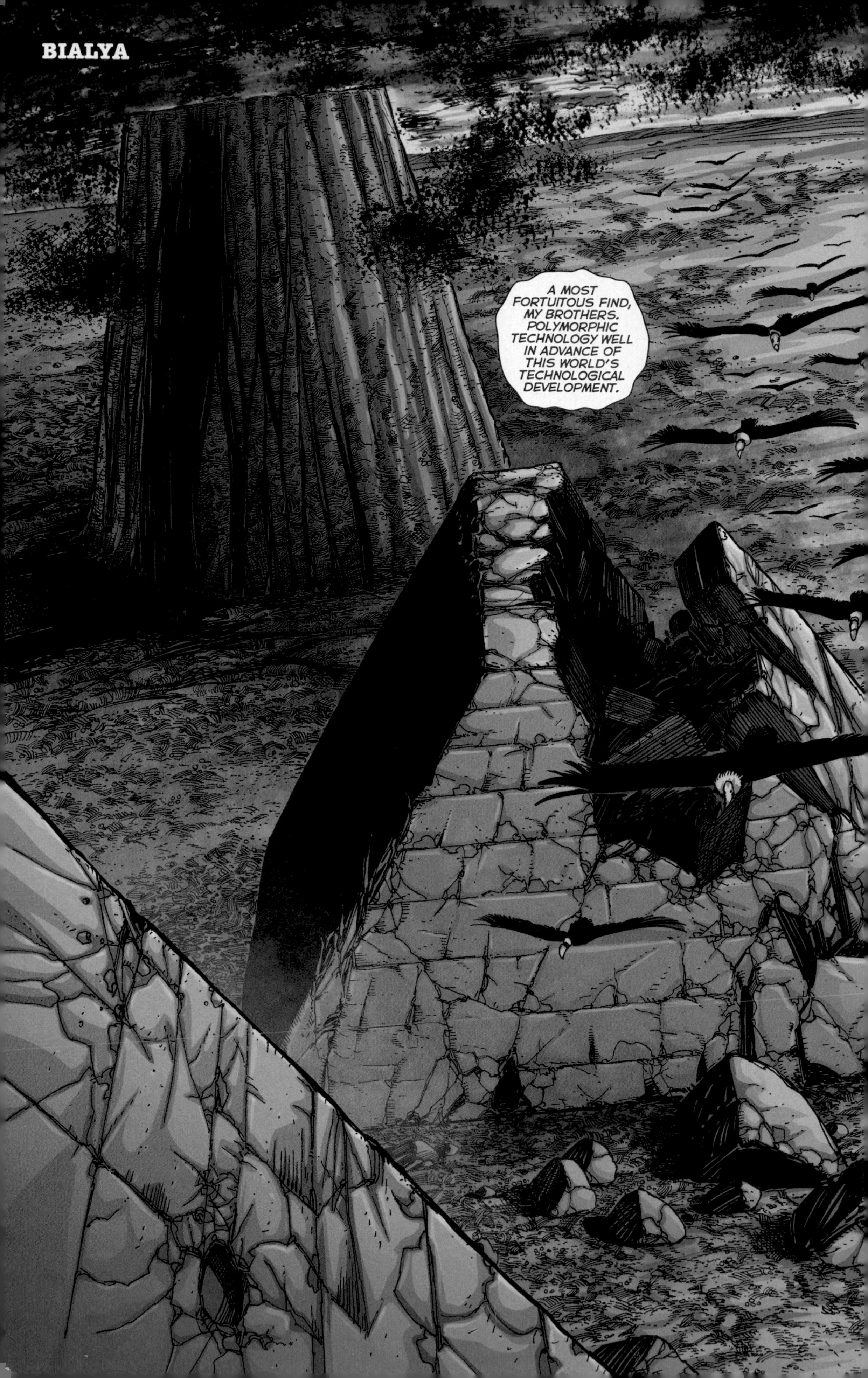
BIALYA
A MOST FORTUITOUS FIND, MY BROTHERS. POLYMORPHIC TECHNOLOGY WELL IN ADVANCE OF THIS WORLD'S TECHNOLOGICAL DEVELOPMENT.

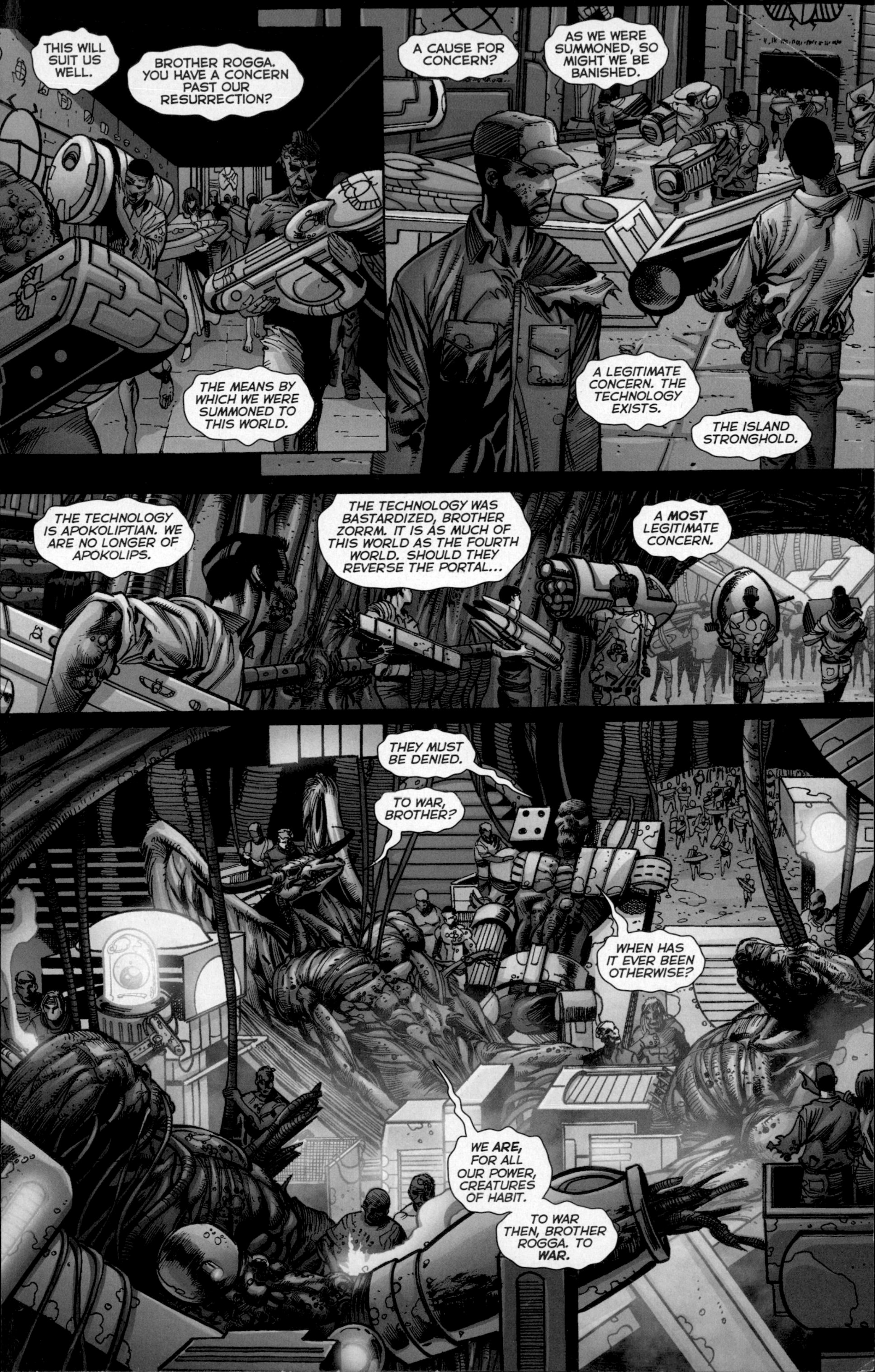
THIS WILL SUIT US WELL.
BROTHER ROGGA. YOU HAVE A CONCERN PAST OUR RESURRECTION?
THE MEANS BY WHICH WE WERE SUMMONED TO THIS WORLD.
A CAUSE FOR CONCERN?
AS WE WERE SUMMONED, SO MIGHT WE BE BANISHED.
A LEGITIMATE CONCERN. THE TECHNOLOGY EXISTS.
THE ISLAND STRONGHOLD.
THE TECHNOLOGY IS APOKOLIPTIAN. WE ARE NO LONGER OF APOKOLIPS.
THE TECHNOLOGY WAS BASTARDIZED, BROTHER ZORRM. IT IS AS MUCH OF THIS WORLD AS THE FOURTH WORLD. SHOULD THEY REVERSE THE PORTAL...
A MOST LEGITIMATE CONCERN.
THEY MUST BE DENIED.
TO WAR, BROTHER?
WHEN HAS IT EVER BEEN OTHERWISE?
WE ARE, FOR ALL OUR POWER, CREATURES OF HABIT.
TO WAR THEN, BROTHER ROGGA. TO WAR.

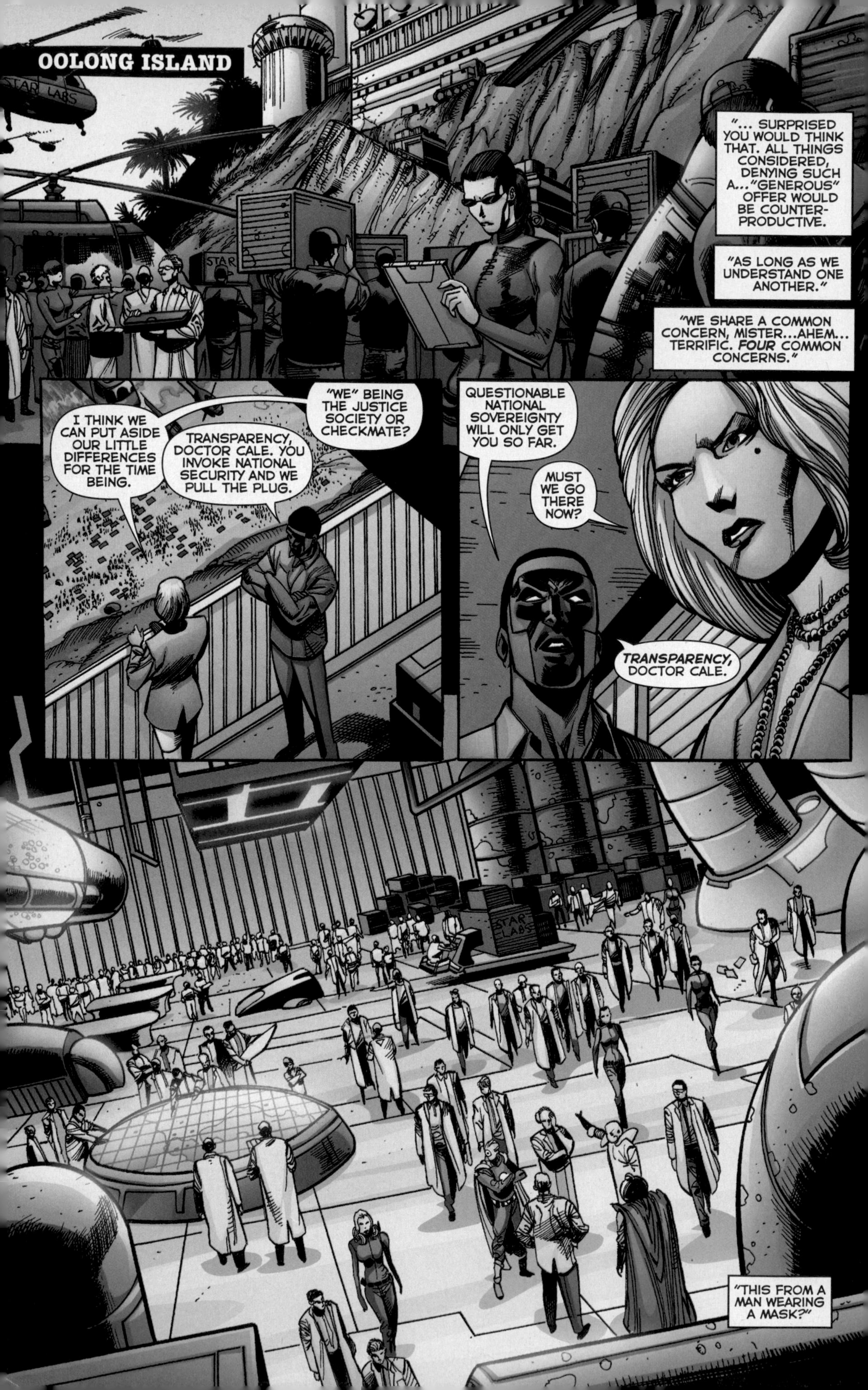
OOLONG ISLAND
"... SURPRISED YOU WOULD THINK THAT. ALL THINGS CONSIDERED, DENYING SUCH A..."GENEROUS" OFFER WOULD BE COUNTER-PRODUCTIVE.
"AS LONG AS WE UNDERSTAND ONE ANOTHER."
"WE SHARE A COMMON CONCERN, MISTER...AHEM... TERRIFIC. FOUR COMMON CONCERNS."
I THINK WE CAN PUT ASIDE OUR LITTLE DIFFERENCES FOR THE TIME BEING.
"WE" BEING THE JUSTICE SOCIETY OR CHECKMATE?
TRANSPARENCY, DOCTOR CALE. YOU INVOKE NATIONAL SECURITY AND WE PULL THE PLUG.
QUESTIONABLE NATIONAL SOVEREIGNTY WILL ONLY GET YOU SO FAR.
MUST WE GO THERE NOW?
TRANSPARENCY, DOCTOR CALE.
"THIS FROM A MAN WEARING A MASK?"

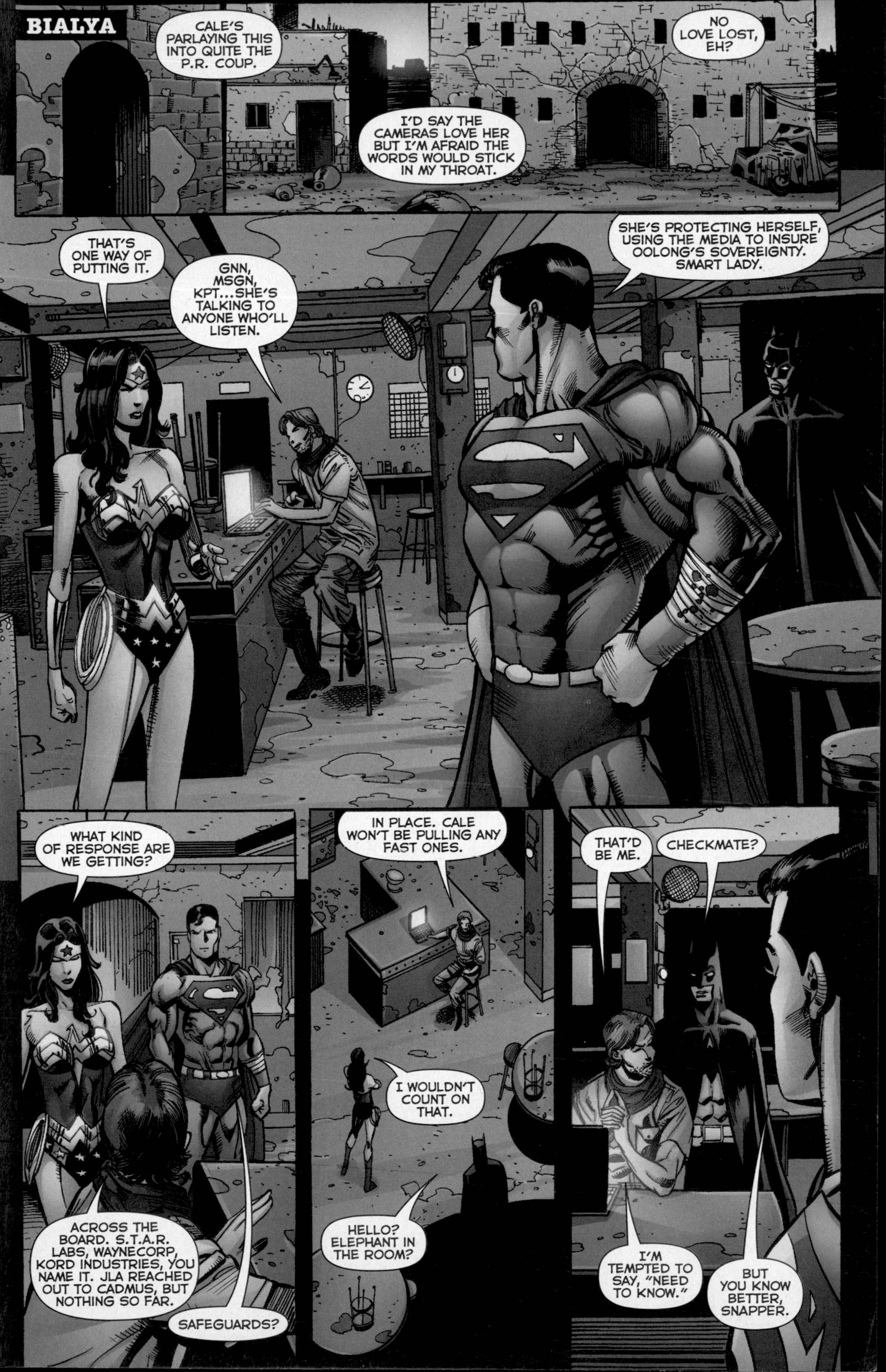
BIALYA
CALE'S PARLAYING THIS INTO QUITE THE P.R. COUP.
I'D SAY THE CAMERAS LOVE HER BUT I'M AFRAID THE WORDS WOULD STICK IN MY THROAT.
NO LOVE LOST, EH?
THAT'S ONE WAY OF PUTTING IT.
GNN, MSGN, KPT...SHE'S TALKING TO ANYONE WHO'LL LISTEN.
SHE'S PROTECTING HERSELF, USING THE MEDIA TO INSURE OOLONG'S SOVEREIGNTY. SMART LADY.
WHAT KIND OF RESPONSE ARE WE GETTING?
ACROSS THE BOARD. S.T.A.R. LABS, WAYNECORP, KORD INDUSTRIES, YOU NAME IT. JLA REACHED OUT TO CADMUS, BUT NOTHING SO FAR.
SAFEGUARDS?
IN PLACE. CALE WON'T BE PULLING ANY FAST ONES.
I WOULDN'T COUNT ON THAT.
HELLO? ELEPHANT IN THE ROOM?
THAT'D BE ME.
CHECKMATE?
I'M TEMPTED TO SAY, "NEED TO KNOW."
BUT YOU KNOW BETTER, SNAPPER.

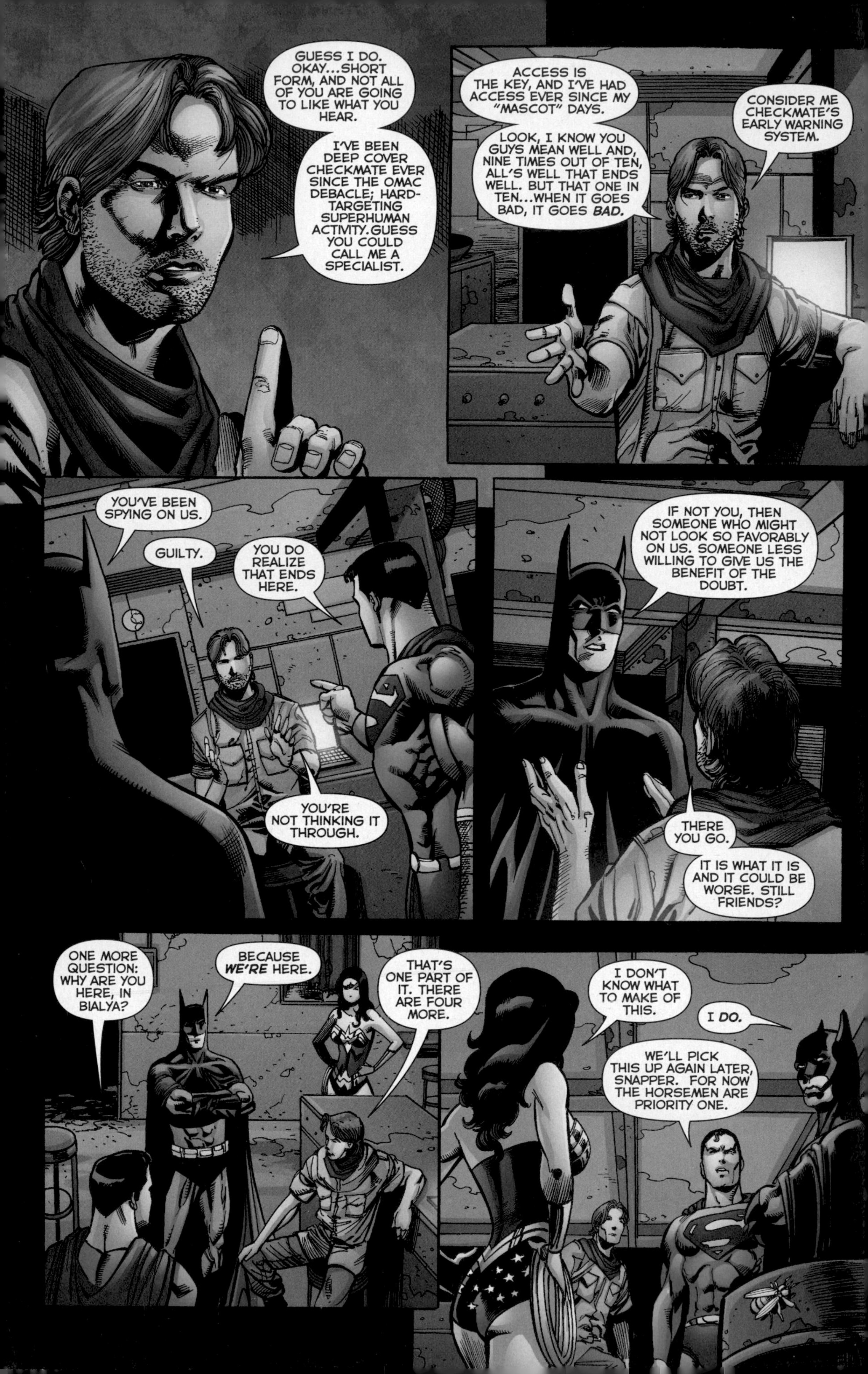
GUESS I DO. OKAY...SHORT FORM, AND NOT ALL OF YOU ARE GOING TO LIKE WHAT YOU HEAR.
I'VE BEEN DEEP COVER CHECKMATE EVER SINCE THE OMAC DEBACLE; HARD-TARGETING SUPERHUMAN ACTIVITY. GUESS YOU COULD CALL ME A SPECIALIST.
ACCESS IS THE KEY, AND I'VE HAD ACCESS EVER SINCE MY "MASCOT" DAYS.
LOOK, I KNOW YOU GUYS MEAN WELL AND, NINE TIMES OUT OF TEN, ALL'S WELL THAT ENDS WELL. BUT THAT ONE IN TEN...WHEN IT GOES BAD, IT GOES *BAD.*
CONSIDER ME CHECKMATE'S EARLY WARNING SYSTEM.
YOU'VE BEEN SPYING ON US.
GUILTY.
YOU DO REALIZE THAT ENDS HERE.
YOU'RE NOT THINKING IT THROUGH.
IF NOT YOU, THEN SOMEONE WHO MIGHT NOT LOOK SO FAVORABLY ON US. SOMEONE LESS WILLING TO GIVE US THE BENEFIT OF THE DOUBT.
THERE YOU GO.
IT IS WHAT IT IS AND IT COULD BE WORSE. STILL FRIENDS?
ONE MORE QUESTION: WHY ARE YOU HERE, IN BIALYA?
BECAUSE *WE'RE* HERE.
THAT'S ONE PART OF IT. THERE ARE FOUR MORE.
I DON'T KNOW WHAT TO MAKE OF THIS.
I *DO.*
WE'LL PICK THIS UP AGAIN LATER, SNAPPER. FOR NOW THE HORSEMEN ARE PRIORITY ONE.

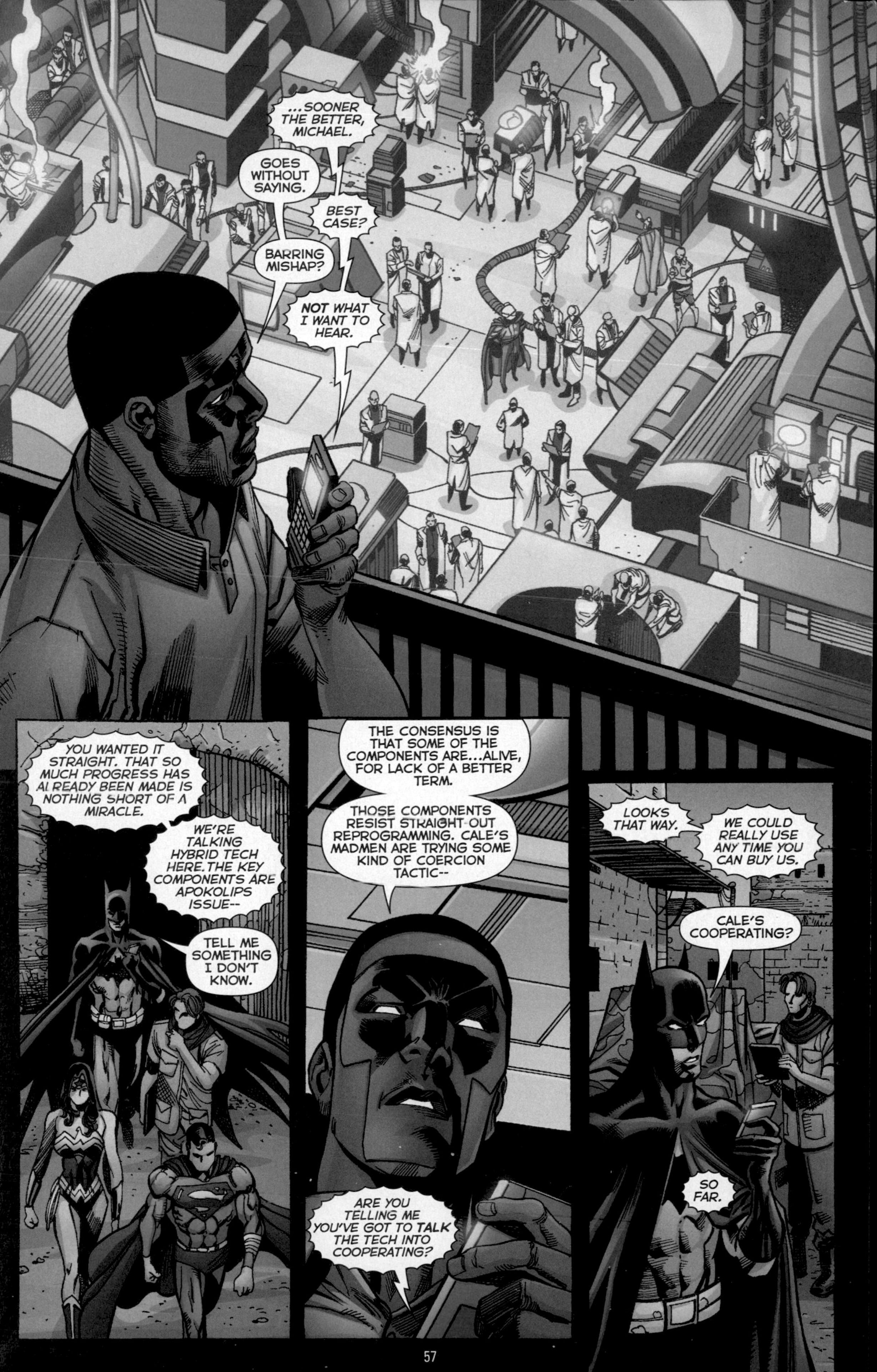
...SOONER THE BETTER, MICHAEL.
GOES WITHOUT SAYING.
BEST CASE?
BARRING MISHAP?
NOT WHAT I WANT TO HEAR.
YOU WANTED IT STRAIGHT. THAT SO MUCH PROGRESS HAS ALREADY BEEN MADE IS NOTHING SHORT OF A MIRACLE.
WE'RE TALKING HYBRID TECH HERE. THE KEY COMPONENTS ARE APOKOLIPS ISSUE--
TELL ME SOMETHING I DON'T KNOW.
THE CONSENSUS IS THAT SOME OF THE COMPONENTS ARE...ALIVE, FOR LACK OF A BETTER TERM.
THOSE COMPONENTS RESIST STRAIGHT-OUT REPROGRAMMING. CALE'S MADMEN ARE TRYING SOME KIND OF COERCION TACTIC--
ARE YOU TELLING ME YOU'VE GOT TO TALK THE TECH INTO COOPERATING?
LOOKS THAT WAY.
WE COULD REALLY USE ANY TIME YOU CAN BUY US.
CALE'S COOPERATING?
SO FAR.

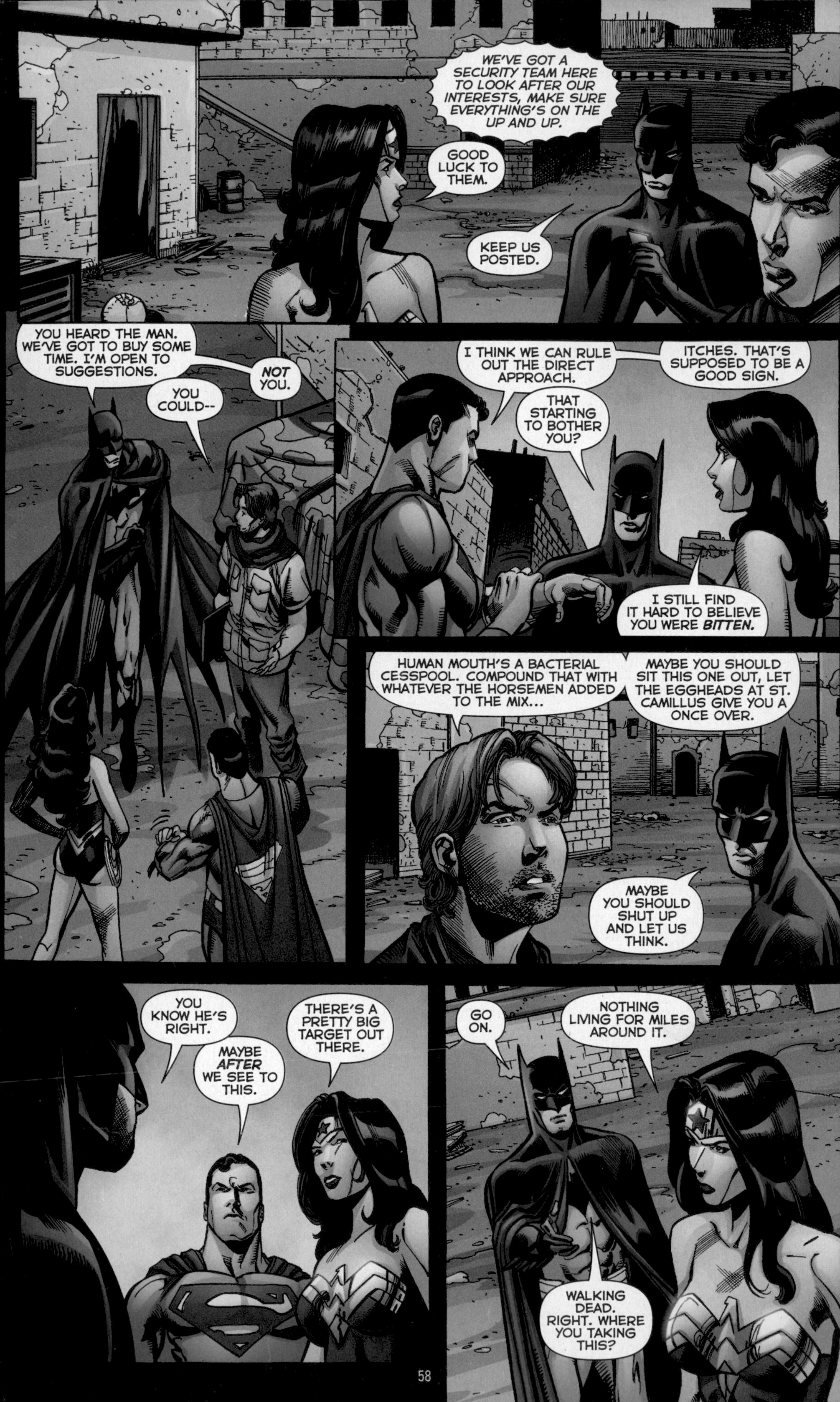
WE'VE GOT A SECURITY TEAM HERE TO LOOK AFTER OUR INTERESTS, MAKE SURE EVERYTHING'S ON THE UP AND UP.
GOOD LUCK TO THEM.
KEEP US POSTED.
YOU HEARD THE MAN. WE'VE GOT TO BUY SOME TIME. I'M OPEN TO SUGGESTIONS.
YOU COULD--
NOT YOU.
I THINK WE CAN RULE OUT THE DIRECT APPROACH.
ITCHES. THAT'S SUPPOSED TO BE A GOOD SIGN.
THAT STARTING TO BOTHER YOU?
I STILL FIND IT HARD TO BELIEVE YOU WERE BITTEN.
HUMAN MOUTH'S A BACTERIAL CESSPOOL. COMPOUND THAT WITH WHATEVER THE HORSEMEN ADDED TO THE MIX...
MAYBE YOU SHOULD SIT THIS ONE OUT, LET THE EGGHEADS AT ST. CAMILLUS GIVE YOU A ONCE OVER.
MAYBE YOU SHOULD SHUT UP AND LET US THINK.
YOU KNOW HE'S RIGHT.
MAYBE AFTER WE SEE TO THIS.
THERE'S A PRETTY BIG TARGET OUT THERE.
GO ON.
NOTHING LIVING FOR MILES AROUND IT.
WALKING DEAD. RIGHT. WHERE YOU TAKING THIS?

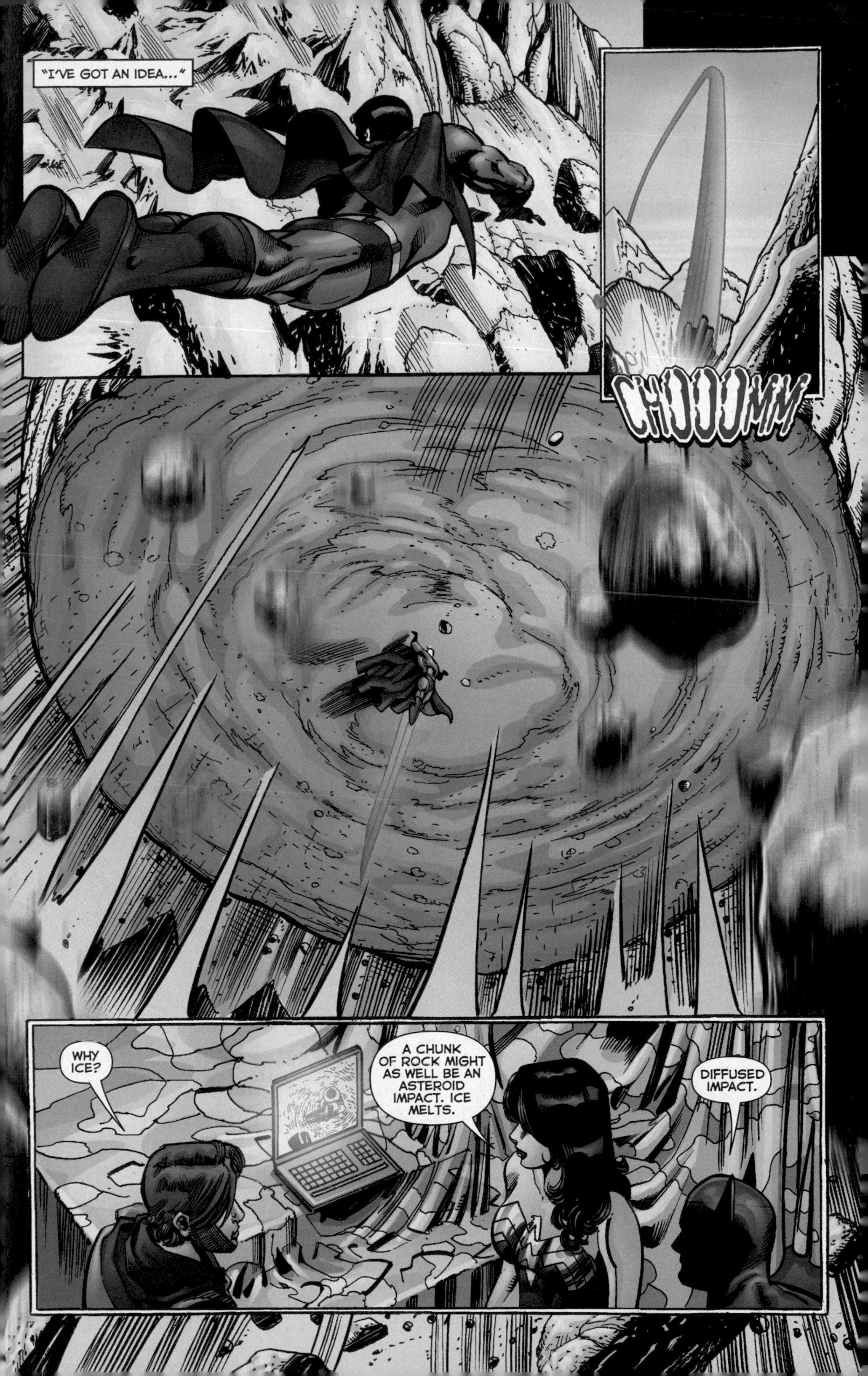
"I'VE GOT AN IDEA..."
CHOOOMM
WHY ICE?
A CHUNK OF ROCK MIGHT AS WELL BE AN ASTEROID IMPACT. ICE MELTS.
DIFFUSED IMPACT.

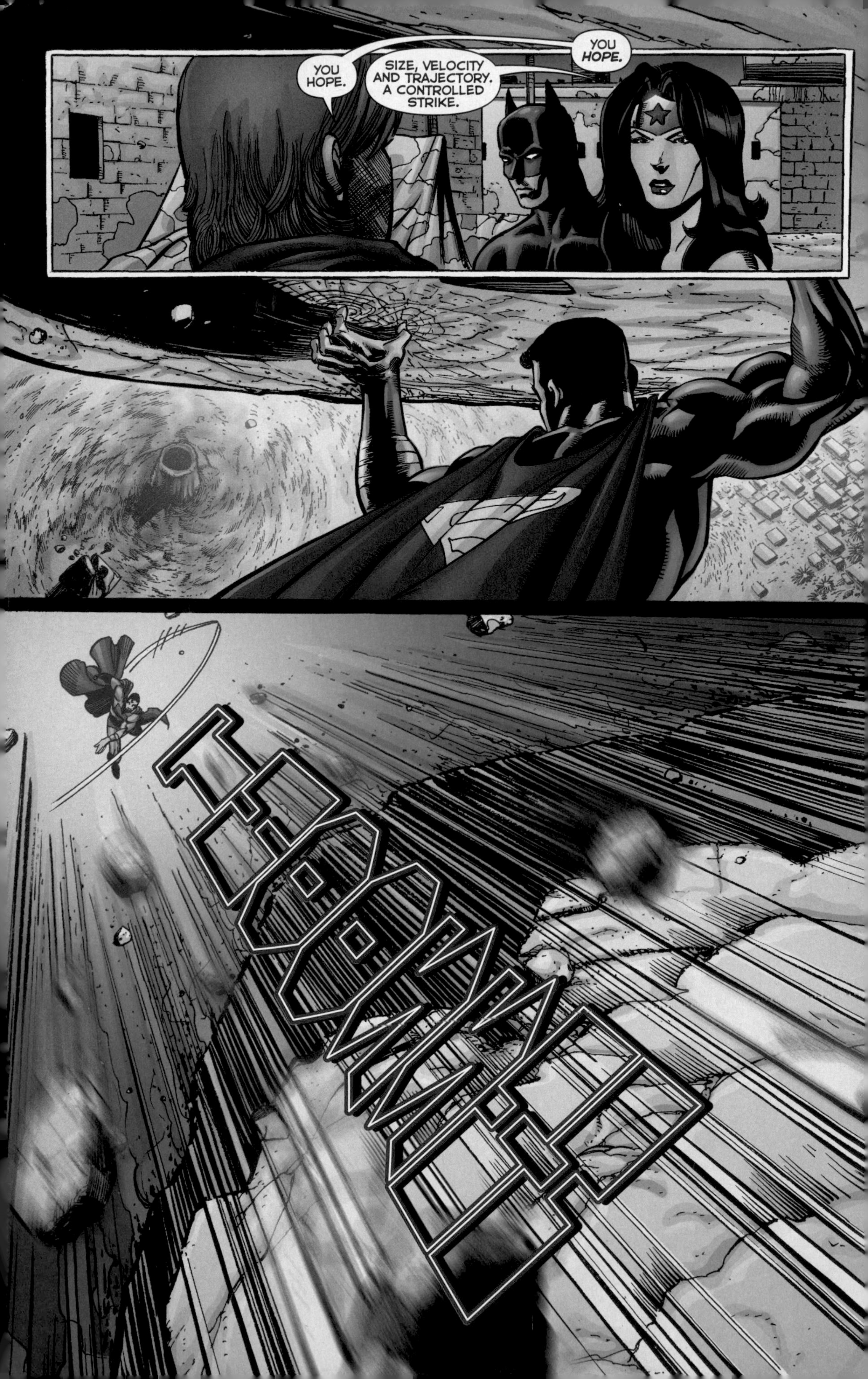
YOU HOPE.
SIZE, VELOCITY AND TRAJECTORY. A CONTROLLED STRIKE.
YOU HOPE.

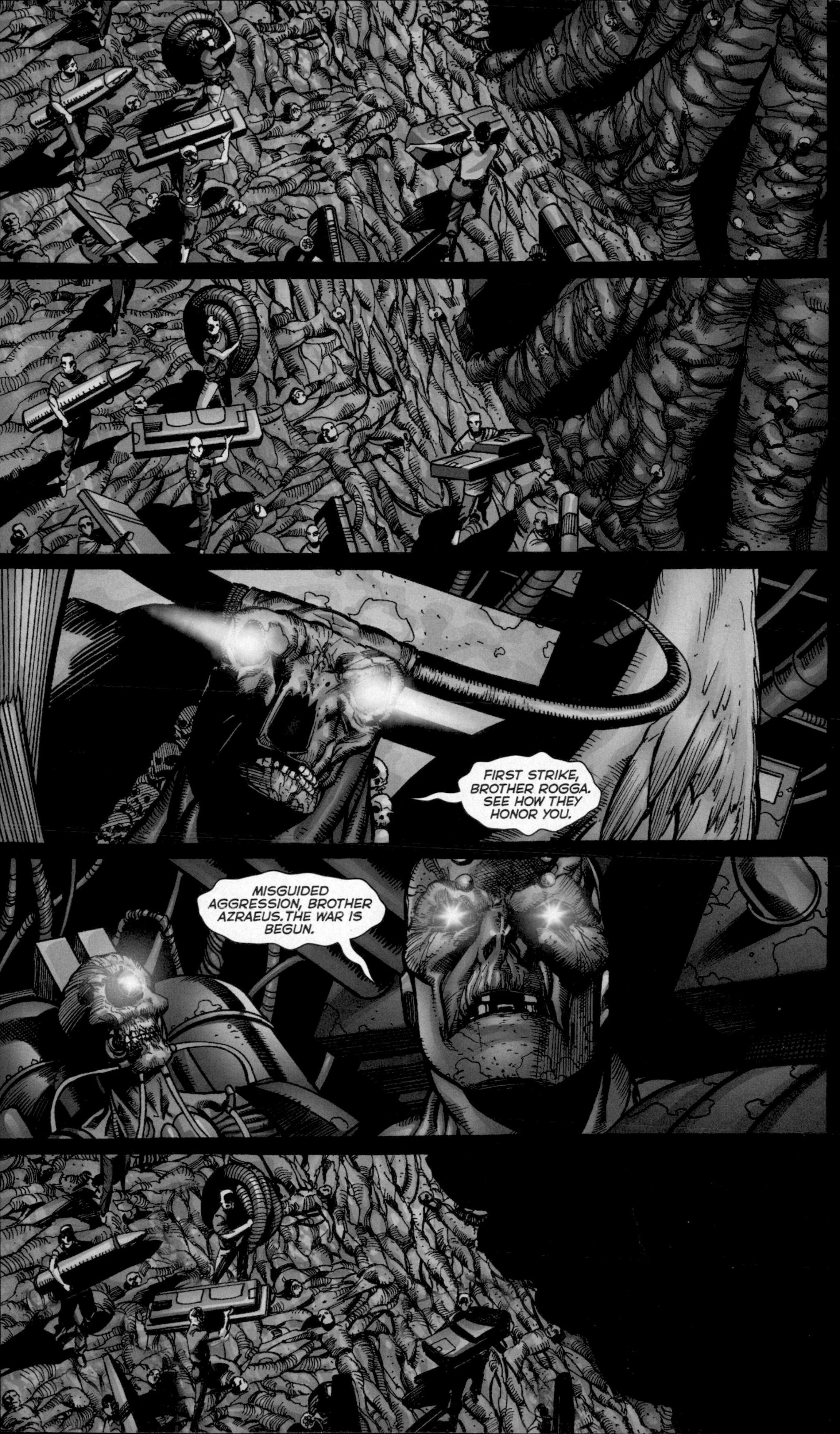
FIRST STRIKE, BROTHER ROGGA. SEE HOW THEY HONOR YOU.
MISGUIDED AGGRESSION, BROTHER AZRAEUS. THE WAR IS BEGUN.

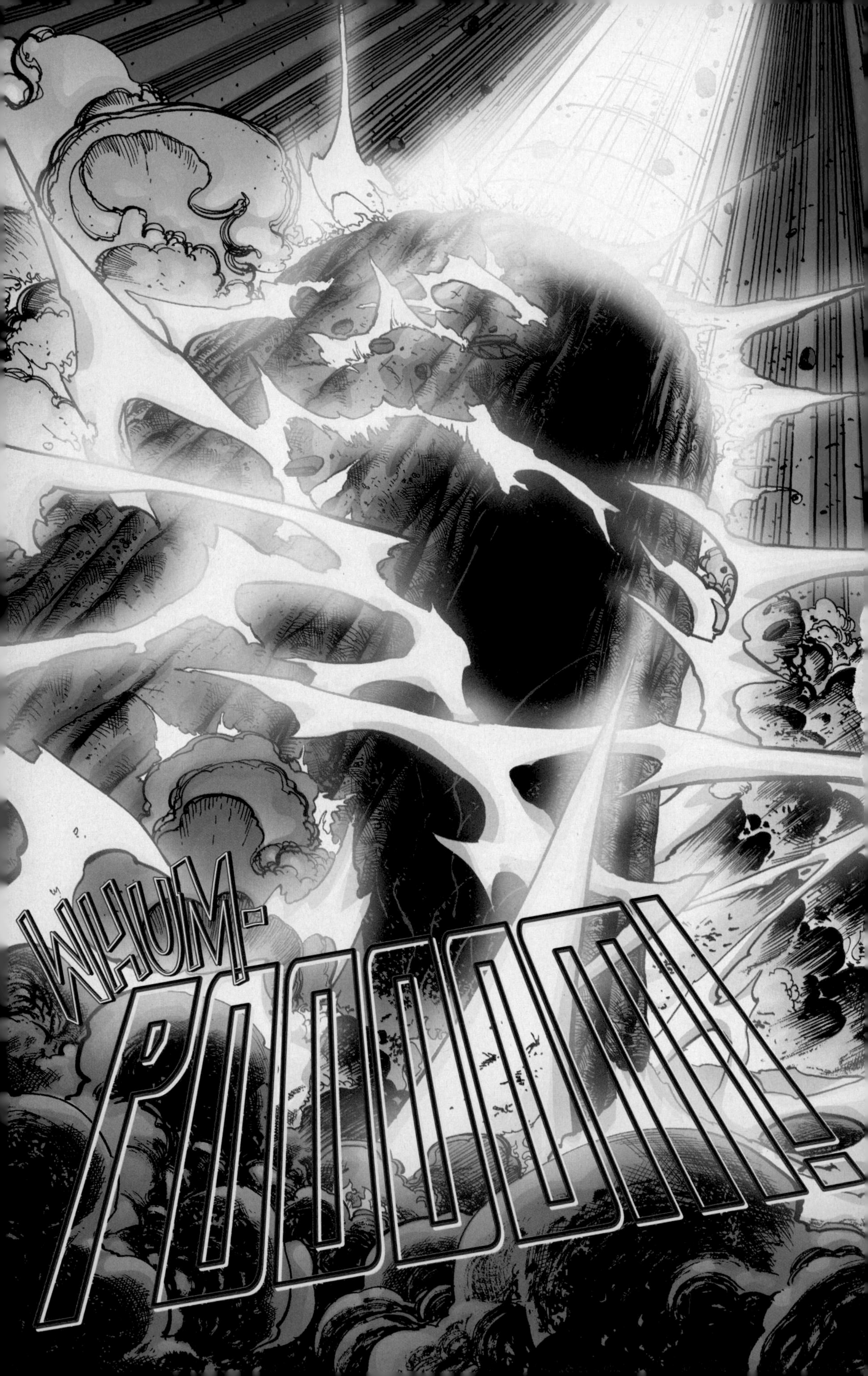
WHUM-
POOOOM!

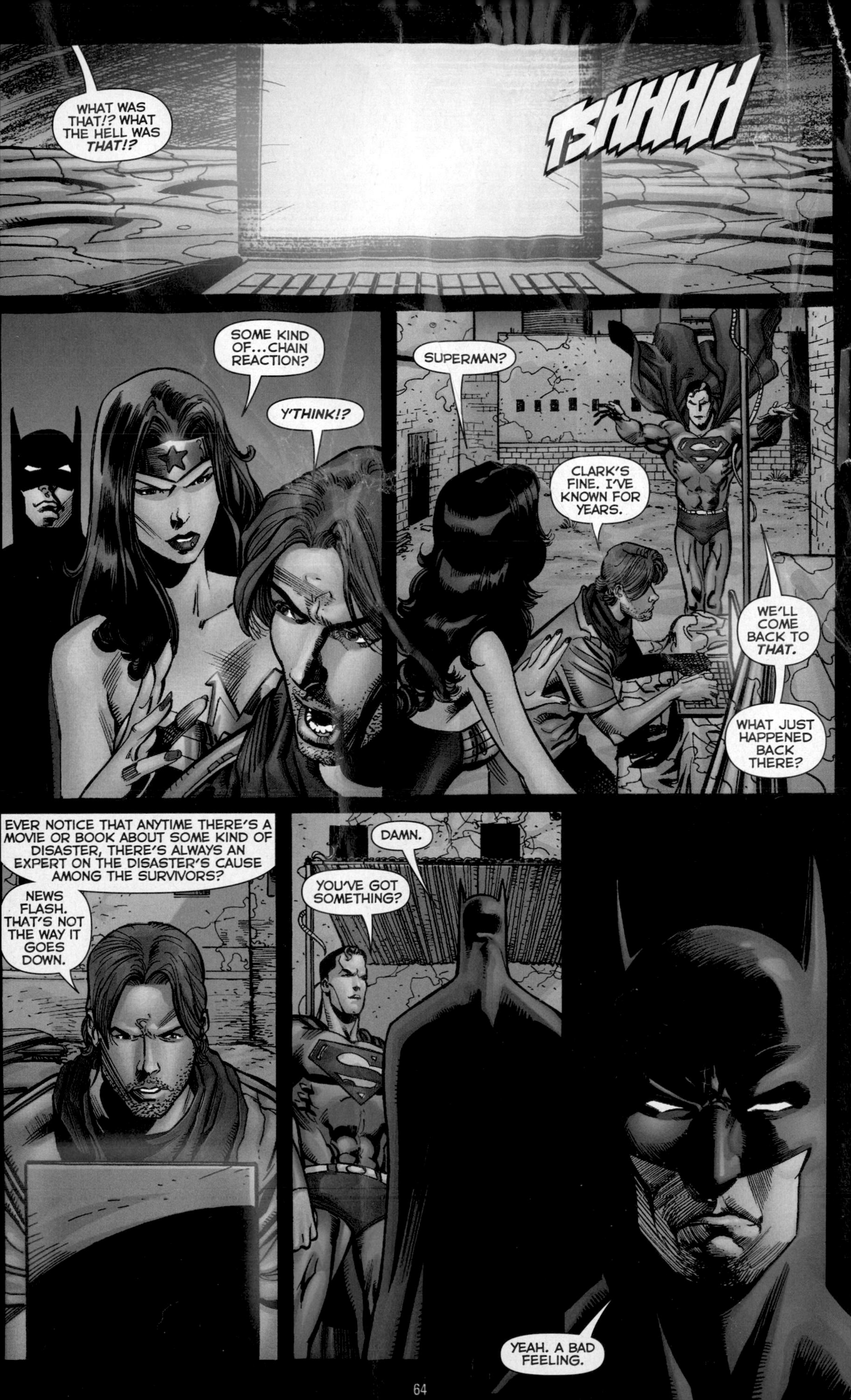
WHAT WAS THAT!? WHAT THE HELL WAS THAT!?
TSHHHH
SOME KIND OF...CHAIN REACTION?
Y'THINK!?
SUPERMAN?
CLARK'S FINE. I'VE KNOWN FOR YEARS.
WE'LL COME BACK TO THAT.
WHAT JUST HAPPENED BACK THERE?
EVER NOTICE THAT ANYTIME THERE'S A MOVIE OR BOOK ABOUT SOME KIND OF DISASTER, THERE'S ALWAYS AN EXPERT ON THE DISASTER'S CAUSE AMONG THE SURVIVORS?
NEWS FLASH. THAT'S NOT THE WAY IT GOES DOWN.
DAMN.
YOU'VE GOT SOMETHING?
YEAH. A BAD FEELING.

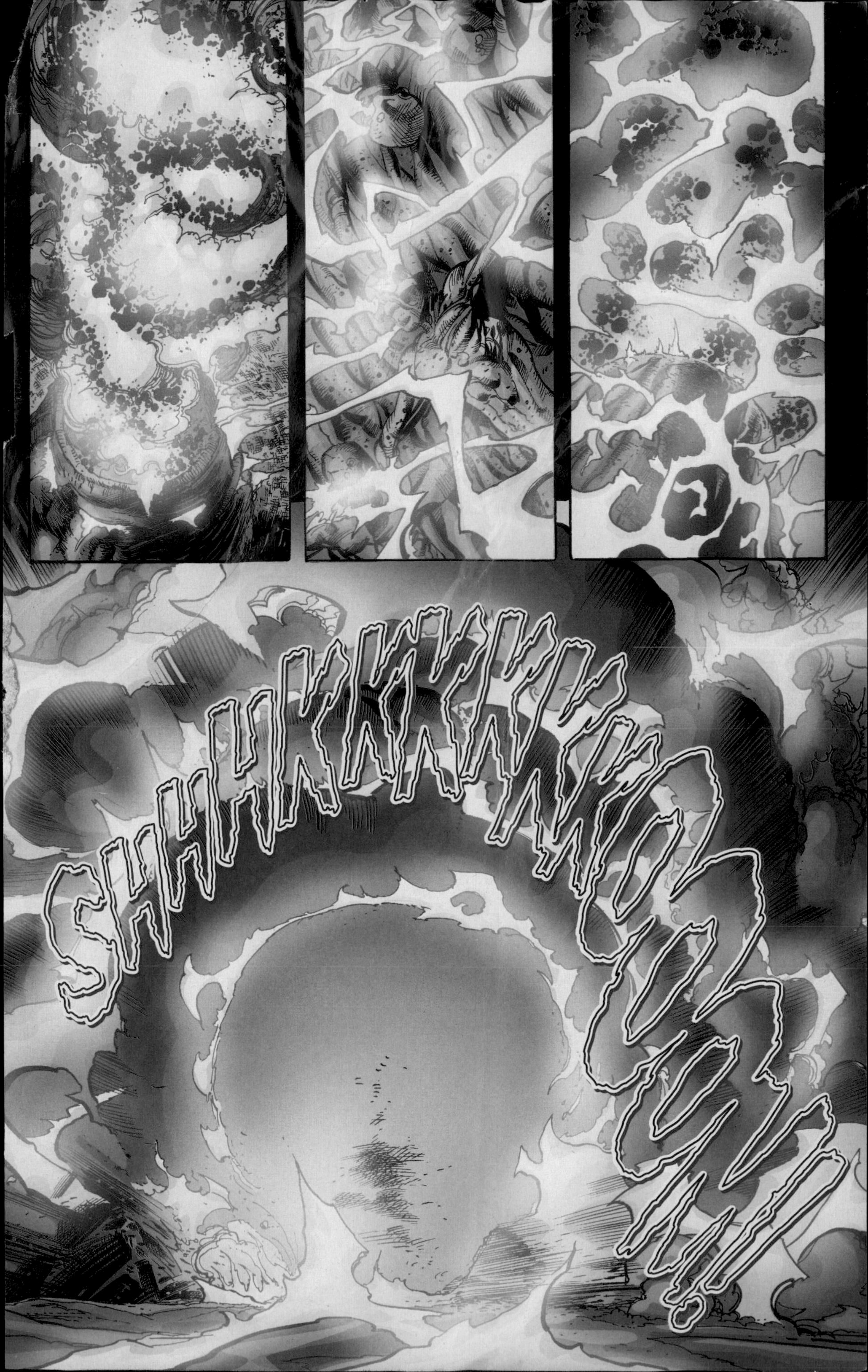
SHHHKKKKWOOOOM!!

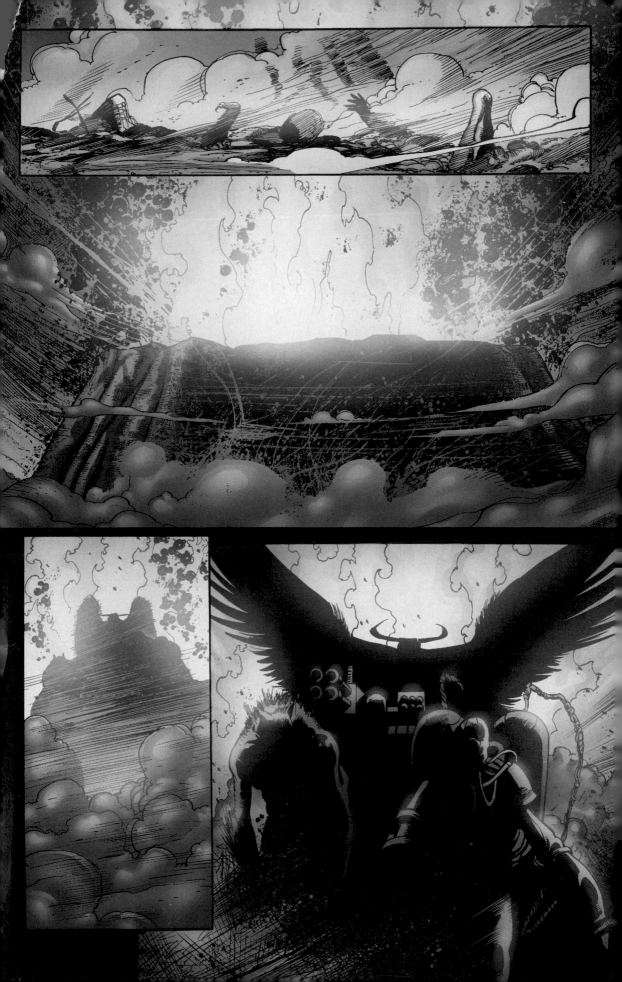

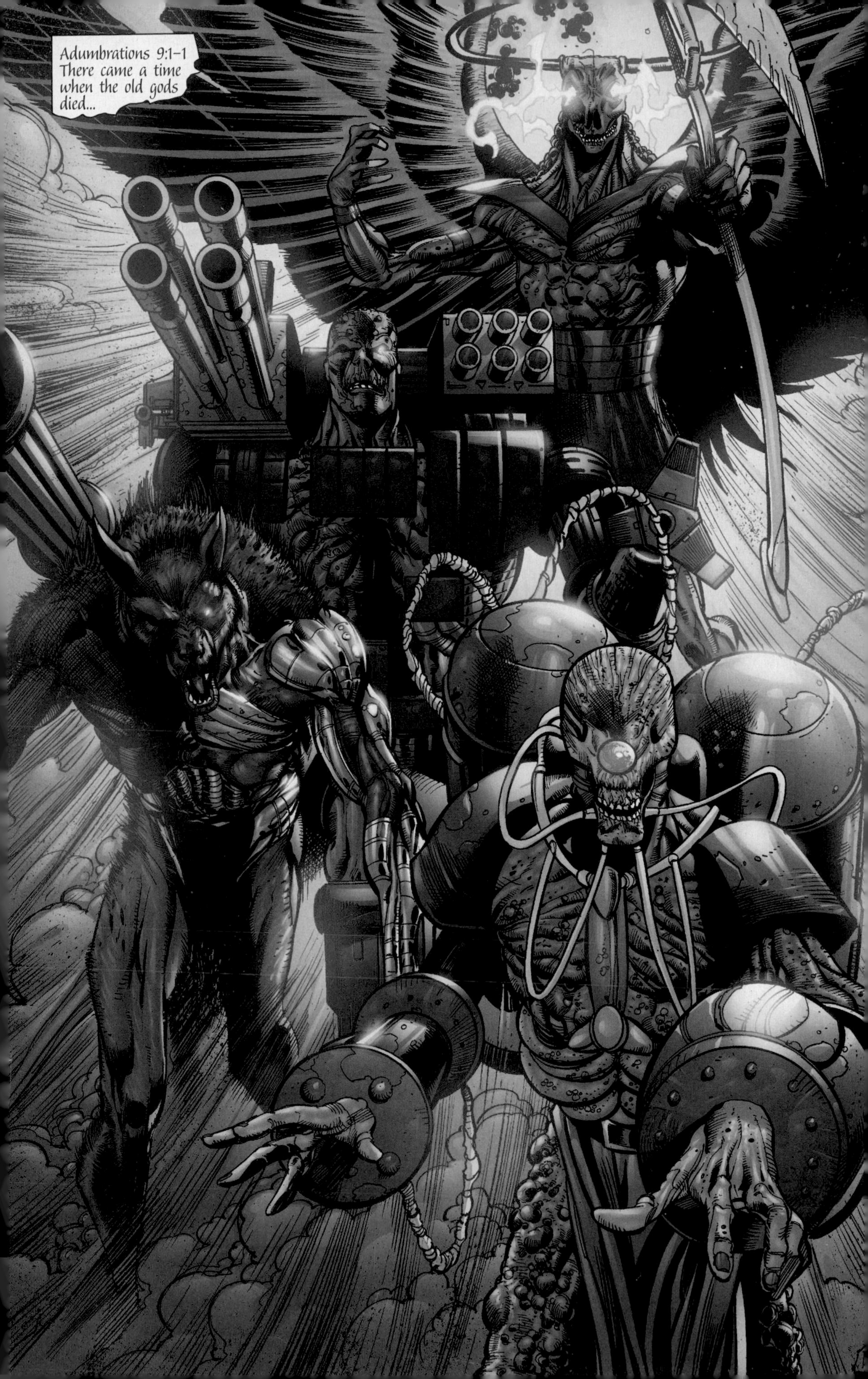
Adumbrations 9:1–1 There came a time when the old gods died...

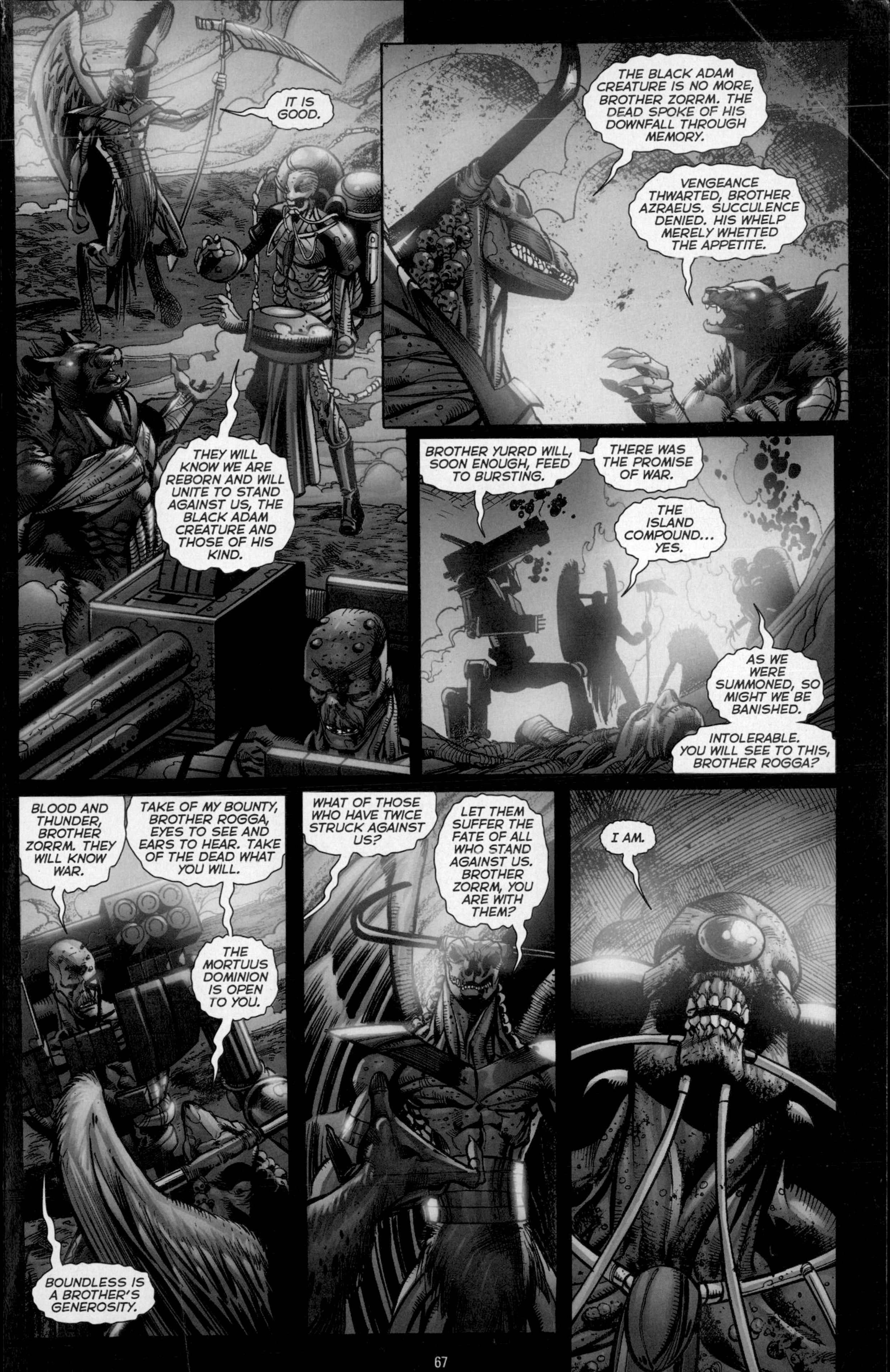

IT IS GOOD.
THEY WILL KNOW WE ARE REBORN AND WILL UNITE TO STAND AGAINST US, THE BLACK ADAM CREATURE AND THOSE OF HIS KIND.
THE BLACK ADAM CREATURE IS NO MORE, BROTHER ZORRM. THE DEAD SPOKE OF HIS DOWNFALL THROUGH MEMORY.
VENGEANCE THWARTED, BROTHER AZRAEUS. SUCCULENCE DENIED. HIS WHELP MERELY WHETTED THE APPETITE.
BROTHER YURRD WILL, SOON ENOUGH, FEED TO BURSTING.
THERE WAS THE PROMISE OF WAR.
THE ISLAND COMPOUND... YES.
AS WE WERE SUMMONED, SO MIGHT WE BE BANISHED.
INTOLERABLE. YOU WILL SEE TO THIS, BROTHER ROGGA?
BLOOD AND THUNDER, BROTHER ZORRM. THEY WILL KNOW WAR.
TAKE OF MY BOUNTY, BROTHER ROGGA, EYES TO SEE AND EARS TO HEAR. TAKE OF THE DEAD WHAT YOU WILL.
THE MORTUUS DOMINION IS OPEN TO YOU.
BOUNDLESS IS A BROTHER'S GENEROSITY.
WHAT OF THOSE WHO HAVE TWICE STRUCK AGAINST US?
LET THEM SUFFER THE FATE OF ALL WHO STAND AGAINST US. BROTHER ZORRM, YOU ARE WITH THEM?
I AM.

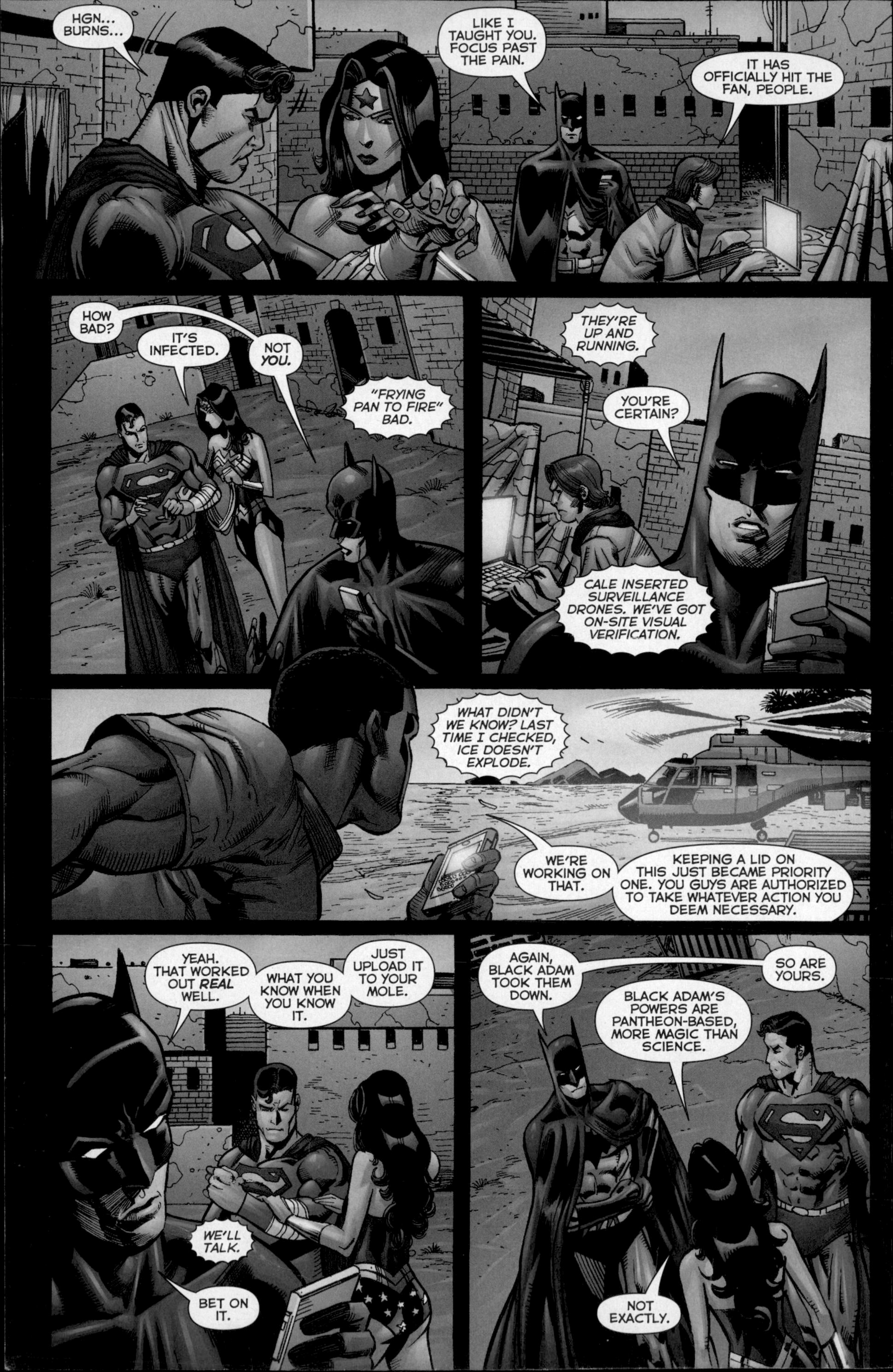
HGN... BURNS...
LIKE I TAUGHT YOU. FOCUS PAST THE PAIN.
IT HAS OFFICIALLY HIT THE FAN, PEOPLE.
HOW BAD?
IT'S INFECTED.
NOT *YOU.*
"FRYING PAN TO FIRE" BAD.
THEY'RE UP AND RUNNING.
YOU'RE CERTAIN?
CALE INSERTED SURVEILLANCE DRONES. WE'VE GOT ON-SITE VISUAL VERIFICATION.
WHAT DIDN'T WE KNOW? LAST TIME I CHECKED, ICE DOESN'T EXPLODE.
WE'RE WORKING ON THAT.
KEEPING A LID ON THIS JUST BECAME PRIORITY ONE. YOU GUYS ARE AUTHORIZED TO TAKE WHATEVER ACTION YOU DEEM NECESSARY.
YEAH. THAT WORKED OUT *REAL* WELL.
WHAT YOU KNOW WHEN YOU KNOW IT.
JUST UPLOAD IT TO YOUR MOLE.
WE'LL TALK.
BET ON IT.
AGAIN, BLACK ADAM TOOK THEM DOWN.
SO ARE YOURS.
BLACK ADAM'S POWERS ARE PANTHEON-BASED, MORE MAGIC THAN SCIENCE.
NOT EXACTLY.

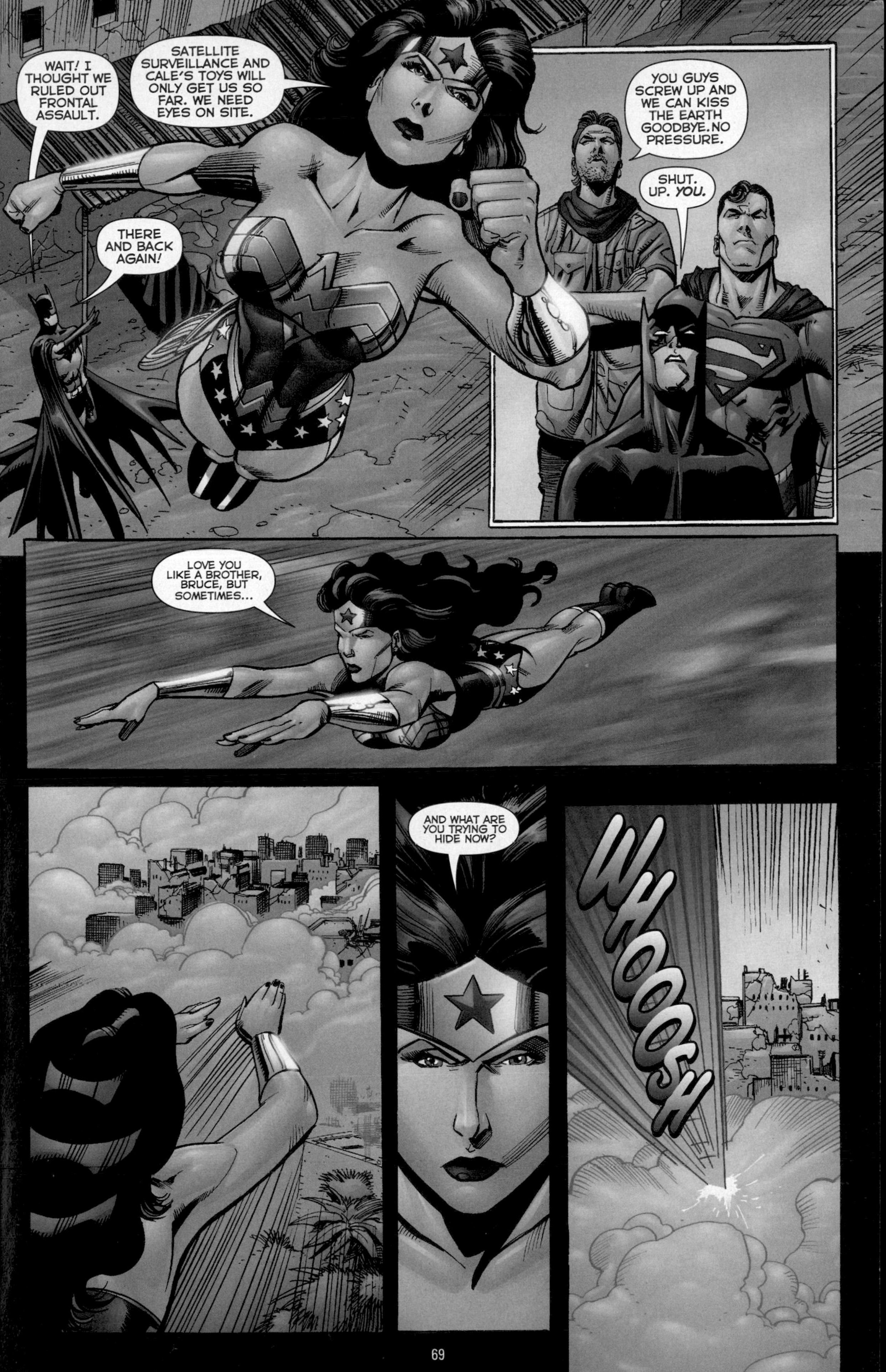
WAIT! I THOUGHT WE RULED OUT FRONTAL ASSAULT.
SATELLITE SURVEILLANCE AND CALE'S TOYS WILL ONLY GET US SO FAR. WE NEED EYES ON SITE.
THERE AND BACK AGAIN!
YOU GUYS SCREW UP AND WE CAN KISS THE EARTH GOODBYE. NO PRESSURE.
SHUT. UP. *YOU.*
LOVE YOU LIKE A BROTHER, BRUCE, BUT SOMETIMES...
AND WHAT ARE YOU TRYING TO HIDE NOW?
WHOOOSH

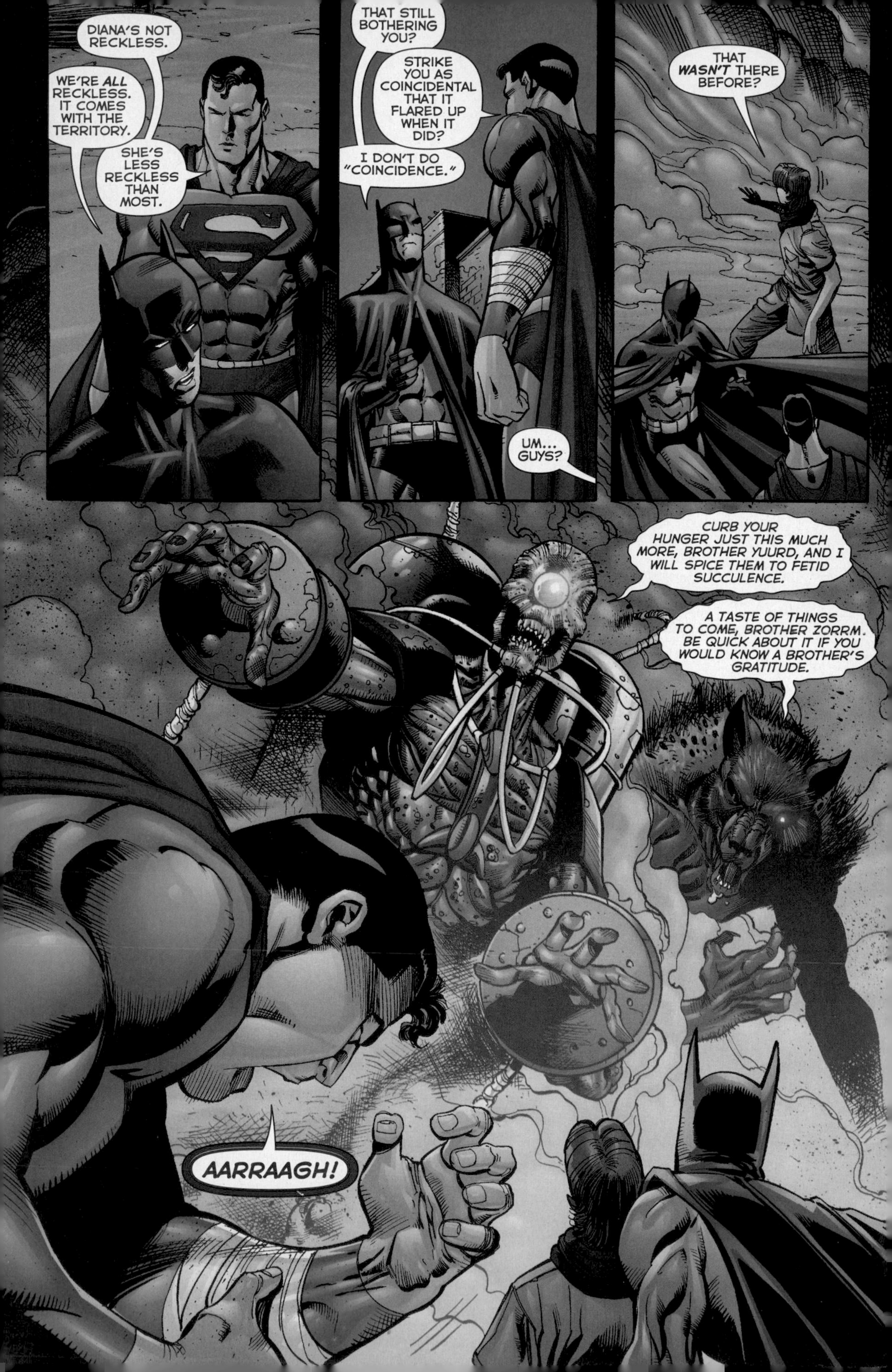

DIANA'S NOT RECKLESS.
WE'RE ALL RECKLESS. IT COMES WITH THE TERRITORY.
SHE'S LESS RECKLESS THAN MOST.
THAT STILL BOTHERING YOU?
STRIKE YOU AS COINCIDENTAL THAT IT FLARED UP WHEN IT DID?
I DON'T DO "COINCIDENCE."
UM... GUYS?
THAT WASN'T THERE BEFORE?
CURB YOUR HUNGER JUST THIS MUCH MORE, BROTHER YUURD, AND I WILL SPICE THEM TO FETID SUCCULENCE.
A TASTE OF THINGS TO COME, BROTHER ZORRM. BE QUICK ABOUT IT IF YOU WOULD KNOW A BROTHER'S GRATITUDE.
AARRAAGH!

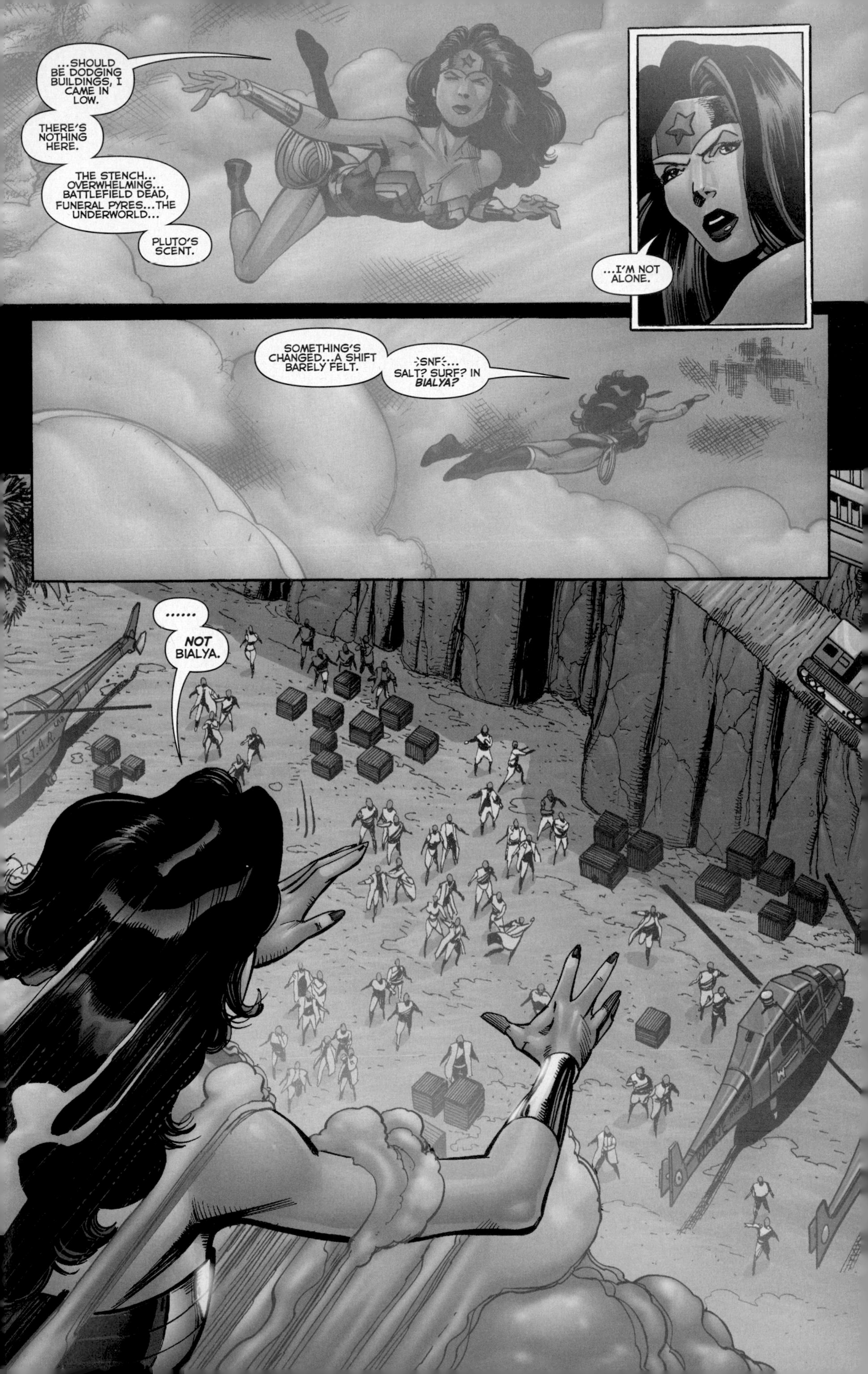

...SHOULD BE DODGING BUILDINGS, I CAME IN LOW.
THERE'S NOTHING HERE.
THE STENCH... OVERWHELMING... BATTLEFIELD DEAD, FUNERAL PYRES...THE UNDERWORLD...
PLUTO'S SCENT.
...I'M NOT ALONE.
SOMETHING'S CHANGED...A SHIFT BARELY FELT.
SNF... SALT? SURF? IN BIALYA?
......
NOT BIALYA.
S.T.A.R. LAB

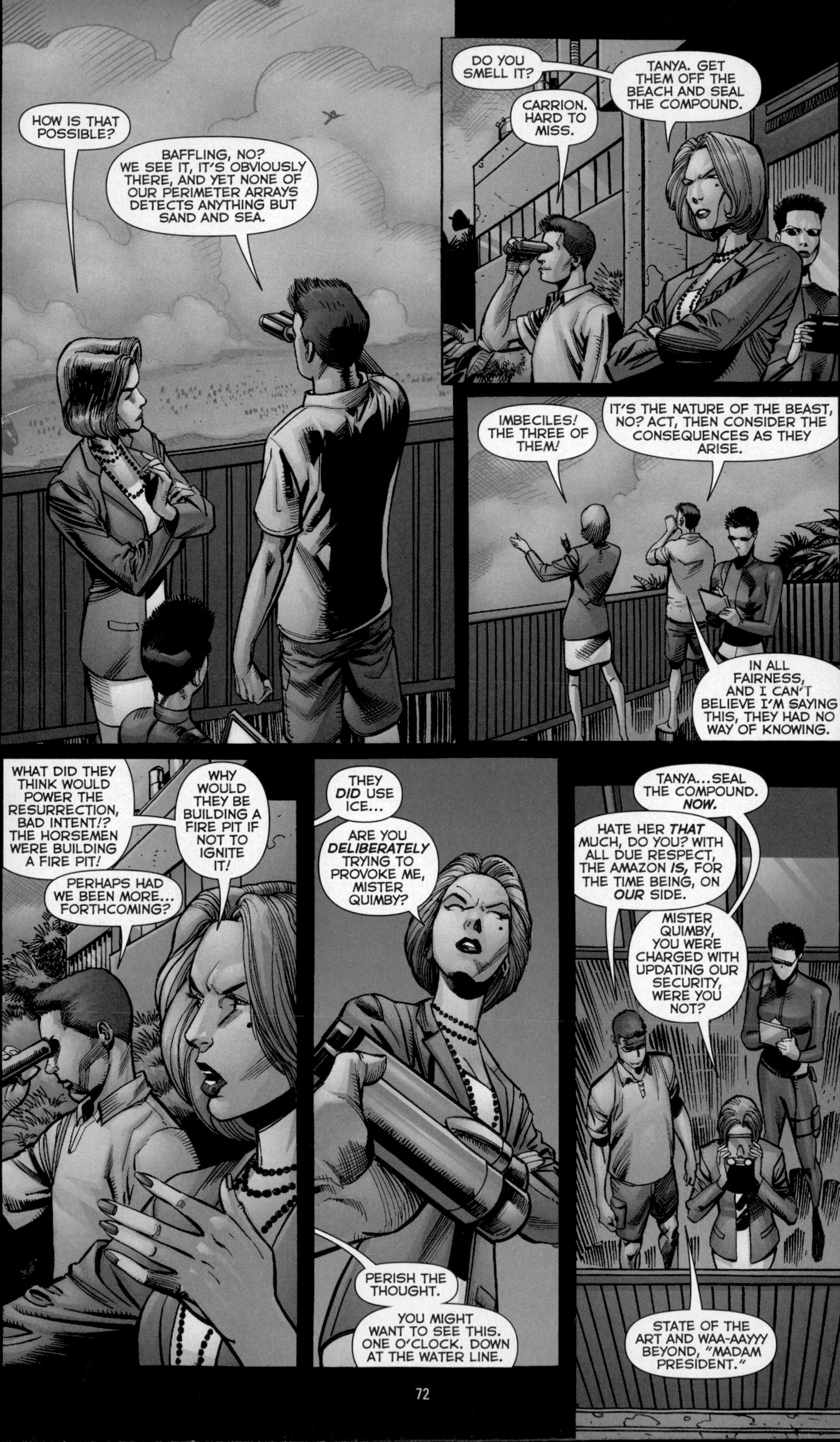
HOW IS THAT POSSIBLE?
BAFFLING, NO? WE SEE IT, IT'S OBVIOUSLY THERE, AND YET NONE OF OUR PERIMETER ARRAYS DETECTS ANYTHING BUT SAND AND SEA.
DO YOU SMELL IT?
CARRION. HARD TO MISS.
TANYA. GET THEM OFF THE BEACH AND SEAL THE COMPOUND.
IMBECILES! THE THREE OF THEM!
IT'S THE NATURE OF THE BEAST, NO? ACT, THEN CONSIDER THE CONSEQUENCES AS THEY ARISE.
IN ALL FAIRNESS, AND I CAN'T BELIEVE I'M SAYING THIS, THEY HAD NO WAY OF KNOWING.
WHAT DID THEY THINK WOULD POWER THE RESURRECTION, BAD INTENT!? THE HORSEMEN WERE BUILDING A FIRE PIT!
WHY WOULD THEY BE BUILDING A FIRE PIT IF NOT TO IGNITE IT!
PERHAPS HAD WE BEEN MORE... FORTHCOMING?
THEY *DID* USE ICE...
ARE YOU ***DELIBERATELY*** TRYING TO PROVOKE ME, MISTER QUIMBY?
PERISH THE THOUGHT.
YOU MIGHT WANT TO SEE THIS. ONE O'CLOCK. DOWN AT THE WATER LINE.
TANYA...SEAL THE COMPOUND. ***NOW.***
HATE HER *THAT* MUCH, DO YOU? WITH ALL DUE RESPECT, THE AMAZON *IS*, FOR THE TIME BEING, ON *OUR* SIDE.
MISTER QUIMBY, YOU WERE CHARGED WITH UPDATING OUR SECURITY, WERE YOU NOT?
STATE OF THE ART AND WAA-AAYYY BEYOND, "MADAM PRESIDENT."

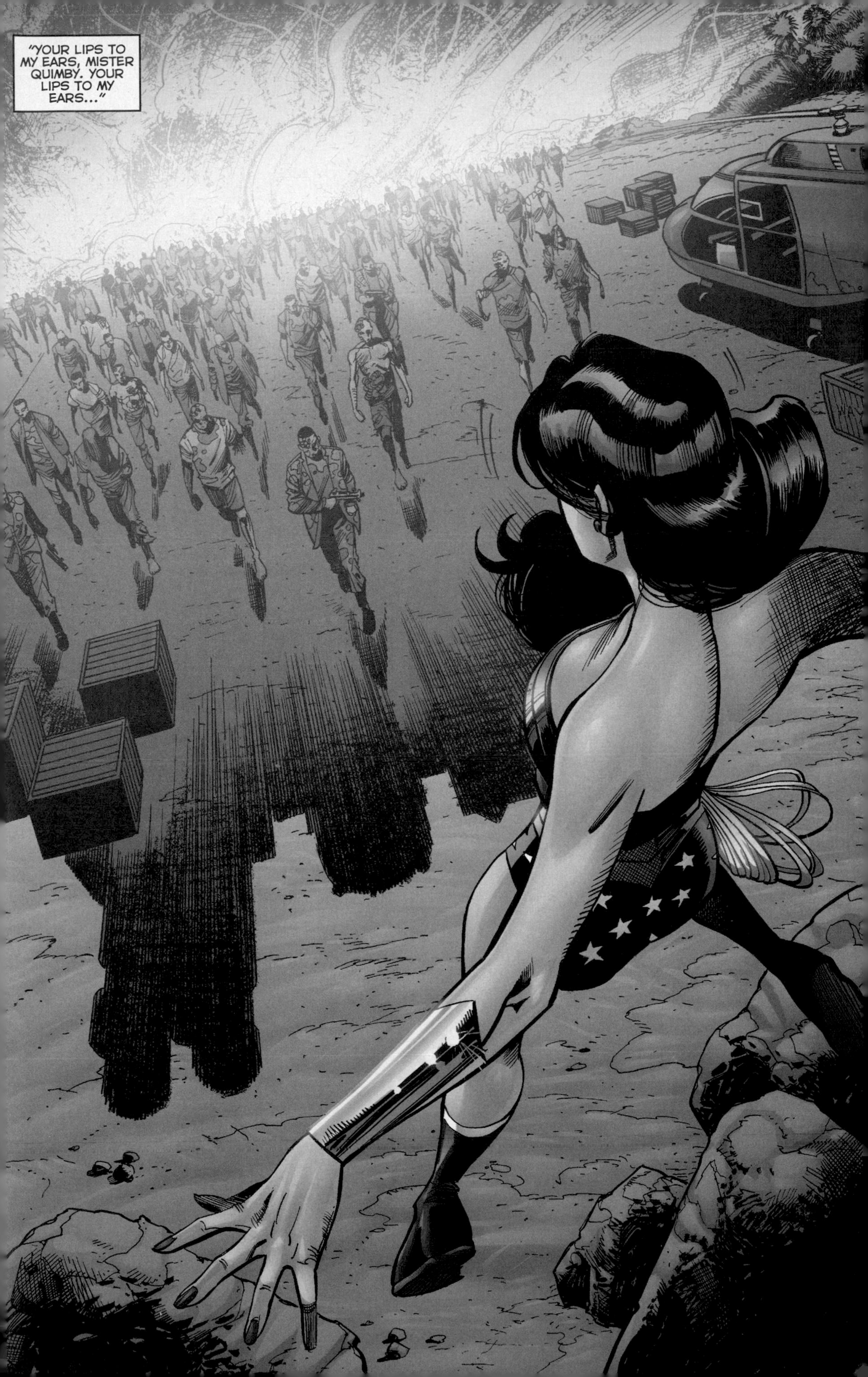
"YOUR LIPS TO MY EARS, MISTER QUIMBY. YOUR LIPS TO MY EARS..."

CHAPTER FOUR

SIEGE

Cover art by ETHAN VAN SCIVER

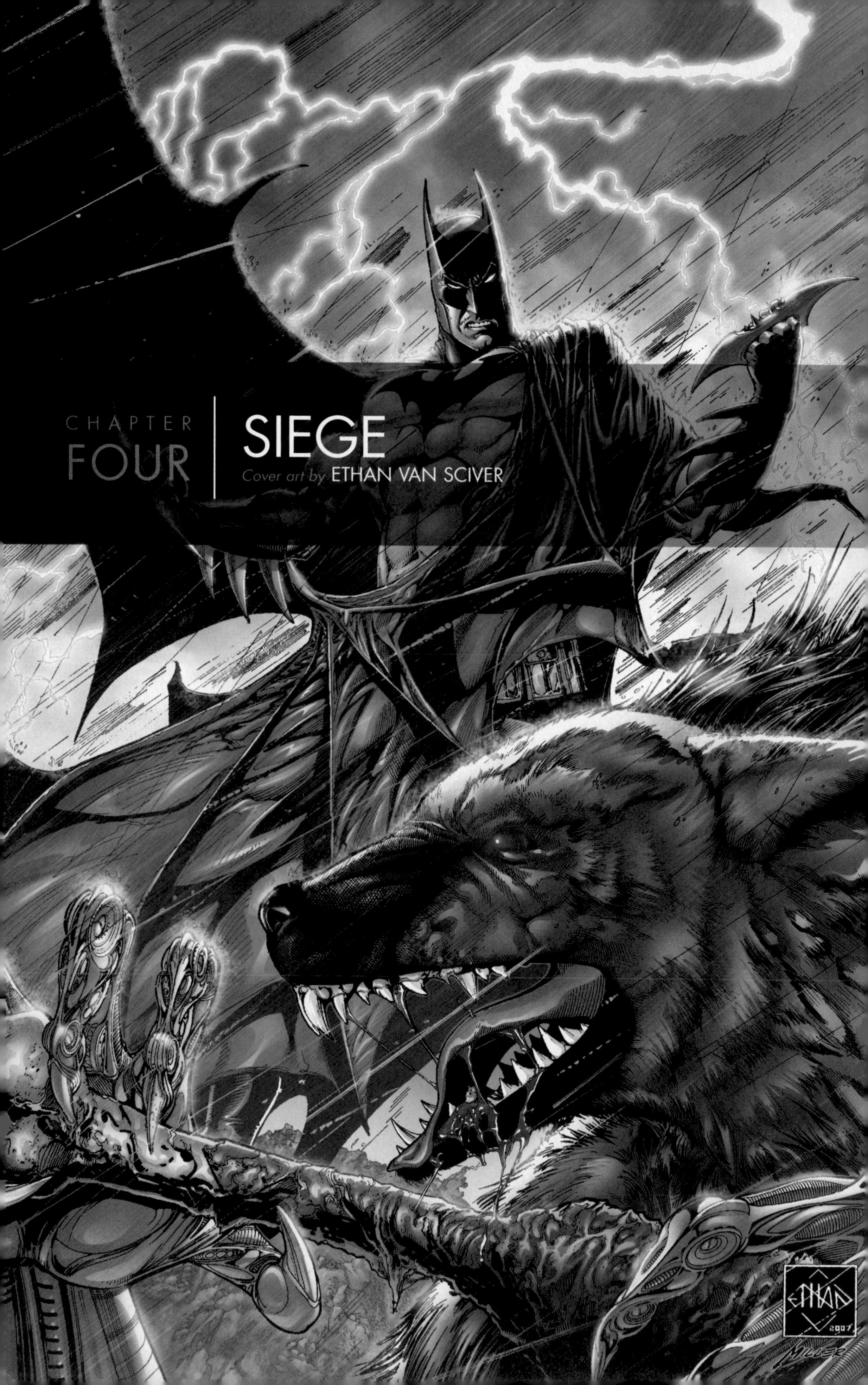

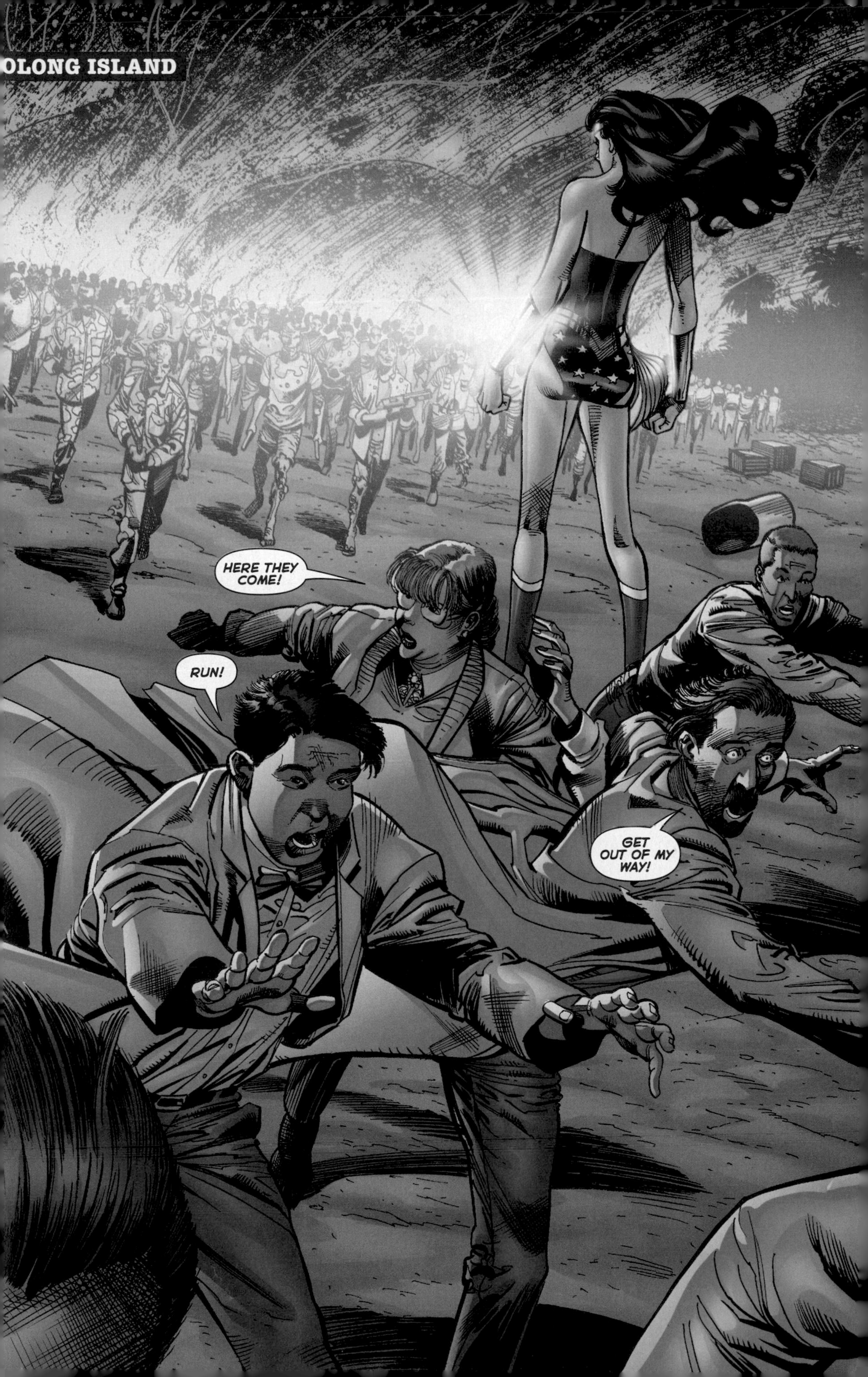

LONG ISLAND
HERE THEY COME!
RUN!
GET OUT OF MY WAY!

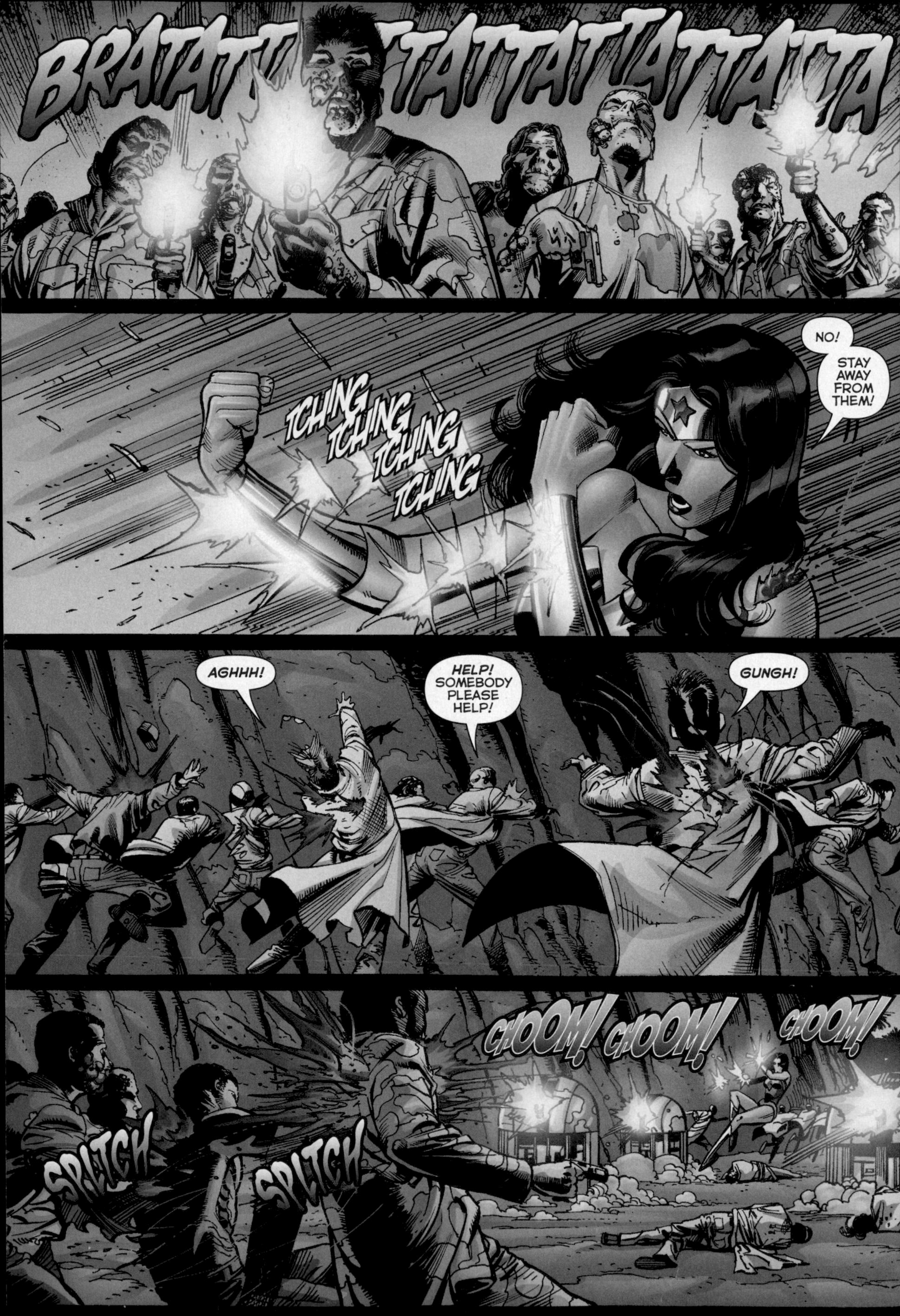
BRATATTATTATTATTATTA
NO!
STAY AWAY FROM THEM!
TCHING TCHING TCHING TCHING
AGHHH!
HELP! SOMEBODY PLEASE HELP!
GUNGH!
CHOOM! CHOOM! CHOOM!
SPLTCH SPLTCH

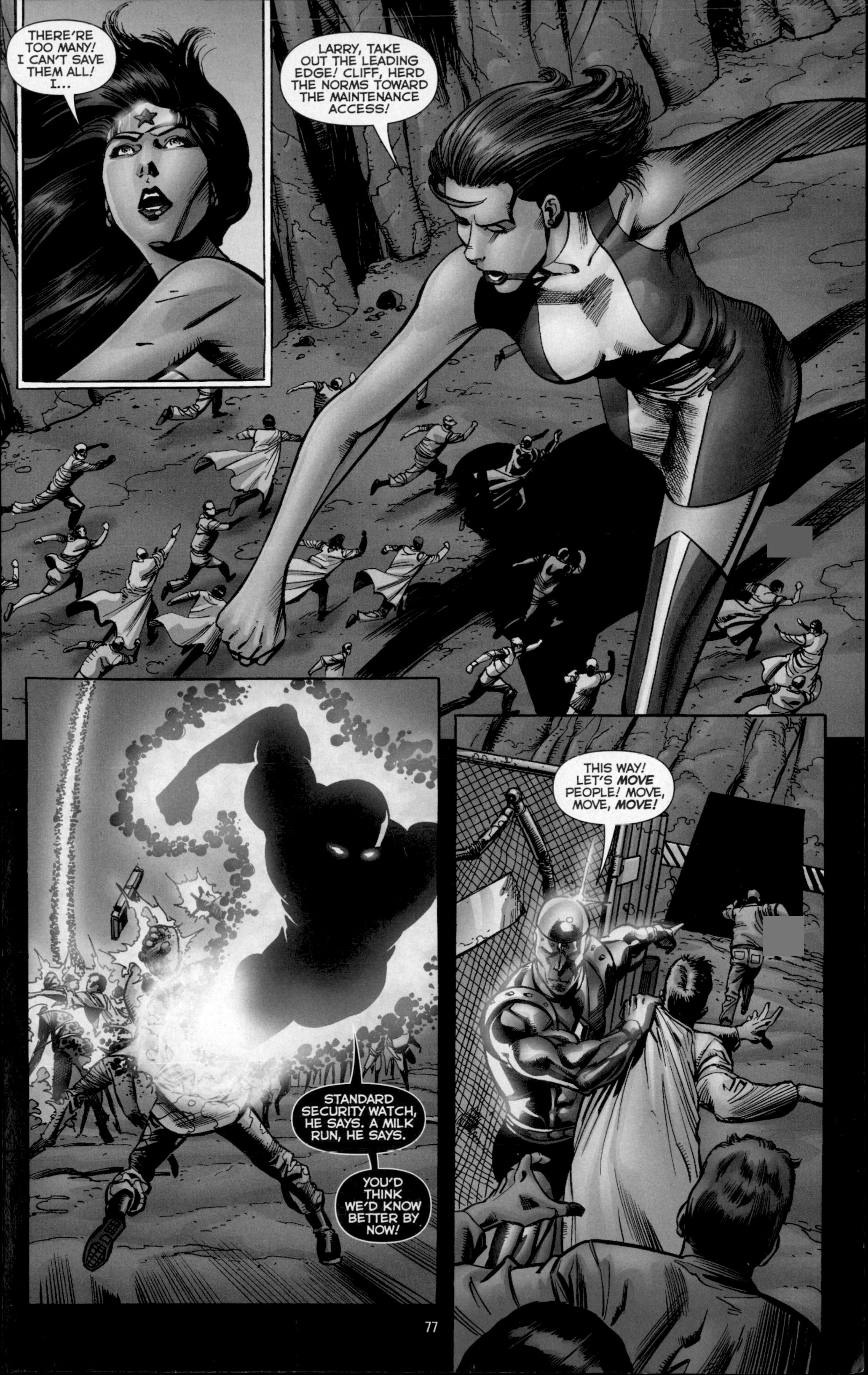
THERE'RE TOO MANY! I CAN'T SAVE THEM ALL! I...
LARRY, TAKE OUT THE LEADING EDGE! CLIFF, HERD THE NORMS TOWARD THE MAINTENANCE ACCESS!
STANDARD SECURITY WATCH, HE SAYS. A MILK RUN, HE SAYS.
YOU'D THINK WE'D KNOW BETTER BY NOW!
THIS WAY! LET'S MOVE PEOPLE! MOVE, MOVE, MOVE!

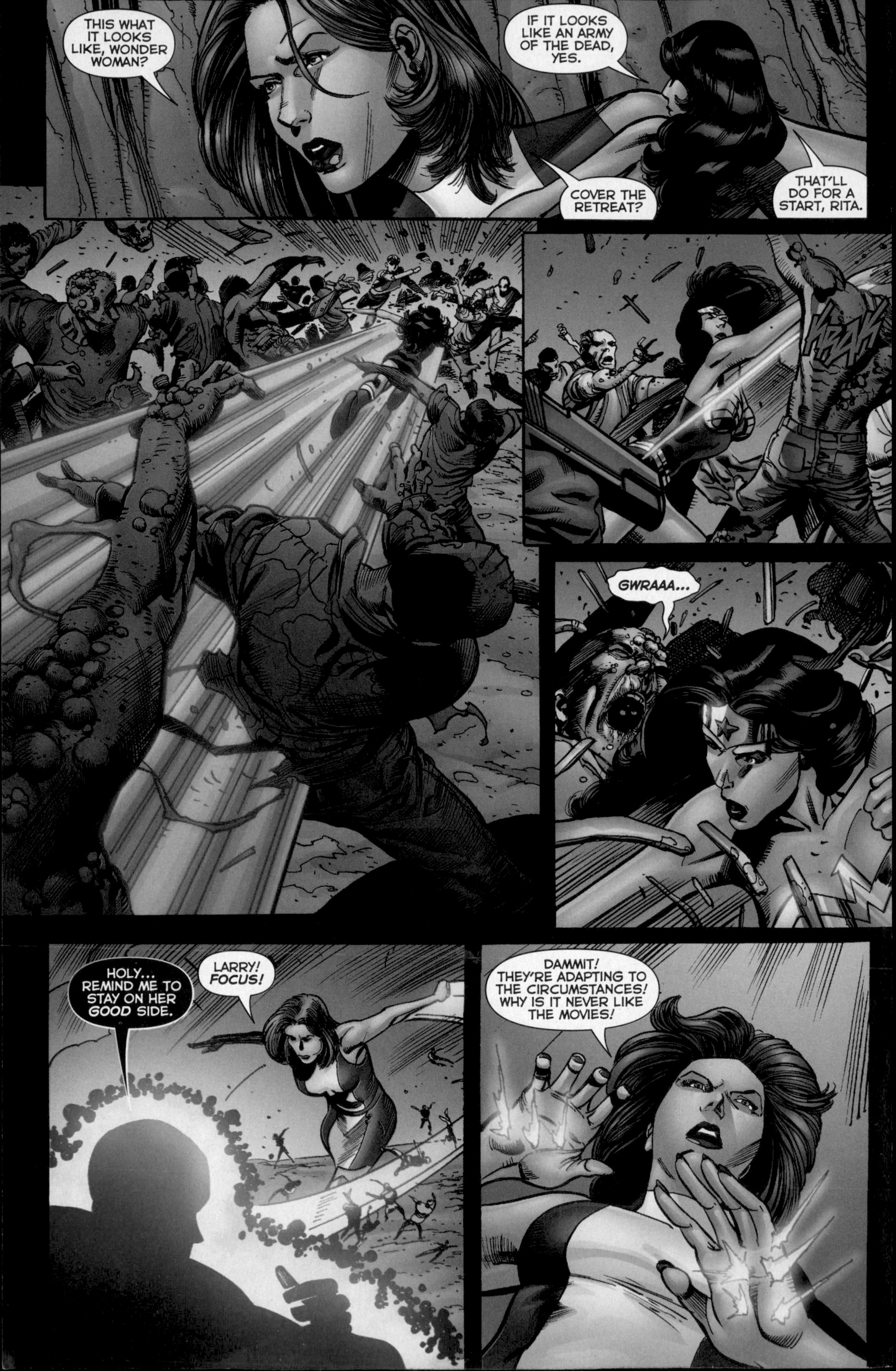
THIS WHAT IT LOOKS LIKE, WONDER WOMAN?
IF IT LOOKS LIKE AN ARMY OF THE DEAD, YES.
COVER THE RETREAT?
THAT'LL DO FOR A START, RITA.
GWRAAA...
HOLY... REMIND ME TO STAY ON HER GOOD SIDE.
LARRY! FOCUS!
DAMMIT! THEY'RE ADAPTING TO THE CIRCUMSTANCES! WHY IS IT NEVER LIKE THE MOVIES!

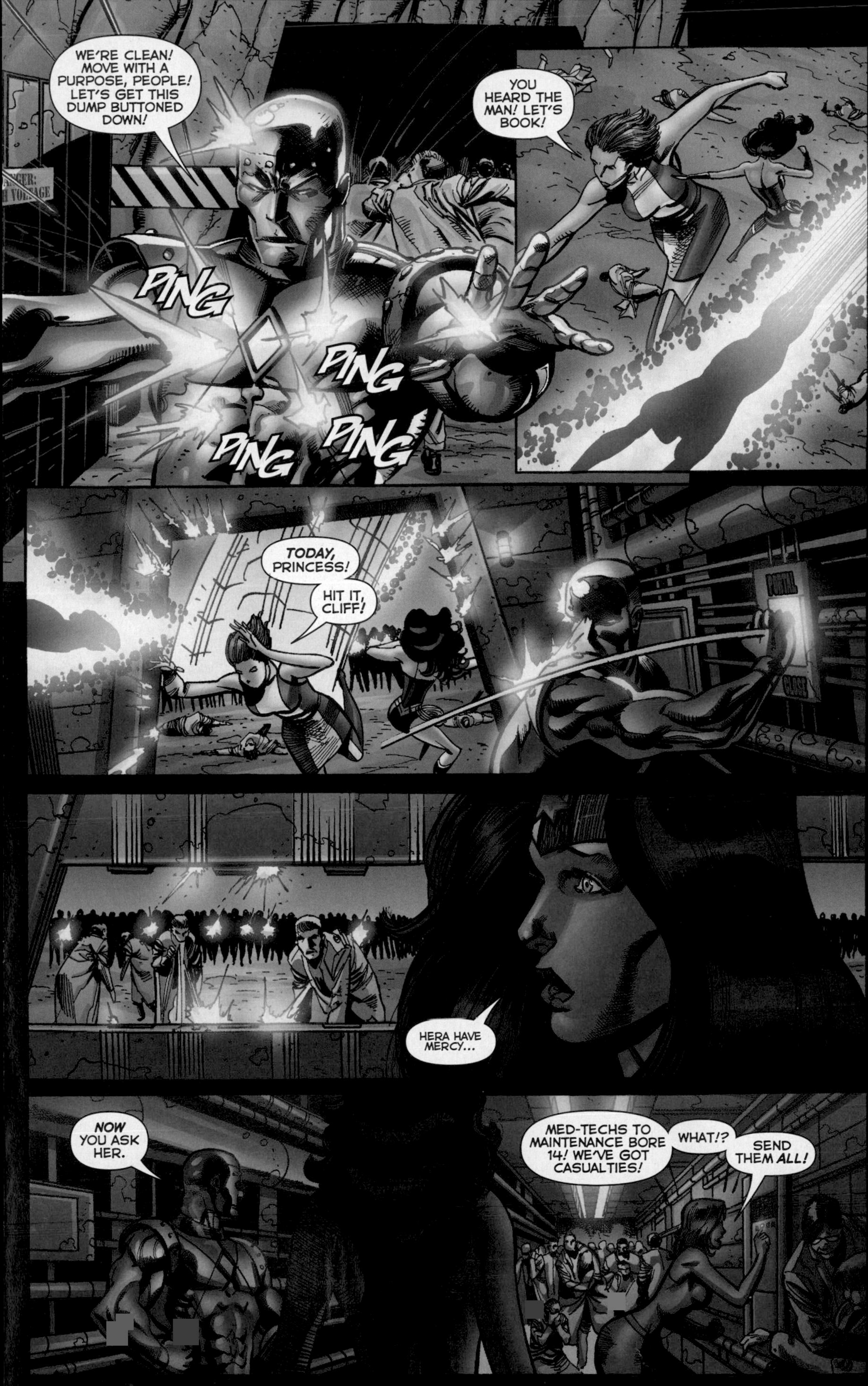
WE'RE CLEAN! MOVE WITH A PURPOSE, PEOPLE! LET'S GET THIS DUMP BUTTONED DOWN!
PING
PING
PING
PING
YOU HEARD THE MAN! LET'S BOOK!
TODAY, PRINCESS!
HIT IT, CLIFF!
PORTAL
CLOSE
HERA HAVE MERCY...
NOW YOU ASK HER.
MED-TECHS TO MAINTENANCE BORE 14! WE'VE GOT CASUALTIES!
WHAT!?
SEND THEM ALL!

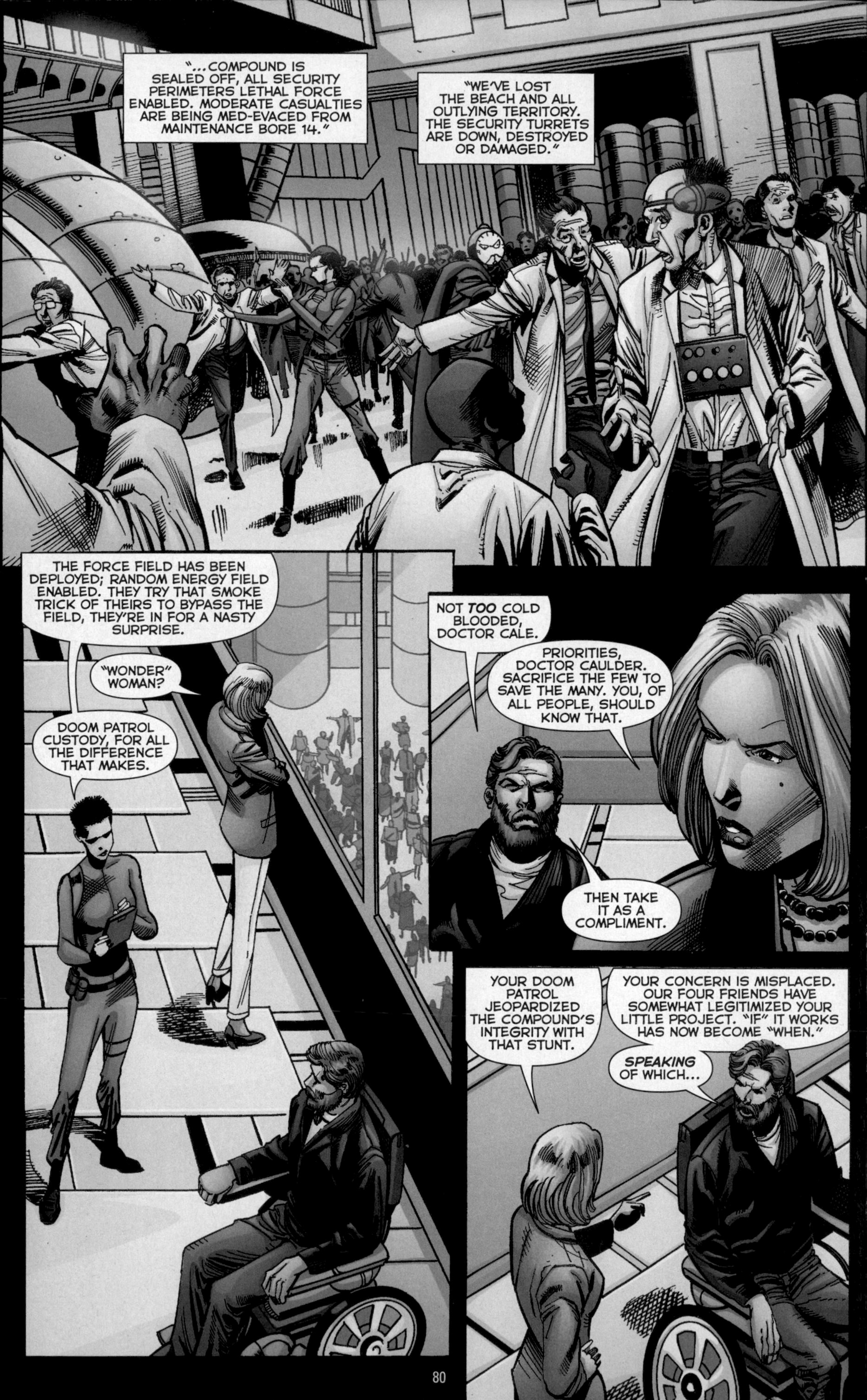
"...COMPOUND IS SEALED OFF, ALL SECURITY PERIMETERS LETHAL FORCE ENABLED. MODERATE CASUALTIES ARE BEING MED-EVACED FROM MAINTENANCE BORE 14."
"WE'VE LOST THE BEACH AND ALL OUTLYING TERRITORY. THE SECURITY TURRETS ARE DOWN, DESTROYED OR DAMAGED."
THE FORCE FIELD HAS BEEN DEPLOYED; RANDOM ENERGY FIELD ENABLED. THEY TRY THAT SMOKE TRICK OF THEIRS TO BYPASS THE FIELD, THEY'RE IN FOR A NASTY SURPRISE.
"WONDER" WOMAN?
DOOM PATROL CUSTODY, FOR ALL THE DIFFERENCE THAT MAKES.
NOT *TOO* COLD BLOODED, DOCTOR CALE.
PRIORITIES, DOCTOR CAULDER. SACRIFICE THE FEW TO SAVE THE MANY. YOU, OF ALL PEOPLE, SHOULD KNOW THAT.
THEN TAKE IT AS A COMPLIMENT.
YOUR DOOM PATROL JEOPARDIZED THE COMPOUND'S INTEGRITY WITH THAT STUNT.
YOUR CONCERN IS MISPLACED. OUR FOUR FRIENDS HAVE SOMEWHAT LEGITIMIZED YOUR LITTLE PROJECT. "IF" IT WORKS HAS NOW BECOME "WHEN."
SPEAKING OF WHICH...

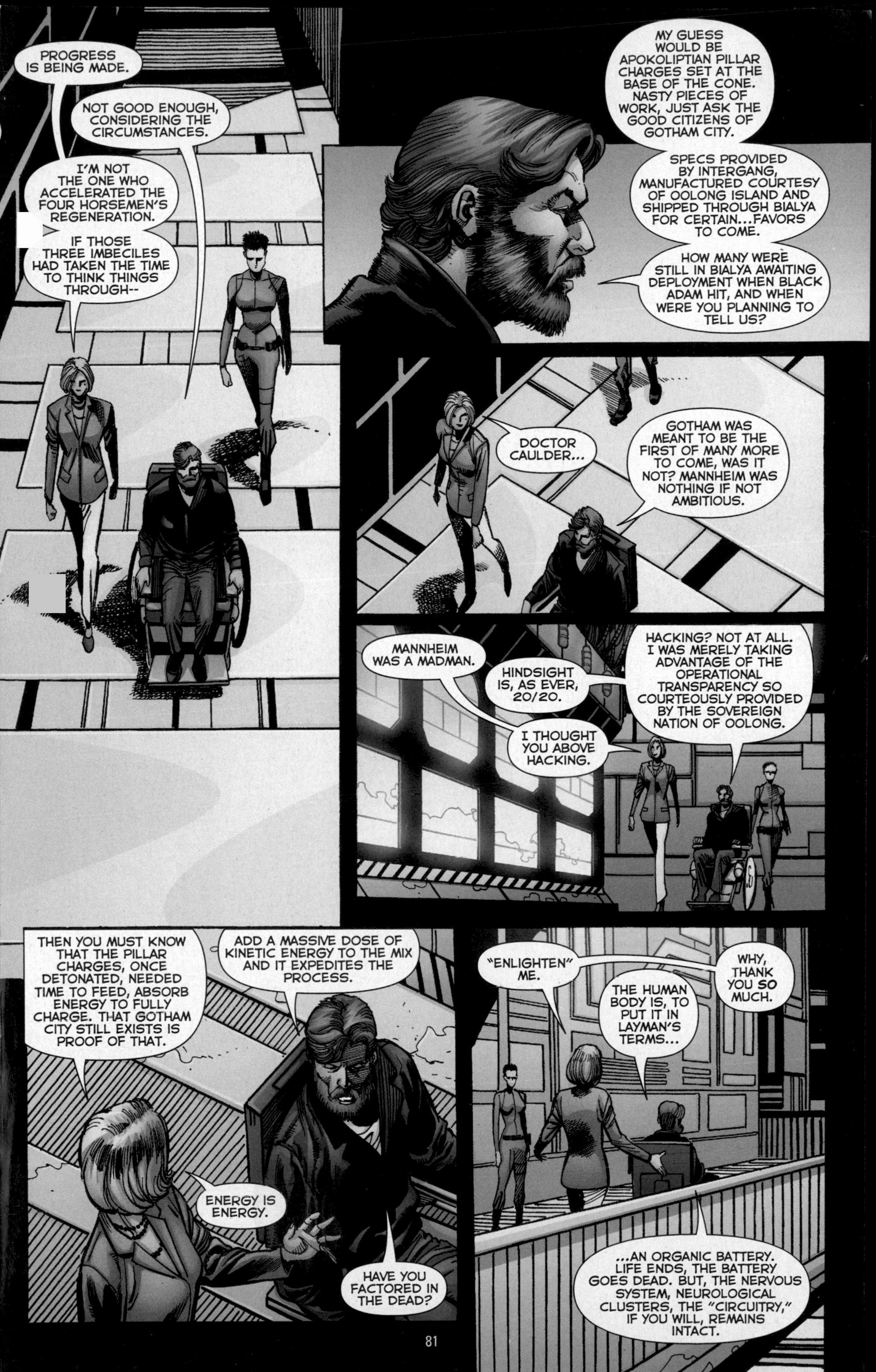
PROGRESS IS BEING MADE.
NOT GOOD ENOUGH, CONSIDERING THE CIRCUMSTANCES.
I'M NOT THE ONE WHO ACCELERATED THE FOUR HORSEMEN'S REGENERATION.
IF THOSE THREE IMBECILES HAD TAKEN THE TIME TO THINK THINGS THROUGH--
MY GUESS WOULD BE APOKOLIPTIAN PILLAR CHARGES SET AT THE BASE OF THE CONE. NASTY PIECES OF WORK, JUST ASK THE GOOD CITIZENS OF GOTHAM CITY.
SPECS PROVIDED BY INTERGANG, MANUFACTURED COURTESY OF OOLONG ISLAND AND SHIPPED THROUGH BIALYA FOR CERTAIN...FAVORS TO COME.
HOW MANY WERE STILL IN BIALYA AWAITING DEPLOYMENT WHEN BLACK ADAM HIT, AND WHEN WERE YOU PLANNING TO TELL US?
DOCTOR CAULDER...
GOTHAM WAS MEANT TO BE THE FIRST OF MANY MORE TO COME, WAS IT NOT? MANNHEIM WAS NOTHING IF NOT AMBITIOUS.
MANNHEIM WAS A MADMAN.
HINDSIGHT IS, AS EVER, 20/20.
I THOUGHT YOU ABOVE HACKING.
HACKING? NOT AT ALL. I WAS MERELY TAKING ADVANTAGE OF THE OPERATIONAL TRANSPARENCY SO COURTEOUSLY PROVIDED BY THE SOVEREIGN NATION OF OOLONG.
THEN YOU MUST KNOW THAT THE PILLAR CHARGES, ONCE DETONATED, NEEDED TIME TO FEED, ABSORB ENERGY TO FULLY CHARGE. THAT GOTHAM CITY STILL EXISTS IS PROOF OF THAT.
ADD A MASSIVE DOSE OF KINETIC ENERGY TO THE MIX AND IT EXPEDITES THE PROCESS.
ENERGY IS ENERGY.
HAVE YOU FACTORED IN THE DEAD?
"ENLIGHTEN" ME.
WHY, THANK YOU SO MUCH.
THE HUMAN BODY IS, TO PUT IT IN LAYMAN'S TERMS...
...AN ORGANIC BATTERY. LIFE ENDS, THE BATTERY GOES DEAD. BUT, THE NERVOUS SYSTEM, NEUROLOGICAL CLUSTERS, THE "CIRCUITRY," IF YOU WILL, REMAINS INTACT.

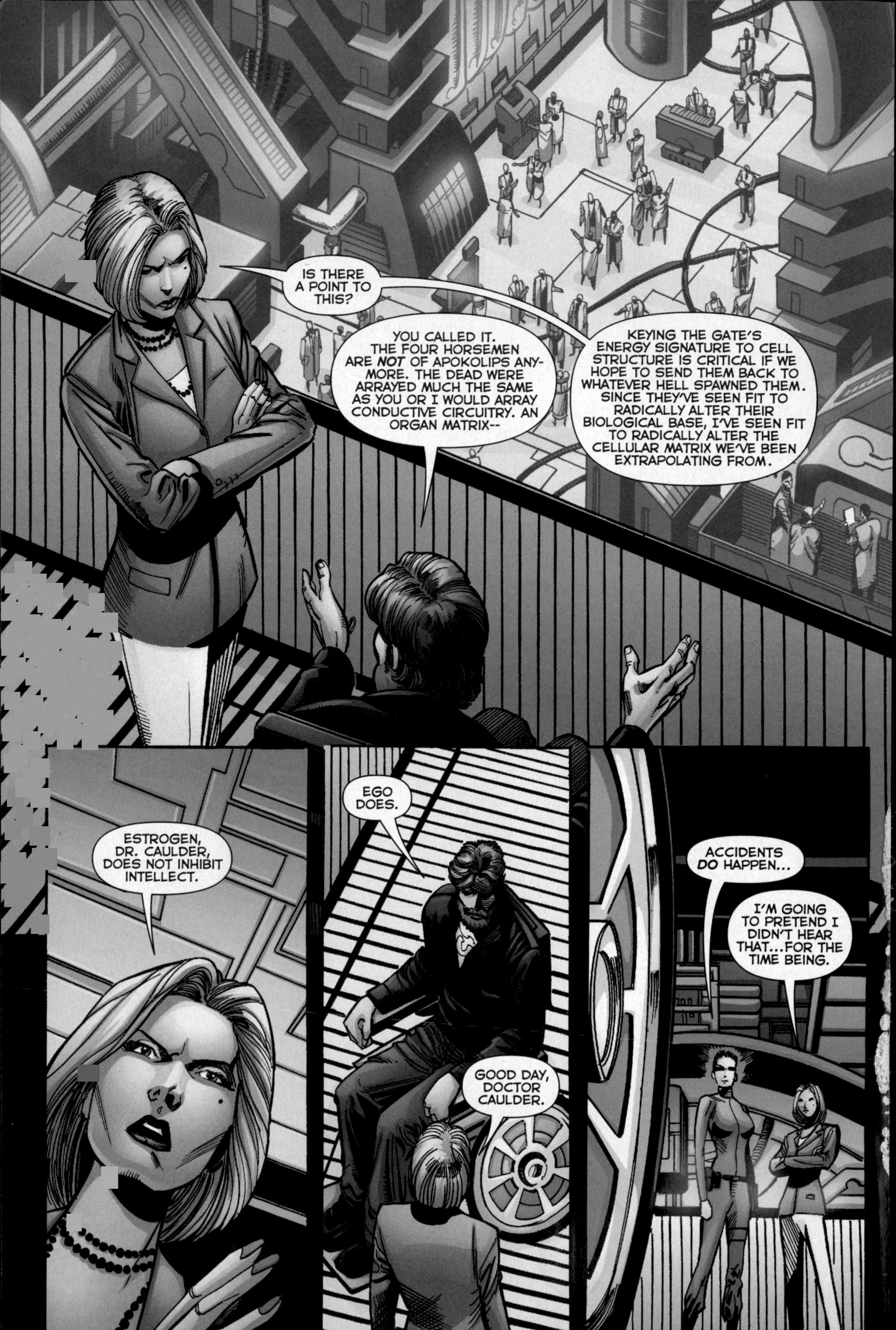
IS THERE A POINT TO THIS?
YOU CALLED IT. THE FOUR HORSEMEN ARE **NOT** OF APOKOLIPS ANYMORE. THE DEAD WERE ARRAYED MUCH THE SAME AS YOU OR I WOULD ARRAY CONDUCTIVE CIRCUITRY. AN ORGAN MATRIX--
KEYING THE GATE'S ENERGY SIGNATURE TO CELL STRUCTURE IS CRITICAL IF WE HOPE TO SEND THEM BACK TO WHATEVER HELL SPAWNED THEM. SINCE THEY'VE SEEN FIT TO RADICALLY ALTER THEIR BIOLOGICAL BASE, I'VE SEEN FIT TO RADICALLY ALTER THE CELLULAR MATRIX WE'VE BEEN EXTRAPOLATING FROM.
ESTROGEN, DR. CAULDER, DOES NOT INHIBIT INTELLECT.
EGO DOES.
GOOD DAY, DOCTOR CAULDER.
ACCIDENTS **DO** HAPPEN...
I'M GOING TO PRETEND I DIDN'T HEAR THAT...FOR THE TIME BEING.

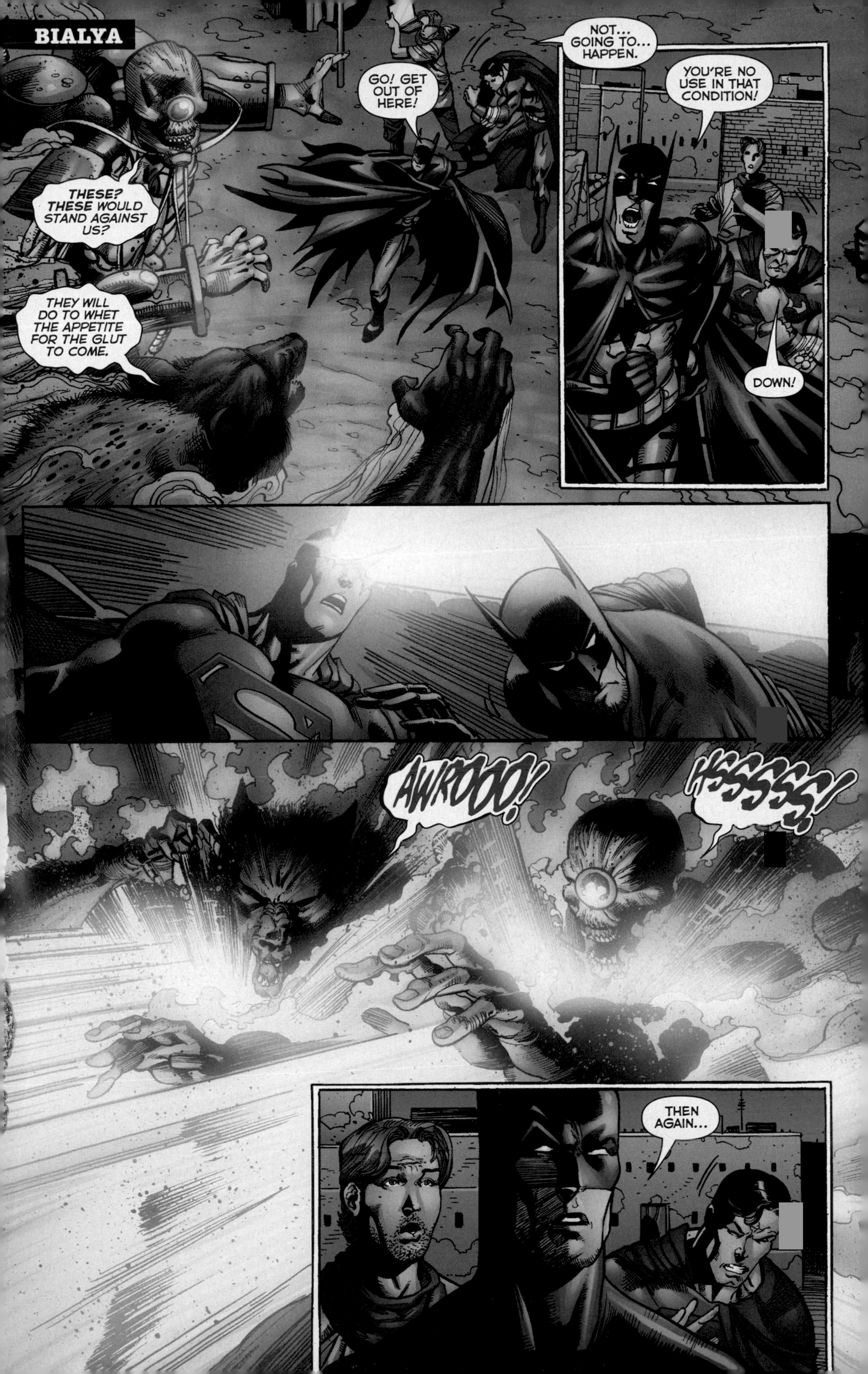
BIALYA
THESE? THESE WOULD STAND AGAINST US?
THEY WILL DO TO WHET THE APPETITE FOR THE GLUT TO COME.
GO! GET OUT OF HERE!
NOT... GOING TO... HAPPEN.
YOU'RE NO USE IN THAT CONDITION!
DOWN!
AWROOO!
HSSSSS!
THEN AGAIN...

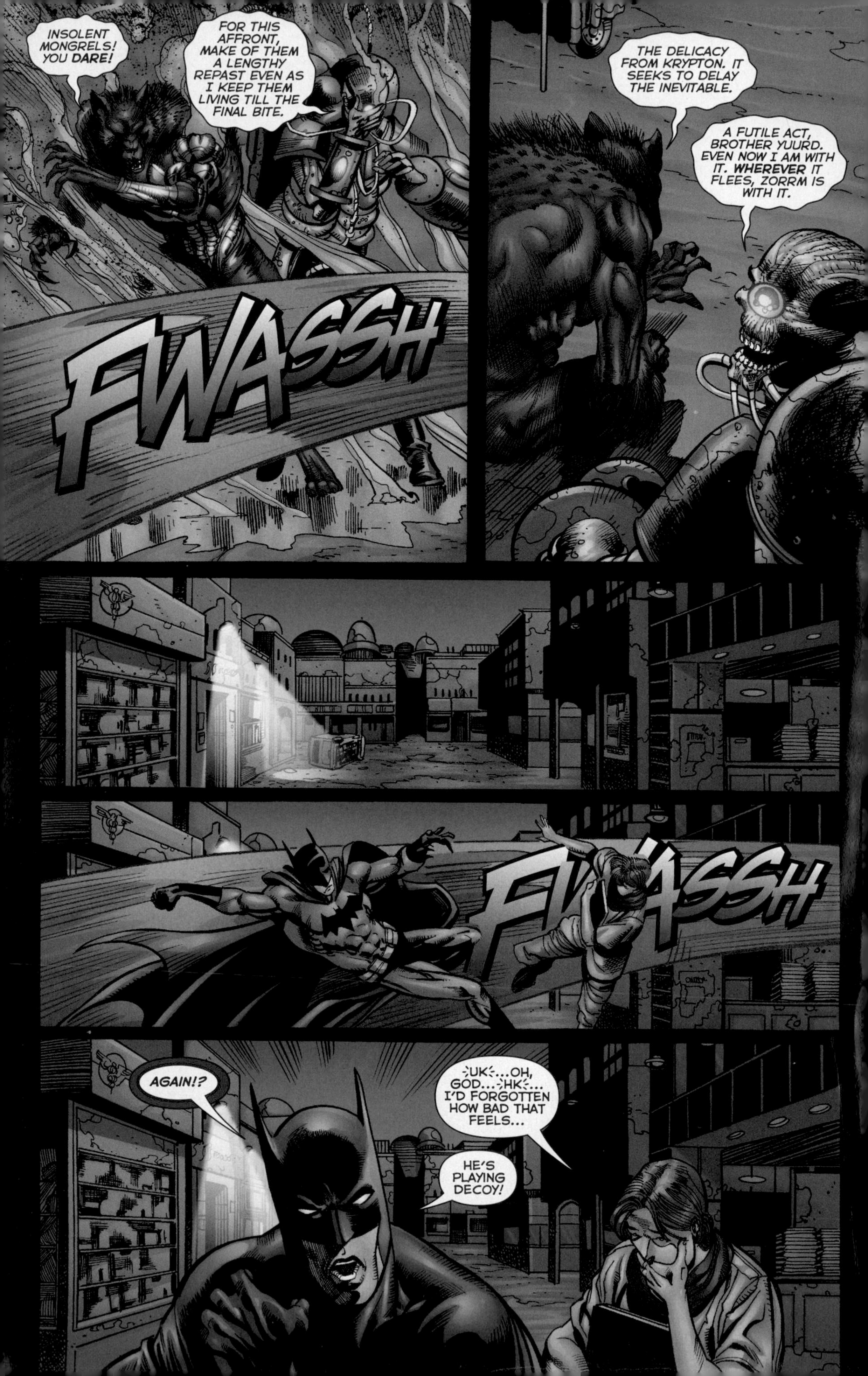
INSOLENT MONGRELS! YOU DARE!
FOR THIS AFFRONT, MAKE OF THEM A LENGTHY REPAST EVEN AS I KEEP THEM LIVING TILL THE FINAL BITE.
FWASSH
THE DELICACY FROM KRYPTON. IT SEEKS TO DELAY THE INEVITABLE.
A FUTILE ACT, BROTHER YUURD. EVEN NOW I AM WITH IT. WHEREVER IT FLEES, ZORRM IS WITH IT.
FWASSH
AGAIN!?
UK...OH, GOD...HK... I'D FORGOTTEN HOW BAD THAT FEELS...
HE'S PLAYING DECOY!

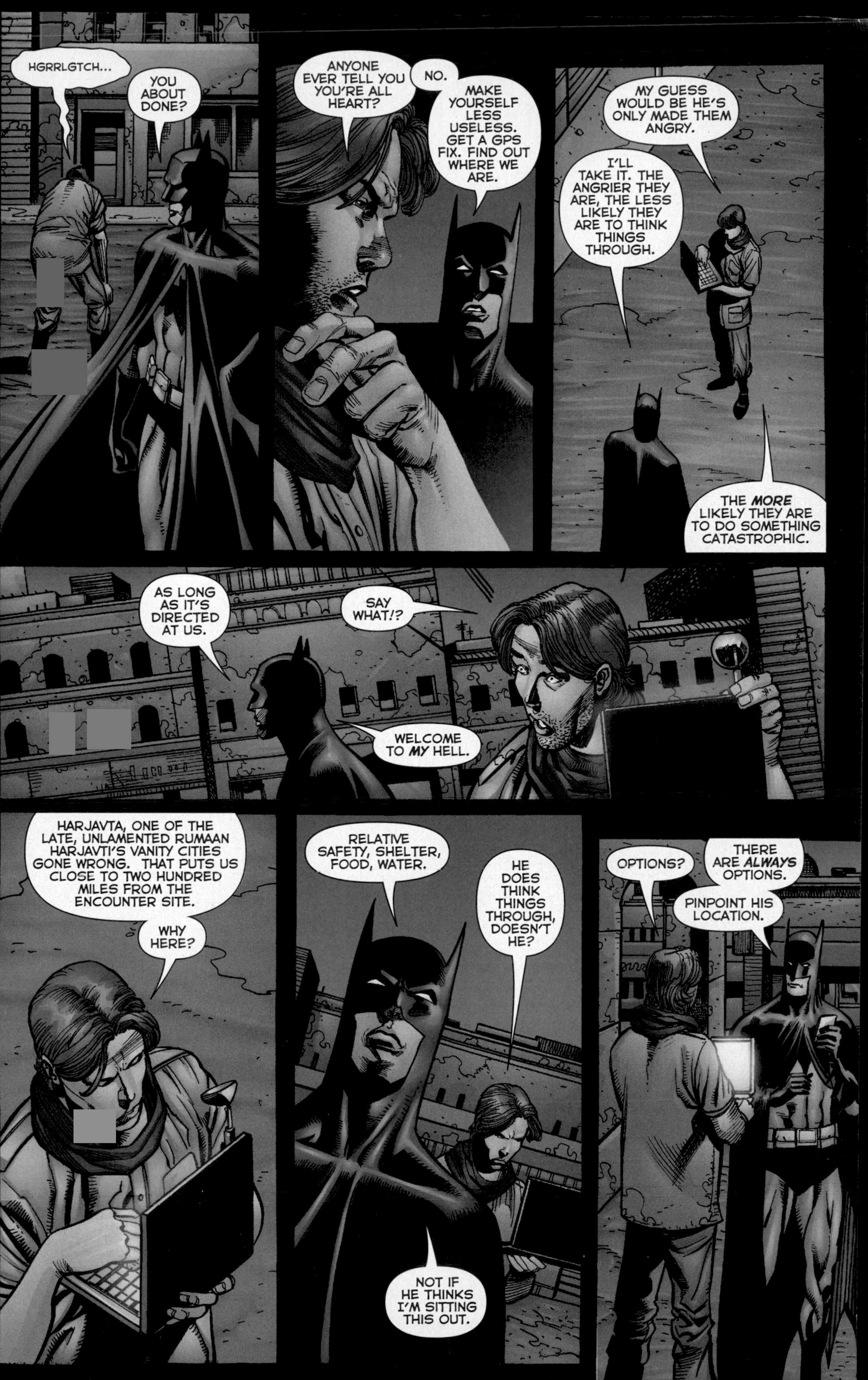
HGRRLGTCH...
YOU ABOUT DONE?
ANYONE EVER TELL YOU YOU'RE ALL HEART?
NO.
MAKE YOURSELF LESS USELESS. GET A GPS FIX. FIND OUT WHERE WE ARE.
MY GUESS WOULD BE HE'S ONLY MADE THEM ANGRY.
I'LL TAKE IT. THE ANGRIER THEY ARE, THE LESS LIKELY THEY ARE TO THINK THINGS THROUGH.
THE *MORE* LIKELY THEY ARE TO DO SOMETHING CATASTROPHIC.
AS LONG AS IT'S DIRECTED AT US.
SAY WHAT!?
WELCOME TO *MY* HELL.
HARJAVTA, ONE OF THE LATE, UNLAMENTED RUMAAN HARJAVTI'S VANITY CITIES GONE WRONG. THAT PUTS US CLOSE TO TWO HUNDRED MILES FROM THE ENCOUNTER SITE.
WHY HERE?
RELATIVE SAFETY, SHELTER, FOOD, WATER.
HE DOES THINK THINGS THROUGH, DOESN'T HE?
NOT IF HE THINKS I'M SITTING THIS OUT.
OPTIONS?
THERE ARE *ALWAYS* OPTIONS.
PINPOINT HIS LOCATION.

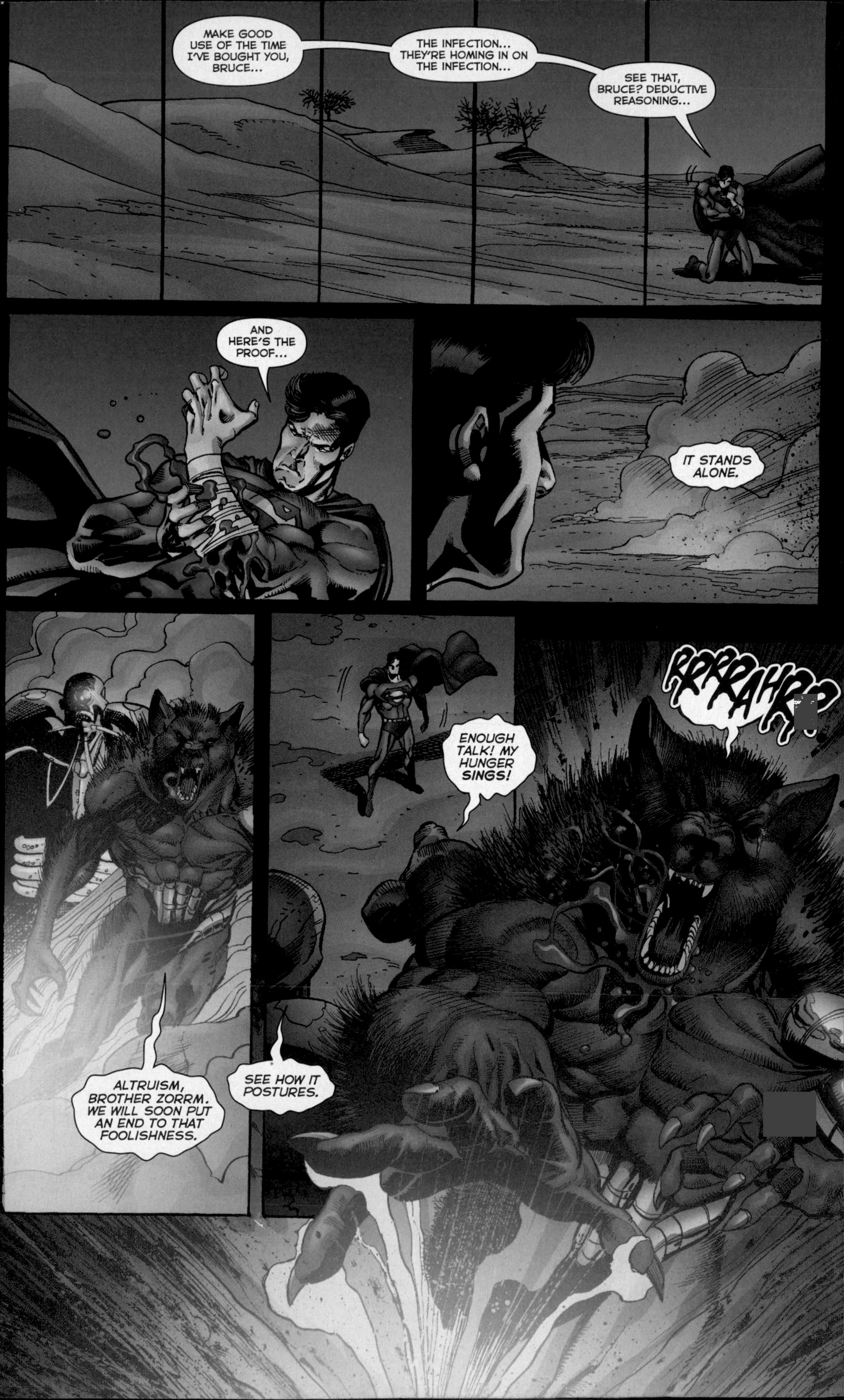
MAKE GOOD USE OF THE TIME I'VE BOUGHT YOU, BRUCE...
THE INFECTION... THEY'RE HOMING IN ON THE INFECTION...
SEE THAT, BRUCE? DEDUCTIVE REASONING...
AND HERE'S THE PROOF...
IT STANDS ALONE.
ENOUGH TALK! MY HUNGER SINGS!
RRRRAHR
ALTRUISM, BROTHER ZORRM. WE WILL SOON PUT AN END TO THAT FOOLISHNESS.
SEE HOW IT POSTURES.

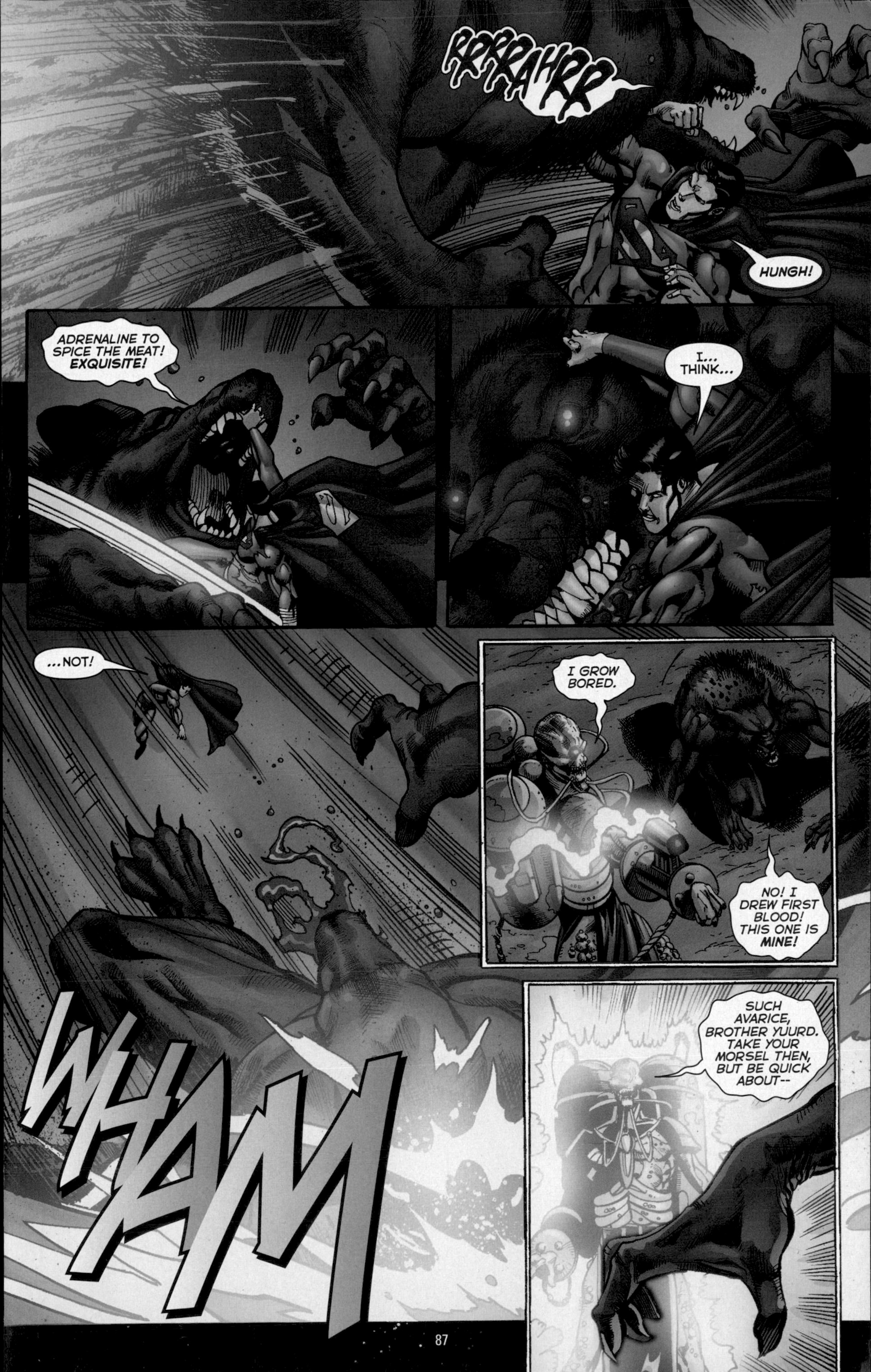
RRRRAHRR
HUNGH!
ADRENALINE TO SPICE THE MEAT! **EXQUISITE!**
I... THINK...
...NOT!
I GROW BORED.
NO! I DREW FIRST BLOOD! THIS ONE IS **MINE!**
SUCH AVARICE, BROTHER YUURD. TAKE YOUR MORSEL THEN, BUT BE QUICK ABOUT--
WHAM

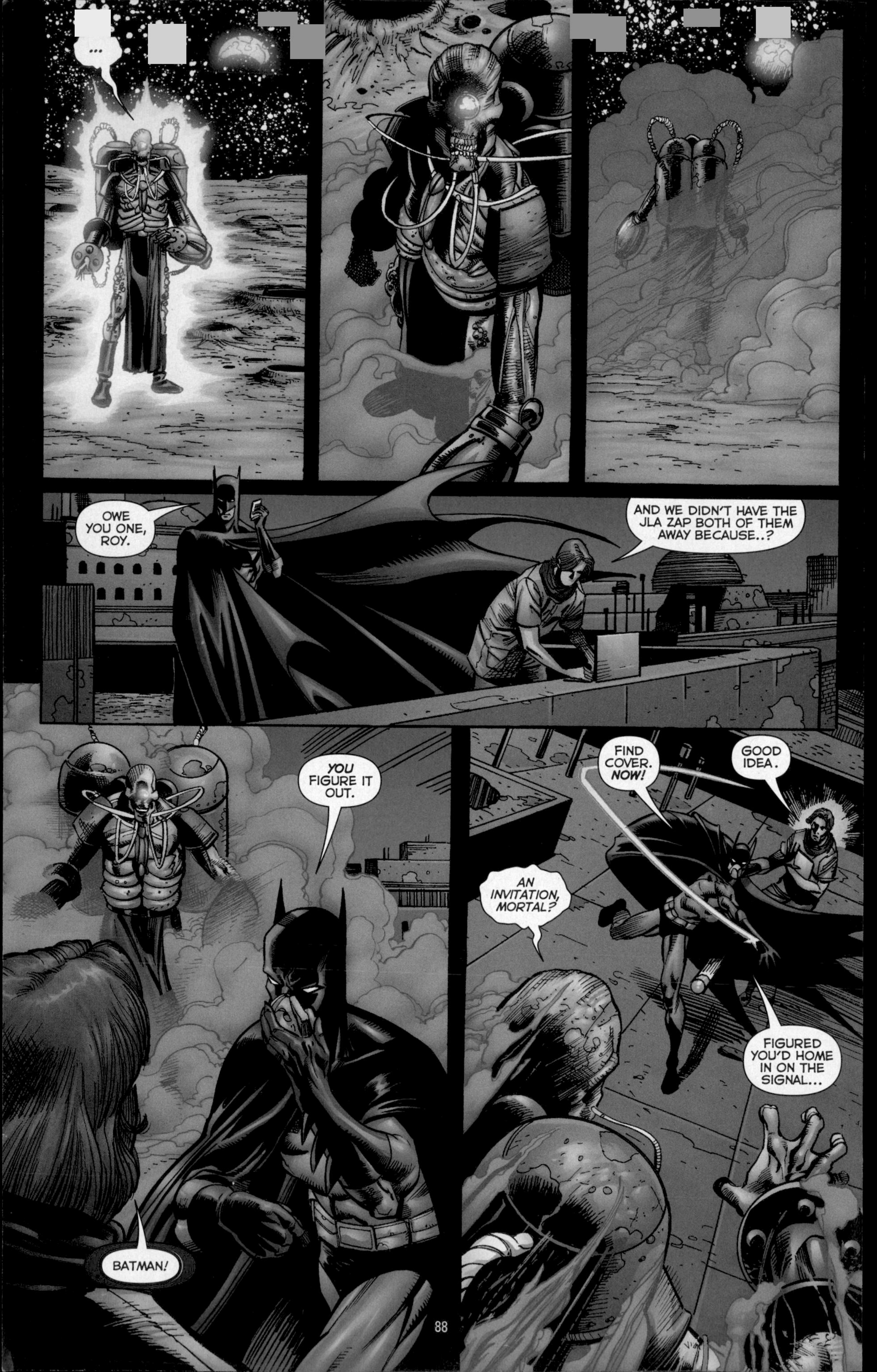
...
OWE YOU ONE, ROY.
AND WE DIDN'T HAVE THE JLA ZAP BOTH OF THEM AWAY BECAUSE..?
YOU FIGURE IT OUT.
BATMAN!
FIND COVER. *NOW!*
GOOD IDEA.
AN INVITATION, MORTAL?
FIGURED YOU'D HOME IN ON THE SIGNAL...

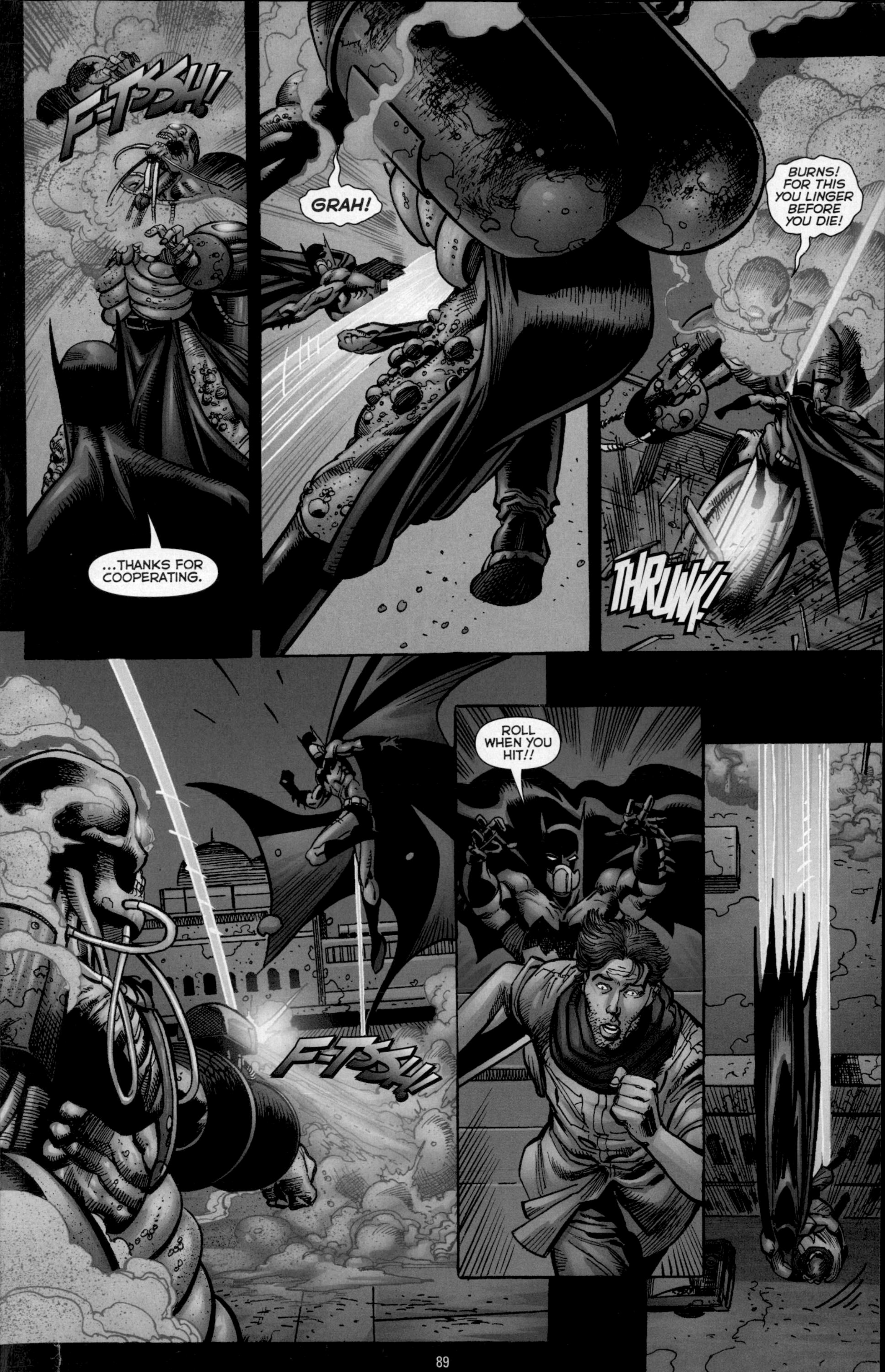
F-TSSH!
...THANKS FOR COOPERATING.
GRAH!
BURNS! FOR THIS YOU LINGER BEFORE YOU DIE!
THRUNK!
F-TSSH!!
ROLL WHEN YOU HIT!!

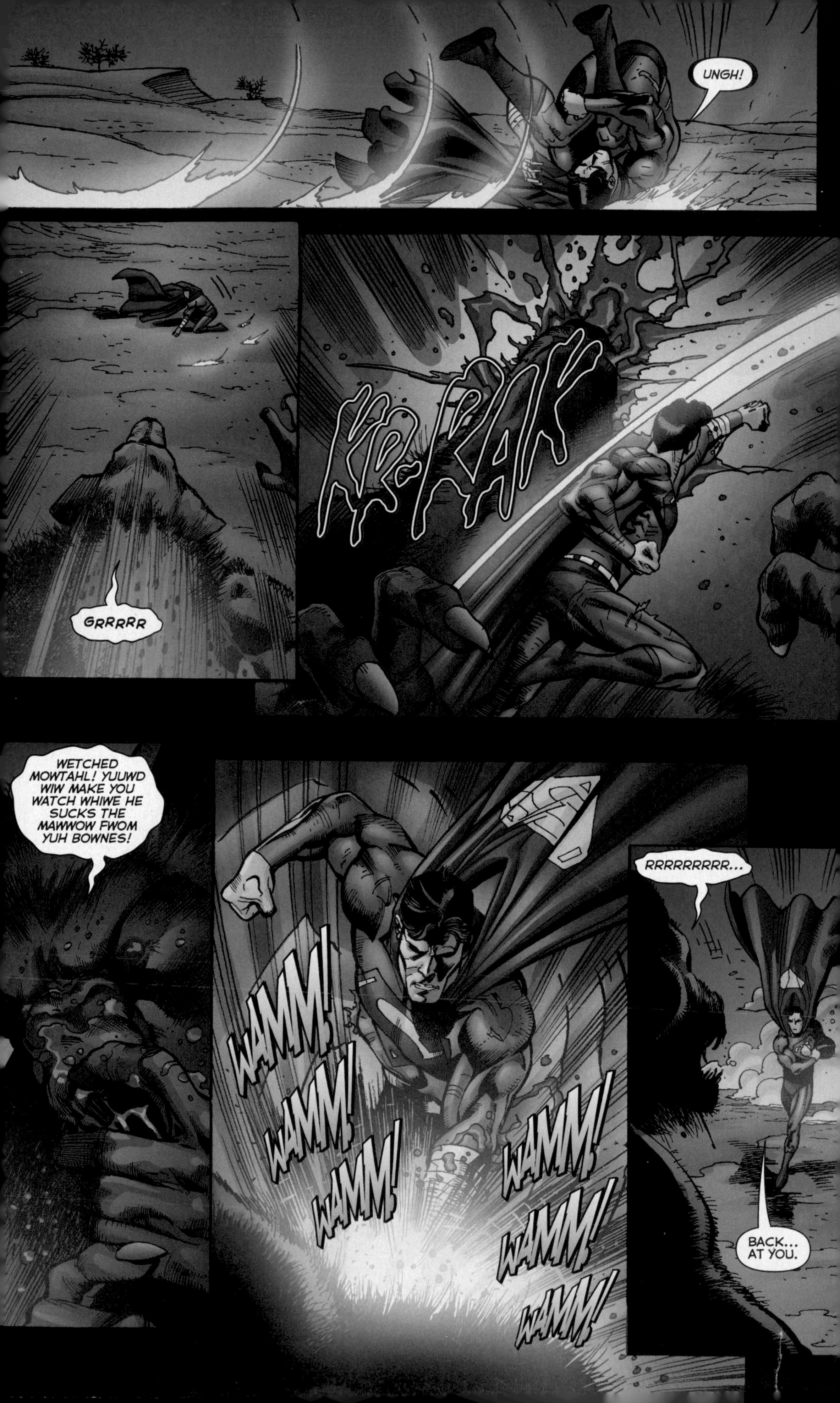
UNGH!
GRRRRR
KRR-RAK
WETCHED MOWTAHL! YUUWD WIW MAKE YOU WATCH WHIWE HE SUCKS THE MAWWOW FWOM YUH BOWNES!
WAMM! WAMM! WAMM! WAMM!
WAMM! WAMM! WAMM!
RRRRRRRRR...
BACK... AT YOU.

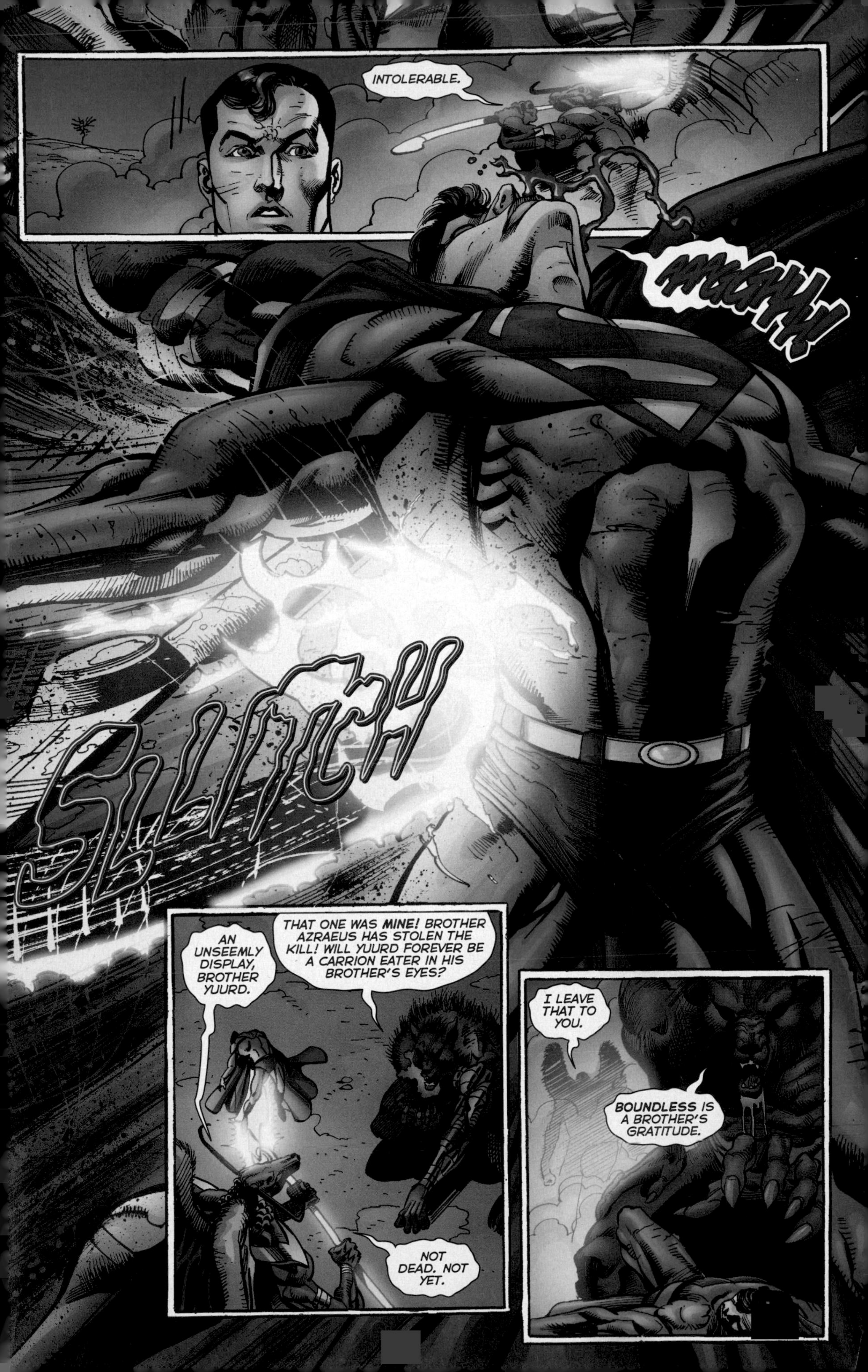
INTOLERABLE.
SSLUNCH
AN UNSEEMLY DISPLAY, BROTHER YUURD.
THAT ONE WAS MINE! BROTHER AZRAEUS HAS STOLEN THE KILL! WILL YUURD FOREVER BE A CARRION EATER IN HIS BROTHER'S EYES?
NOT DEAD. NOT YET.
I LEAVE THAT TO YOU.
BOUNDLESS IS A BROTHER'S GRATITUDE.

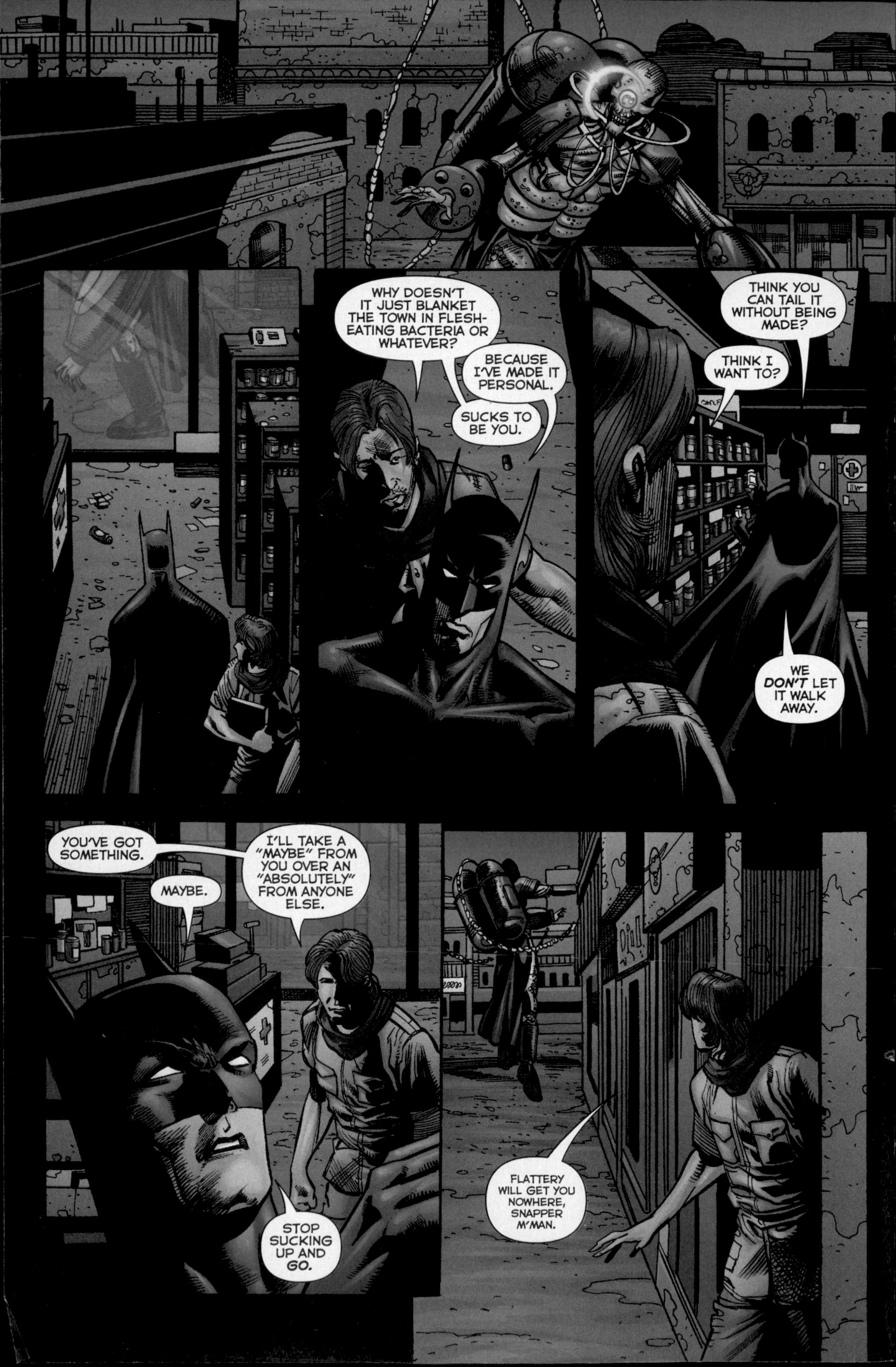
WHY DOESN'T IT JUST BLANKET THE TOWN IN FLESH-EATING BACTERIA OR WHATEVER?
BECAUSE I'VE MADE IT PERSONAL.
SUCKS TO BE YOU.
THINK YOU CAN TAIL IT WITHOUT BEING MADE?
THINK I WANT TO?
WE DON'T LET IT WALK AWAY.
YOU'VE GOT SOMETHING.
MAYBE.
I'LL TAKE A "MAYBE" FROM YOU OVER AN "ABSOLUTELY" FROM ANYONE ELSE.
STOP SUCKING UP AND GO.
FLATTERY WILL GET YOU NOWHERE, SNAPPER M'MAN.

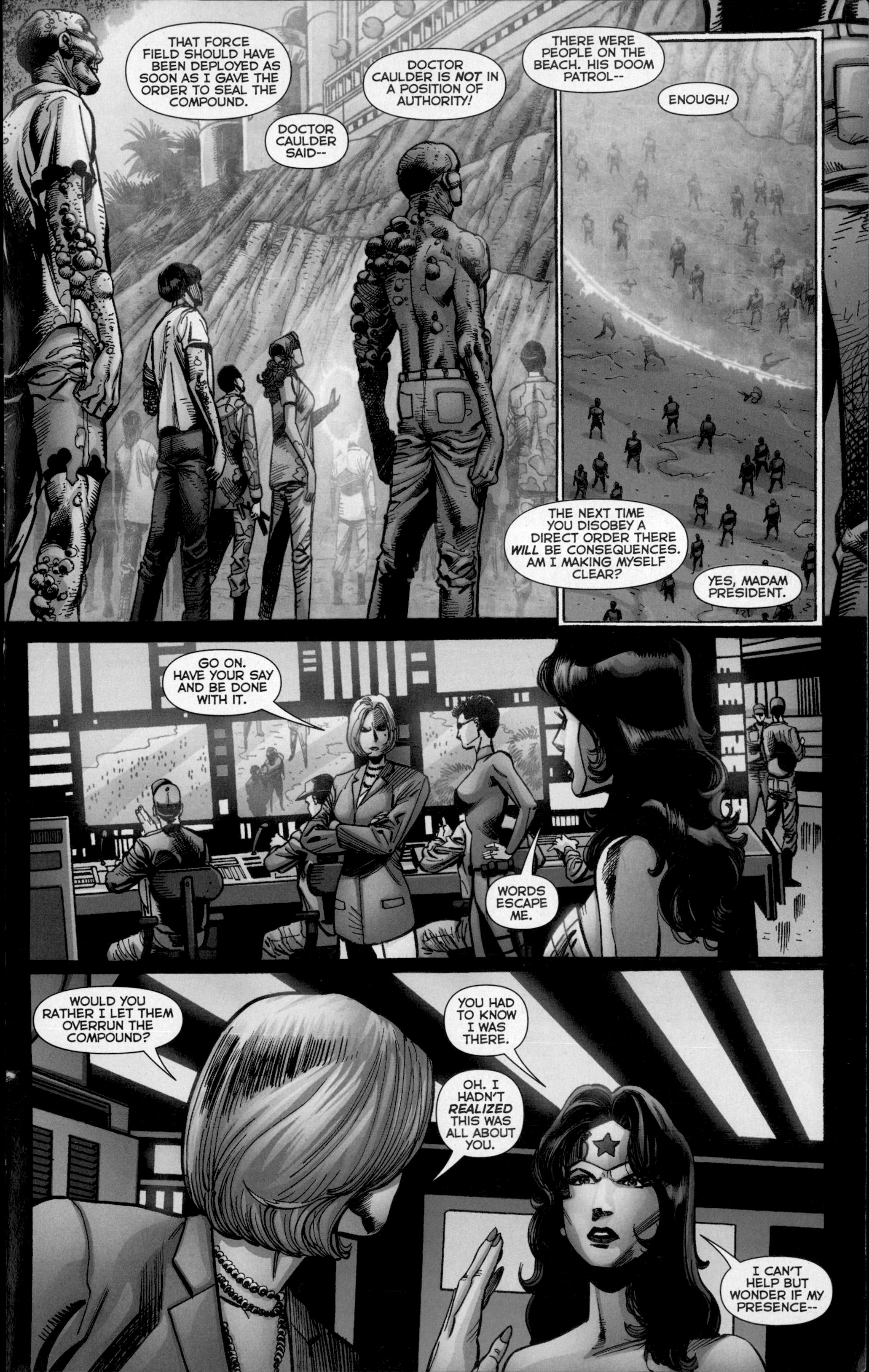
THAT FORCE FIELD SHOULD HAVE BEEN DEPLOYED AS SOON AS I GAVE THE ORDER TO SEAL THE COMPOUND.
DOCTOR CAULDER SAID--
DOCTOR CAULDER IS NOT IN A POSITION OF AUTHORITY!
THERE WERE PEOPLE ON THE BEACH. HIS DOOM PATROL--
ENOUGH!
THE NEXT TIME YOU DISOBEY A DIRECT ORDER THERE WILL BE CONSEQUENCES. AM I MAKING MYSELF CLEAR?
YES, MADAM PRESIDENT.
GO ON. HAVE YOUR SAY AND BE DONE WITH IT.
WORDS ESCAPE ME.
WOULD YOU RATHER I LET THEM OVERRUN THE COMPOUND?
YOU HAD TO KNOW I WAS THERE.
OH. I HADN'T REALIZED THIS WAS ALL ABOUT YOU.
I CAN'T HELP BUT WONDER IF MY PRESENCE--

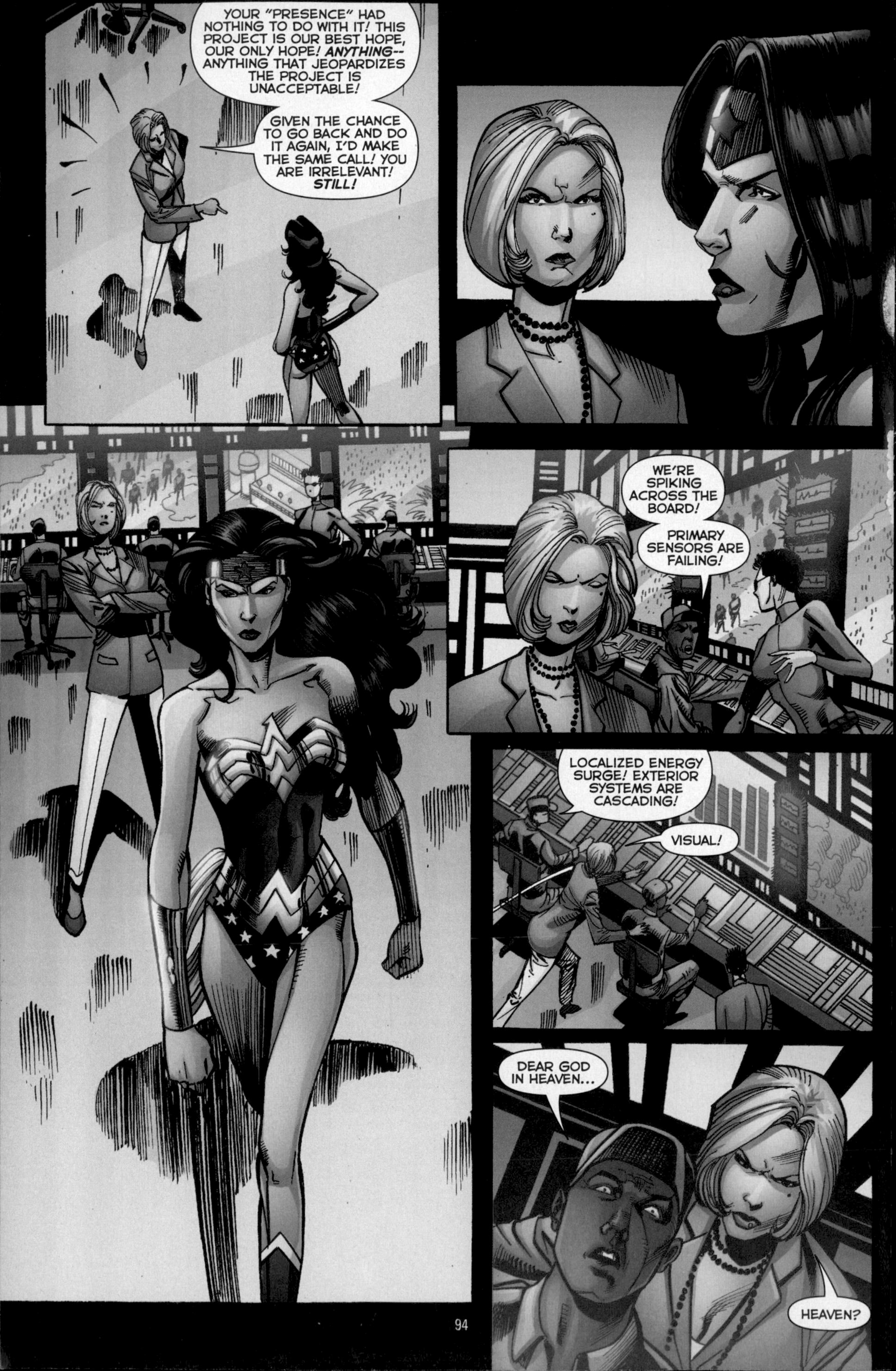
YOUR "PRESENCE" HAD NOTHING TO DO WITH IT! THIS PROJECT IS OUR BEST HOPE, OUR ONLY HOPE! ANYTHING-- ANYTHING THAT JEOPARDIZES THE PROJECT IS UNACCEPTABLE!
GIVEN THE CHANCE TO GO BACK AND DO IT AGAIN, I'D MAKE THE SAME CALL! YOU ARE IRRELEVANT! STILL!
WE'RE SPIKING ACROSS THE BOARD!
PRIMARY SENSORS ARE FAILING!
LOCALIZED ENERGY SURGE! EXTERIOR SYSTEMS ARE CASCADING!
VISUAL!
DEAR GOD IN HEAVEN...
HEAVEN?

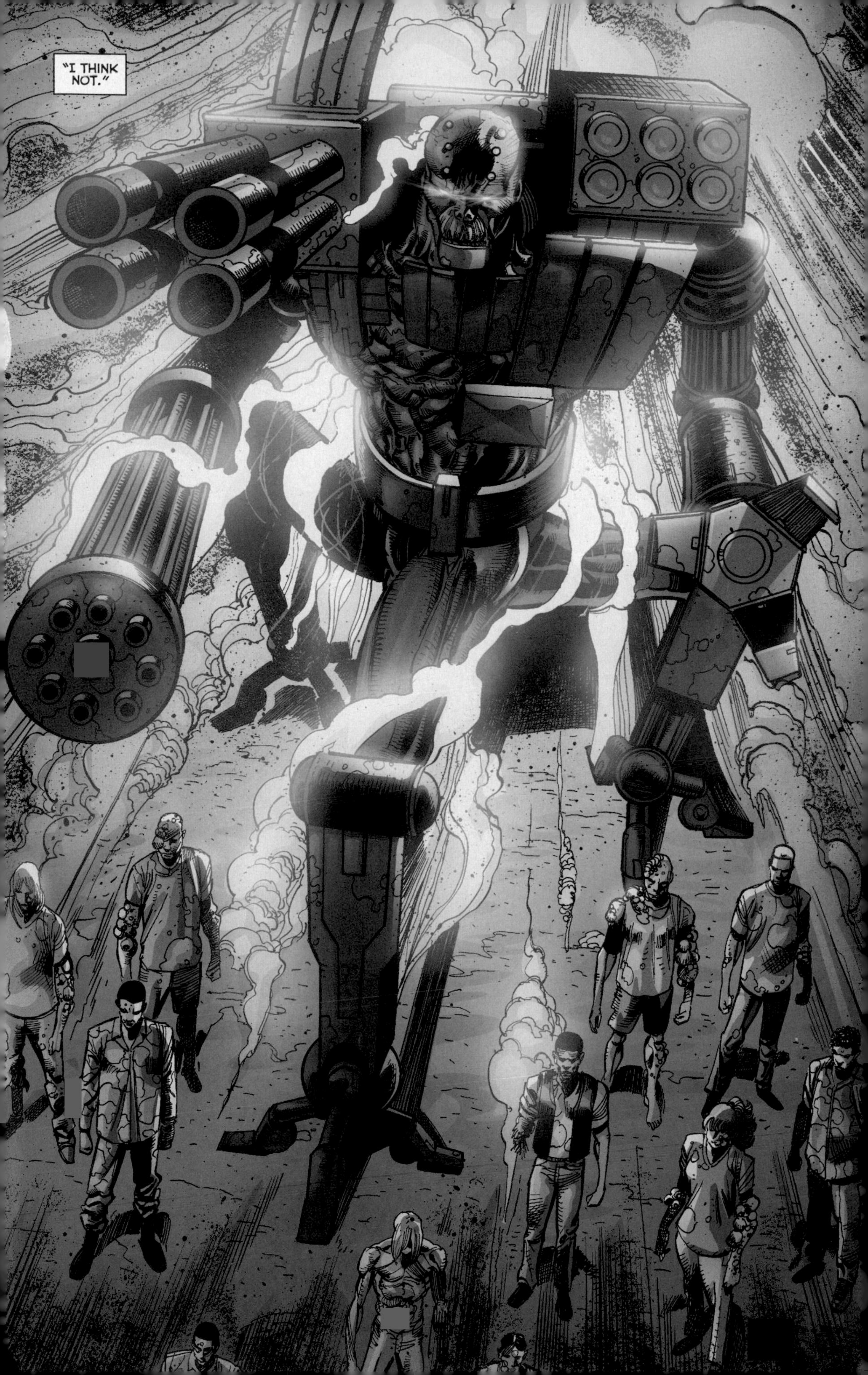
"I THINK NOT."

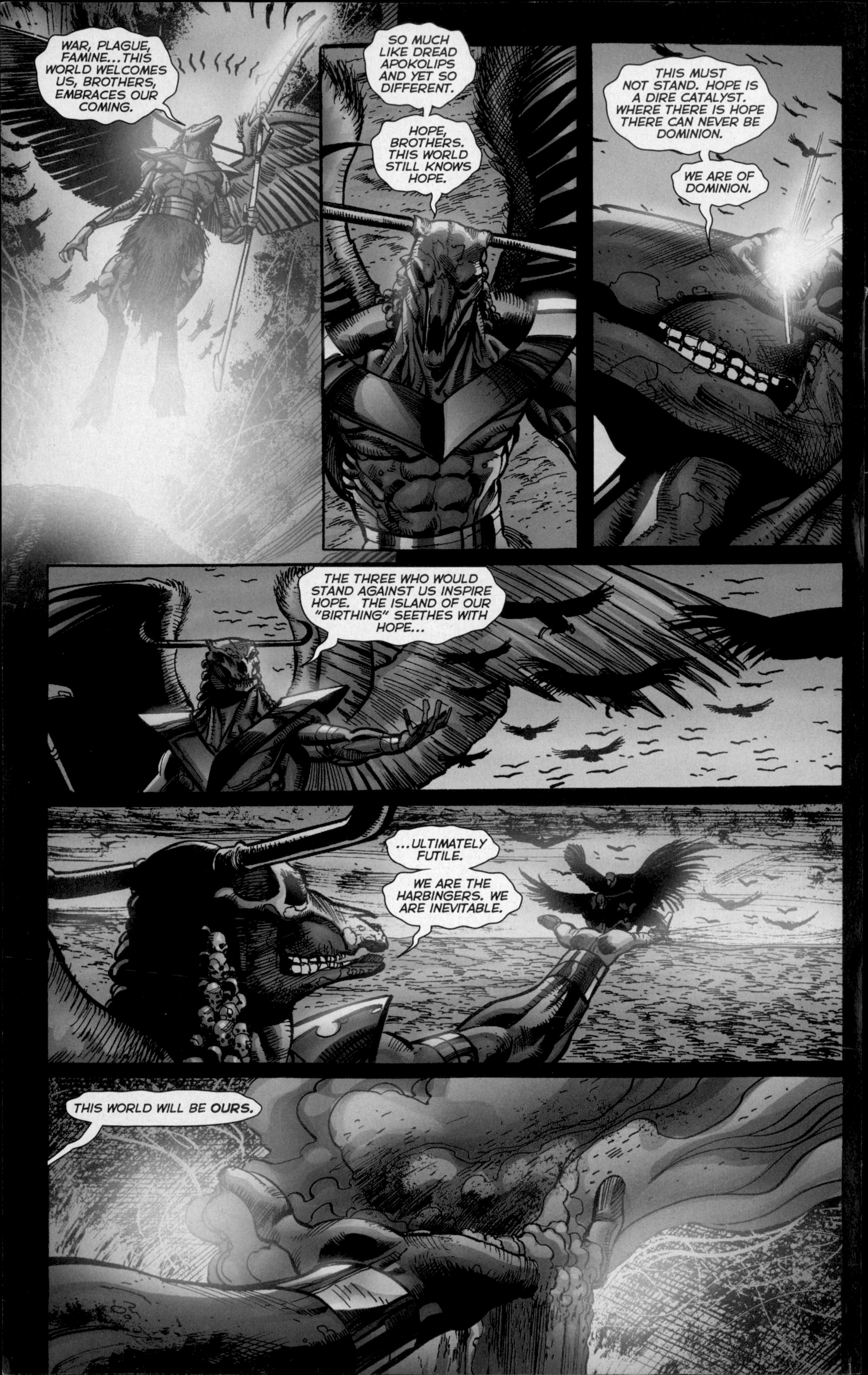
WAR, PLAGUE, FAMINE...THIS WORLD WELCOMES US, BROTHERS, EMBRACES OUR COMING.
SO MUCH LIKE DREAD APOKOLIPS AND YET SO DIFFERENT.
HOPE, BROTHERS. THIS WORLD STILL KNOWS HOPE.
THIS MUST NOT STAND. HOPE IS A DIRE CATALYST. WHERE THERE IS HOPE THERE CAN NEVER BE DOMINION.
WE ARE OF DOMINION.
THE THREE WHO WOULD STAND AGAINST US INSPIRE HOPE. THE ISLAND OF OUR "BIRTHING" SEETHES WITH HOPE...
...ULTIMATELY FUTILE.
WE ARE THE HARBINGERS. WE ARE INEVITABLE.
THIS WORLD WILL BE **OURS.**

DEAD RECKONING

CHAPTER FIVE

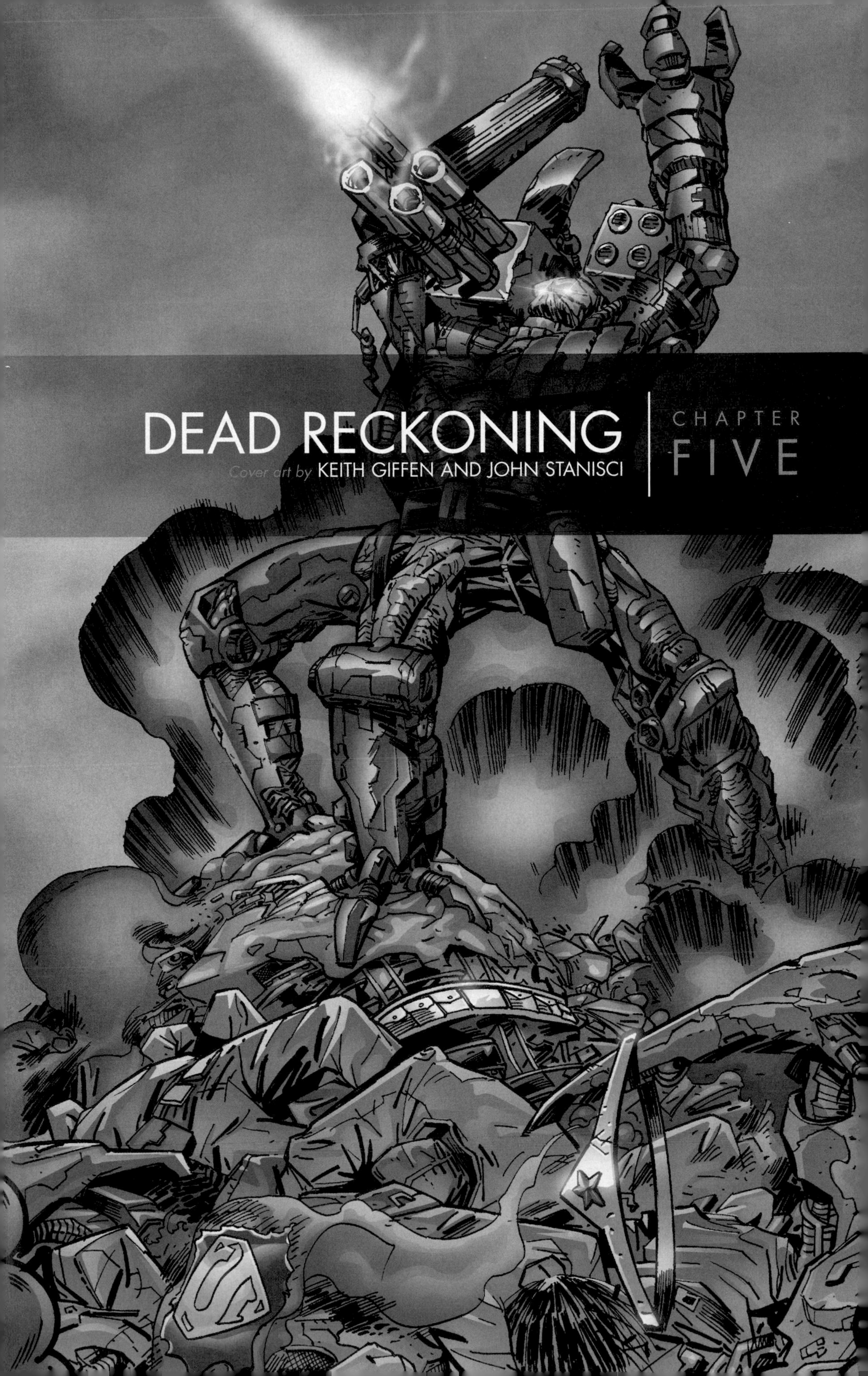

Cover art by KEITH GIFFEN AND JOHN STANISCI

DEATH
PESTILENCE
FAMINE
WAR

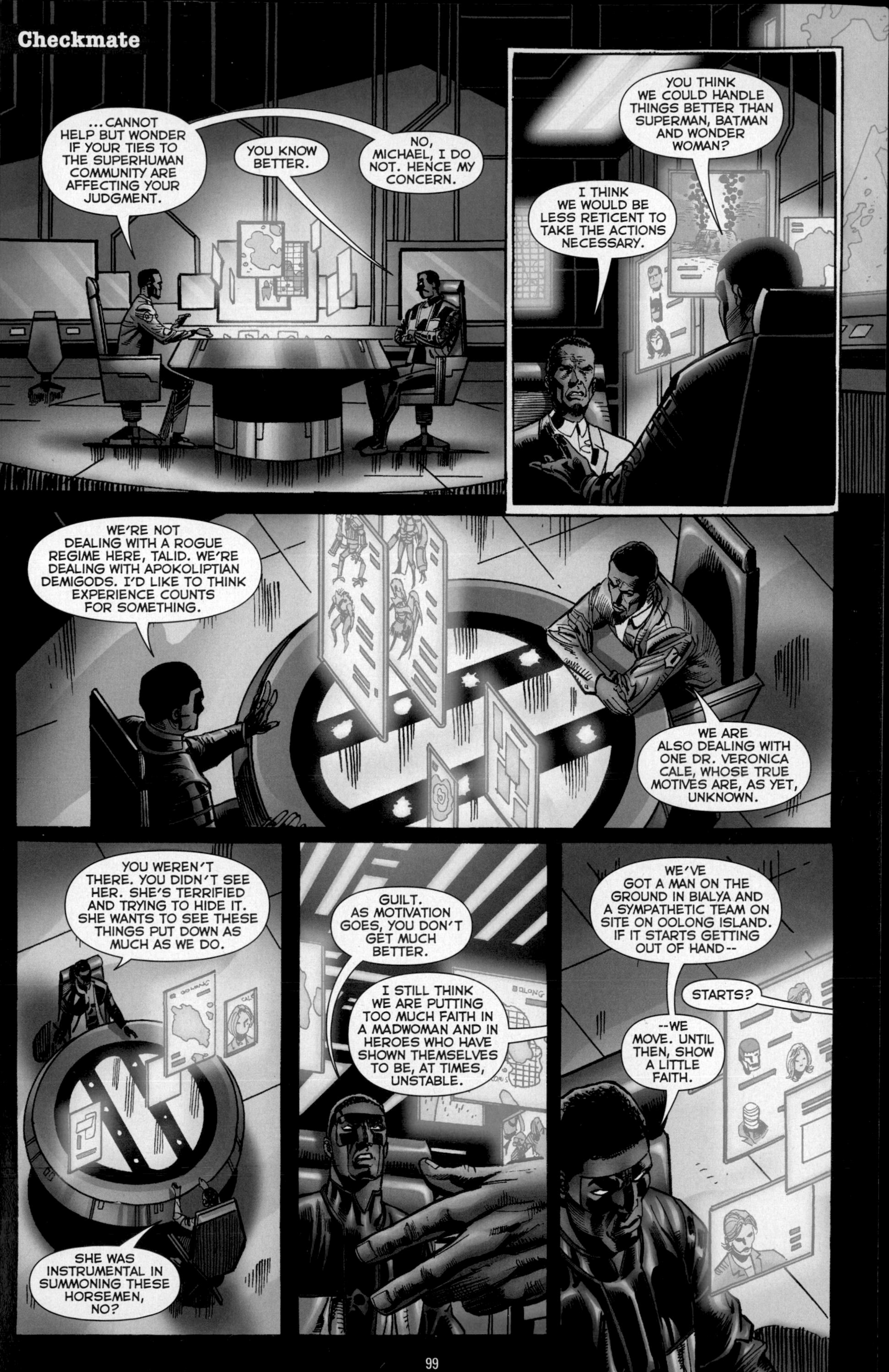
...CANNOT HELP BUT WONDER IF YOUR TIES TO THE SUPERHUMAN COMMUNITY ARE AFFECTING YOUR JUDGMENT.
YOU KNOW BETTER.
NO, MICHAEL, I DO NOT. HENCE MY CONCERN.
YOU THINK WE COULD HANDLE THINGS BETTER THAN SUPERMAN, BATMAN AND WONDER WOMAN?
I THINK WE WOULD BE LESS RETICENT TO TAKE THE ACTIONS NECESSARY.
WE'RE NOT DEALING WITH A ROGUE REGIME HERE, TALID. WE'RE DEALING WITH APOKOLIPTIAN DEMIGODS. I'D LIKE TO THINK EXPERIENCE COUNTS FOR SOMETHING.
WE ARE ALSO DEALING WITH ONE DR. VERONICA CALE, WHOSE TRUE MOTIVES ARE, AS YET, UNKNOWN.
YOU WEREN'T THERE. YOU DIDN'T SEE HER. SHE'S TERRIFIED AND TRYING TO HIDE IT. SHE WANTS TO SEE THESE THINGS PUT DOWN AS MUCH AS WE DO.
SHE WAS INSTRUMENTAL IN SUMMONING THESE HORSEMEN, NO?
GUILT. AS MOTIVATION GOES, YOU DON'T GET MUCH BETTER.
I STILL THINK WE ARE PUTTING TOO MUCH FAITH IN A MADWOMAN AND IN HEROES WHO HAVE SHOWN THEMSELVES TO BE, AT TIMES, UNSTABLE.
WE'VE GOT A MAN ON THE GROUND IN BIALYA AND A SYMPATHETIC TEAM ON SITE ON OOLONG ISLAND. IF IT STARTS GETTING OUT OF HAND--
STARTS?
--WE MOVE. UNTIL THEN, SHOW A LITTLE FAITH.

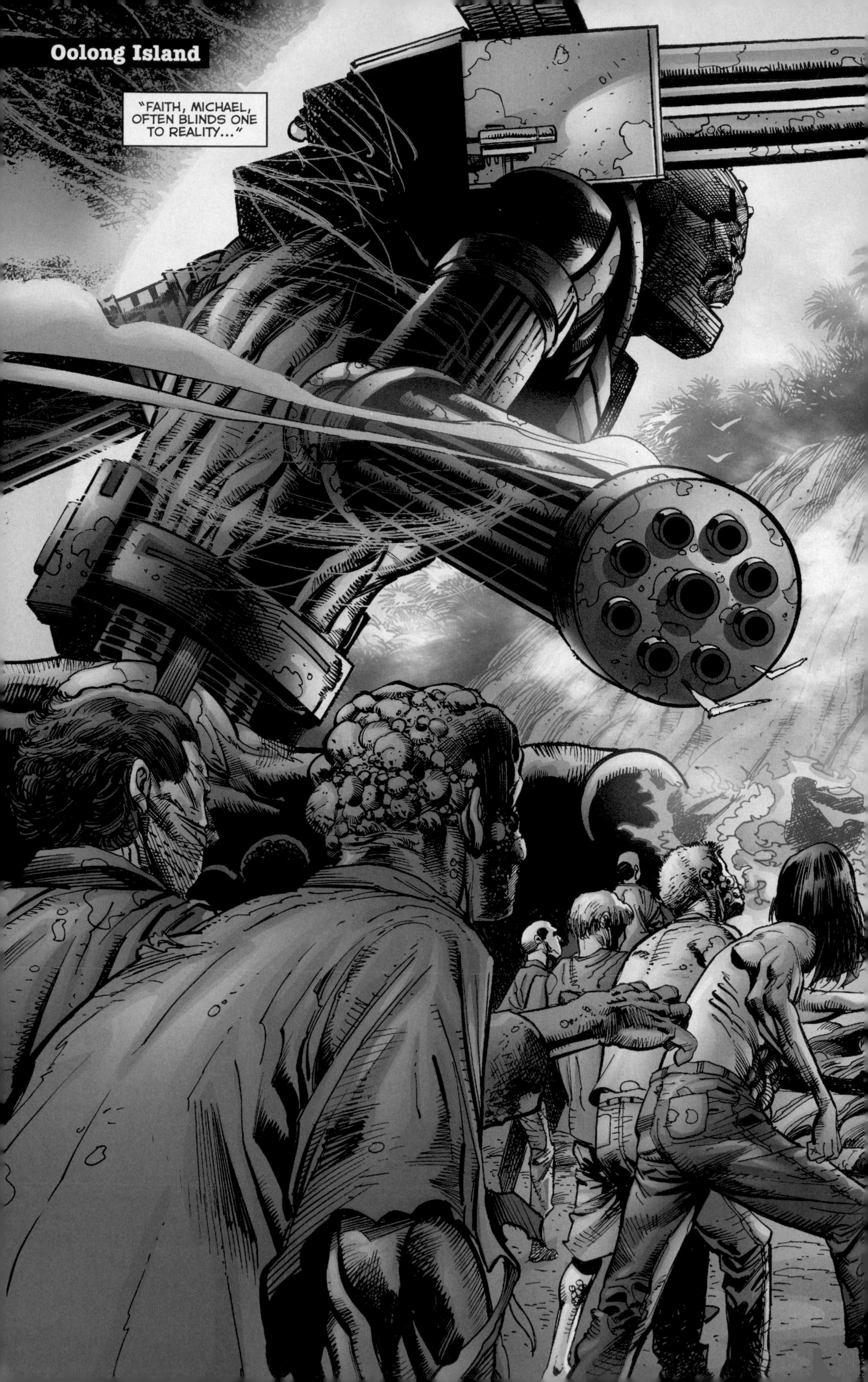
Oolong Island
"FAITH, MICHAEL, OFTEN BLINDS ONE TO REALITY..."

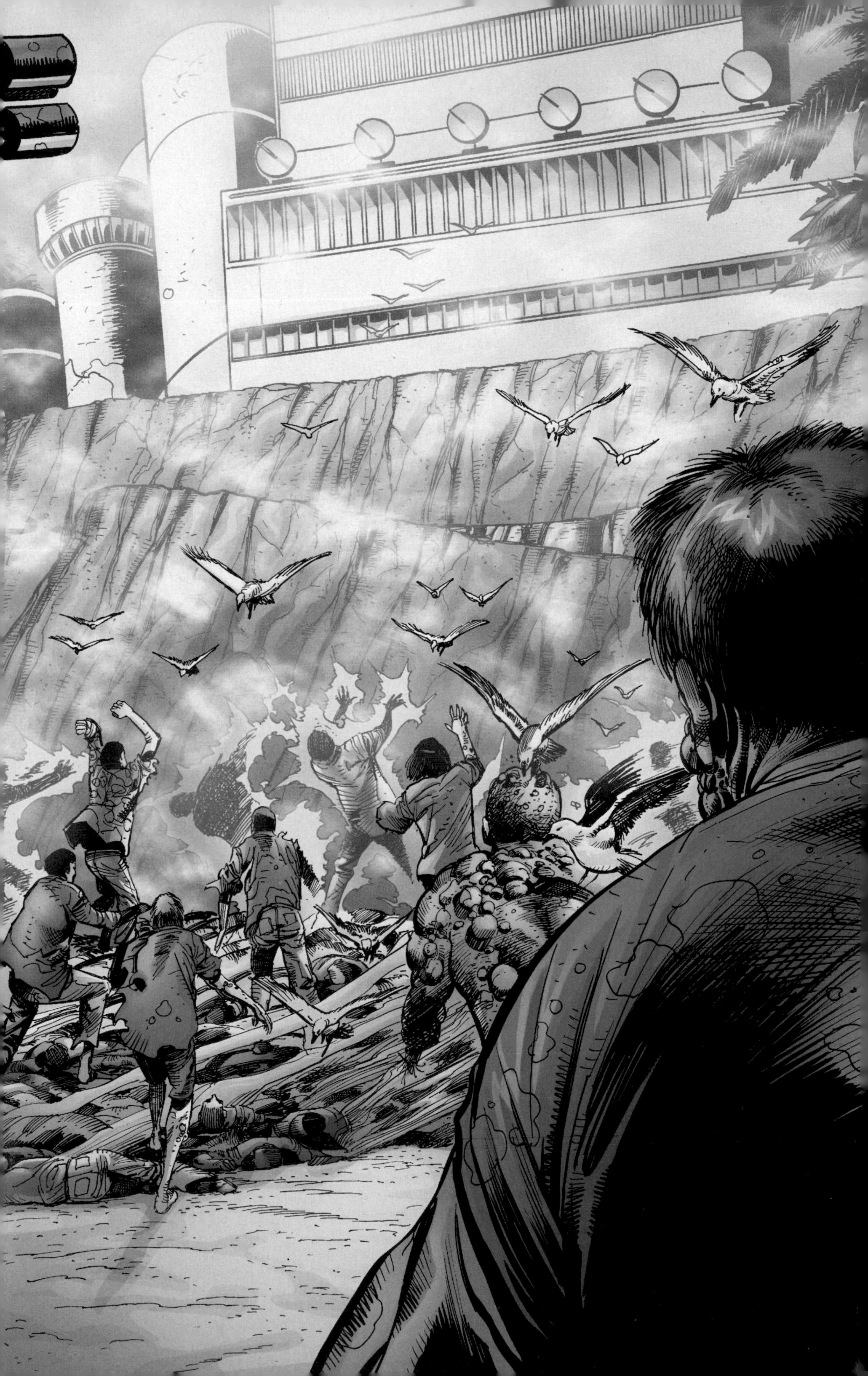

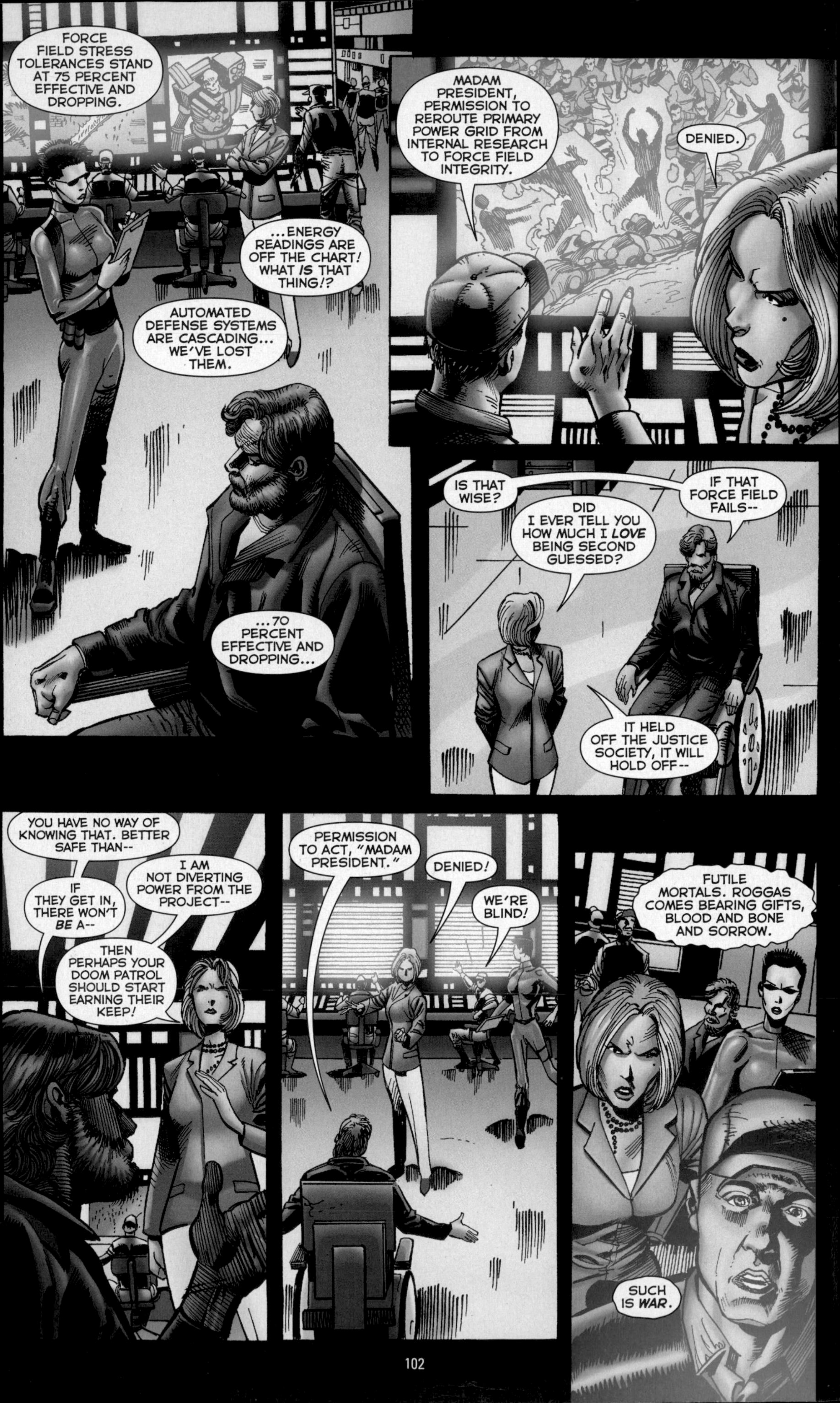
FORCE FIELD STRESS TOLERANCES STAND AT 75 PERCENT EFFECTIVE AND DROPPING.
...ENERGY READINGS ARE OFF THE CHART! WHAT IS THAT THING!?
AUTOMATED DEFENSE SYSTEMS ARE CASCADING... WE'VE LOST THEM.
...70 PERCENT EFFECTIVE AND DROPPING...
MADAM PRESIDENT, PERMISSION TO REROUTE PRIMARY POWER GRID FROM INTERNAL RESEARCH TO FORCE FIELD INTEGRITY.
DENIED.
IS THAT WISE?
IF THAT FORCE FIELD FAILS--
DID I EVER TELL YOU HOW MUCH I LOVE BEING SECOND GUESSED?
IT HELD OFF THE JUSTICE SOCIETY, IT WILL HOLD OFF--
YOU HAVE NO WAY OF KNOWING THAT. BETTER SAFE THAN--
I AM NOT DIVERTING POWER FROM THE PROJECT--
IF THEY GET IN, THERE WON'T BE A--
THEN PERHAPS YOUR DOOM PATROL SHOULD START EARNING THEIR KEEP!
PERMISSION TO ACT, "MADAM PRESIDENT."
DENIED!
WE'RE BLIND!
FUTILE MORTALS. ROGGAS COMES BEARING GIFTS, BLOOD AND BONE AND SORROW.
SUCH IS WAR.

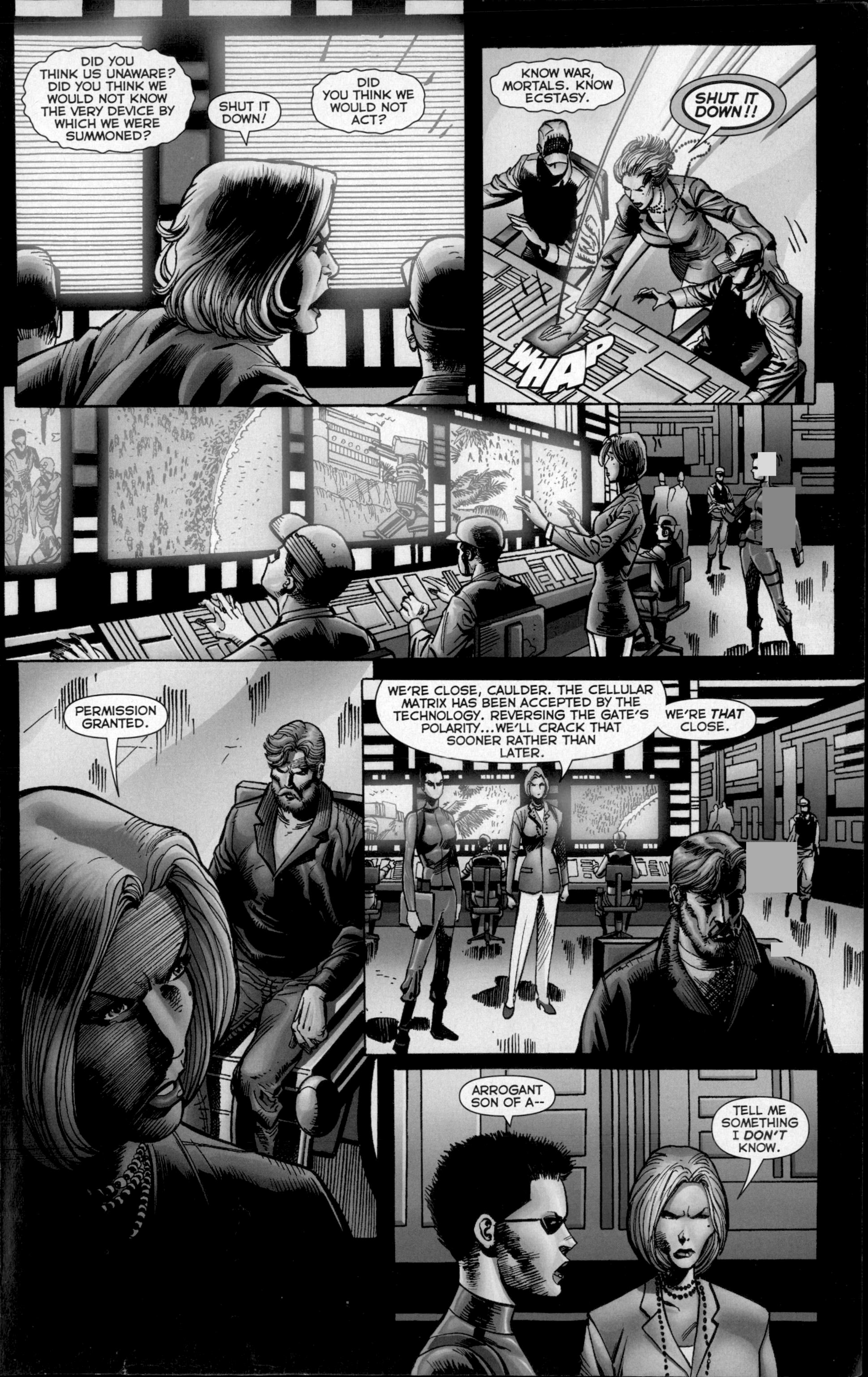
DID YOU THINK US UNAWARE? DID YOU THINK WE WOULD NOT KNOW THE VERY DEVICE BY WHICH WE WERE SUMMONED?
SHUT IT DOWN!
DID YOU THINK WE WOULD NOT ACT?
KNOW WAR, MORTALS. KNOW ECSTASY.
SHUT IT DOWN!!
WHAP
PERMISSION GRANTED.
WE'RE CLOSE, CAULDER. THE CELLULAR MATRIX HAS BEEN ACCEPTED BY THE TECHNOLOGY. REVERSING THE GATE'S POLARITY...WE'LL CRACK THAT SOONER RATHER THAN LATER.
WE'RE *THAT* CLOSE.
ARROGANT SON OF A--
TELL ME SOMETHING I *DON'T* KNOW.

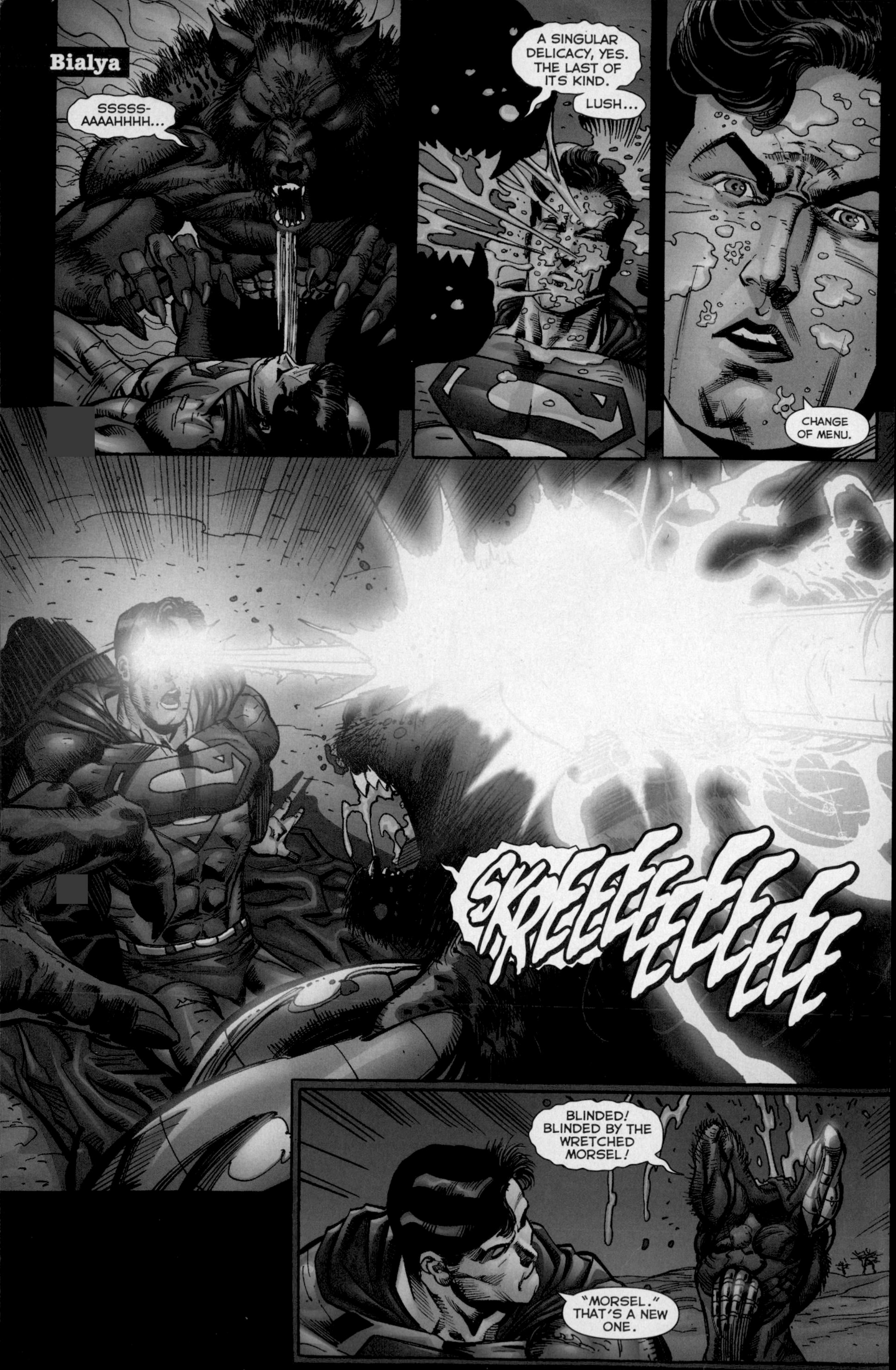
Bialya
SSSSS-AAAAHHHH...
A SINGULAR DELICACY, YES. THE LAST OF ITS KIND.
LUSH...
CHANGE OF MENU.
SKREEEEEEEEEEE
BLINDED! BLINDED BY THE WRETCHED MORSEL!
"MORSEL." THAT'S A NEW ONE.

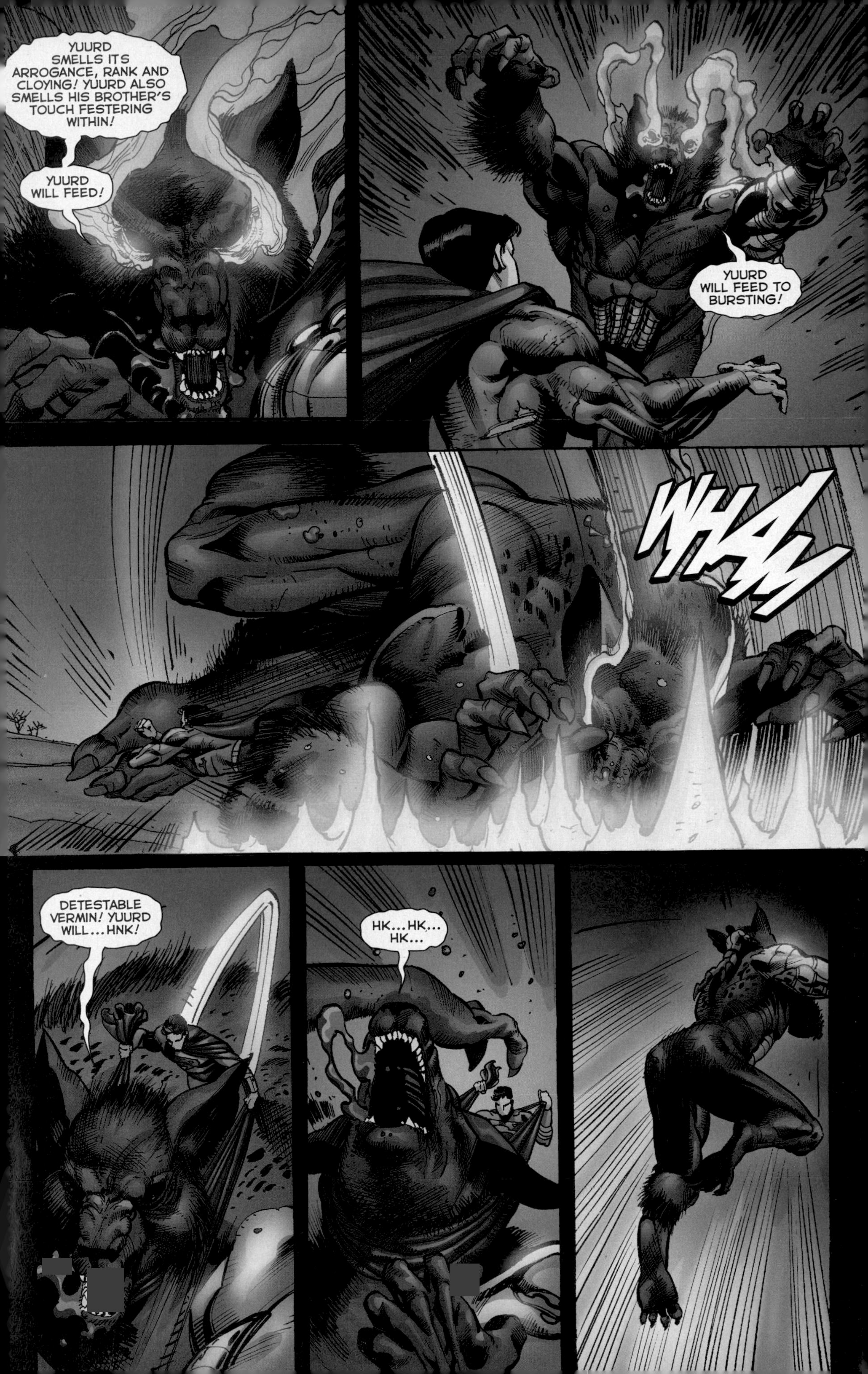
YUURD SMELLS ITS ARROGANCE, RANK AND CLOYING! YUURD ALSO SMELLS HIS BROTHER'S TOUCH FESTERING WITHIN!
YUURD WILL FEED!
YUURD WILL FEED TO BURSTING!
WHAM
DETESTABLE VERMIN! YUURD WILL...HNK!
HK...HK... HK...

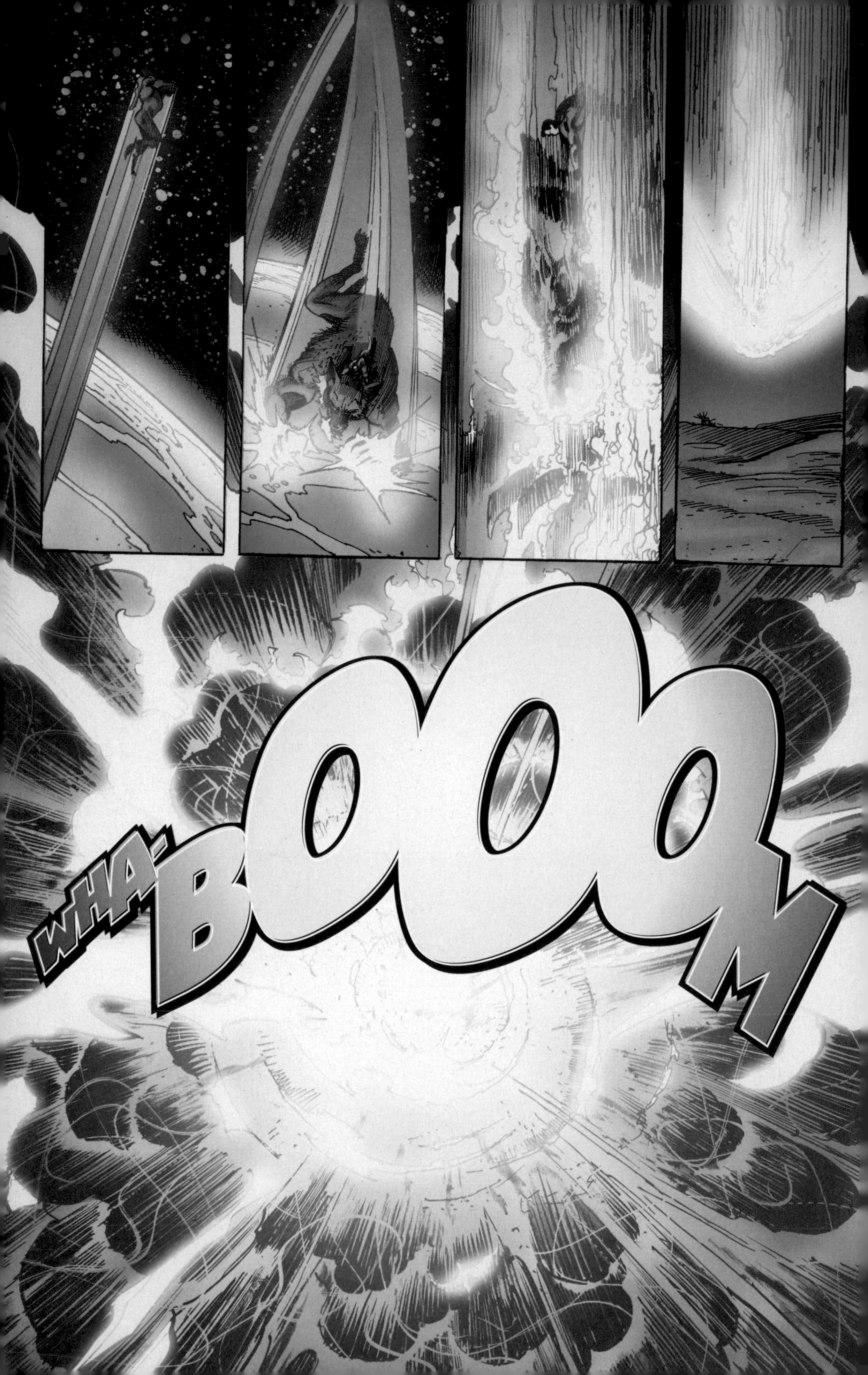
WHA-BOOOM

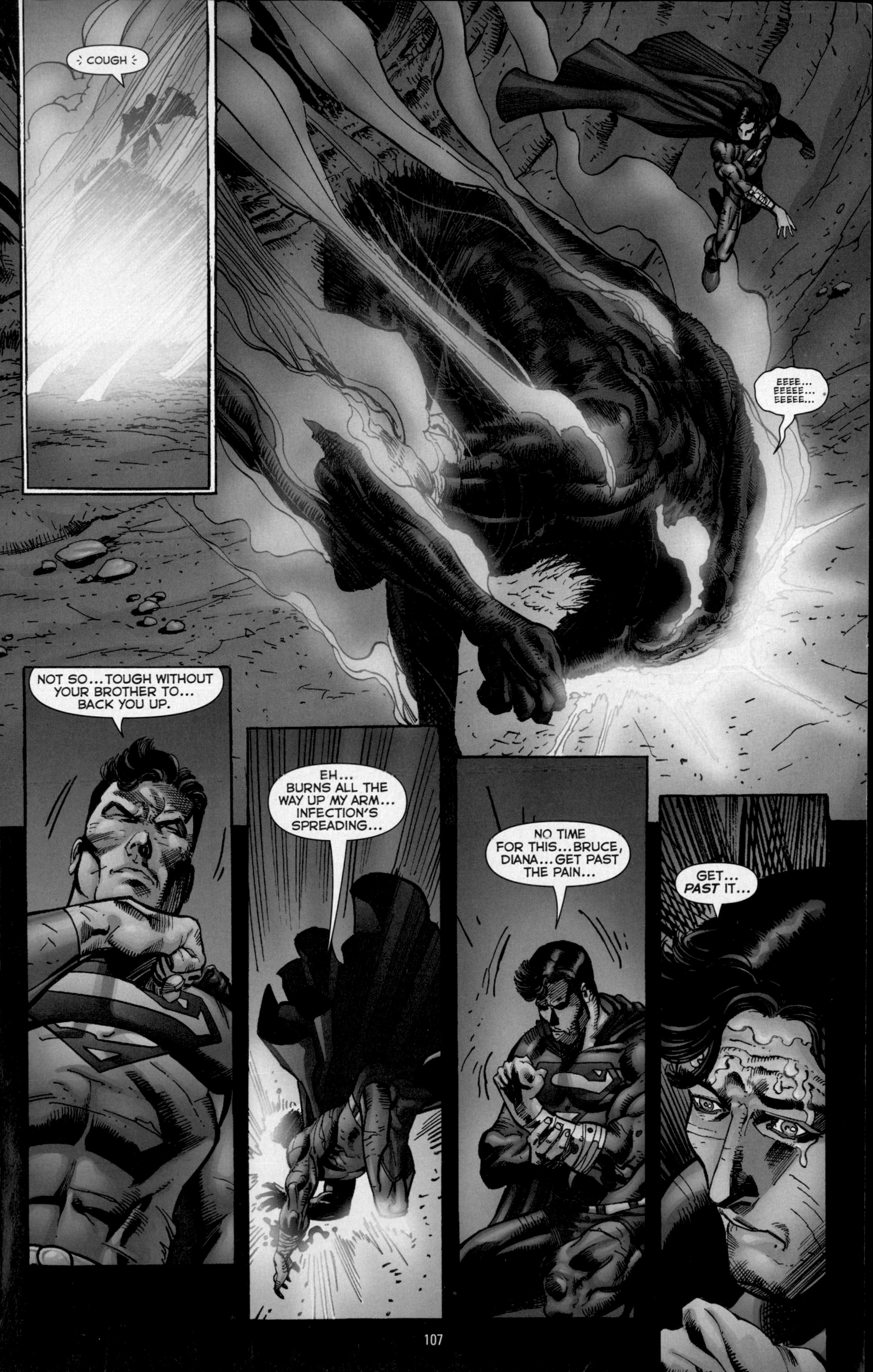
COUGH
EEEE... EEEEE... EEEEE...
NOT SO...TOUGH WITHOUT YOUR BROTHER TO... BACK YOU UP.
EH... BURNS ALL THE WAY UP MY ARM... INFECTION'S SPREADING...
NO TIME FOR THIS...BRUCE, DIANA...GET PAST THE PAIN...
GET... *PAST* IT...

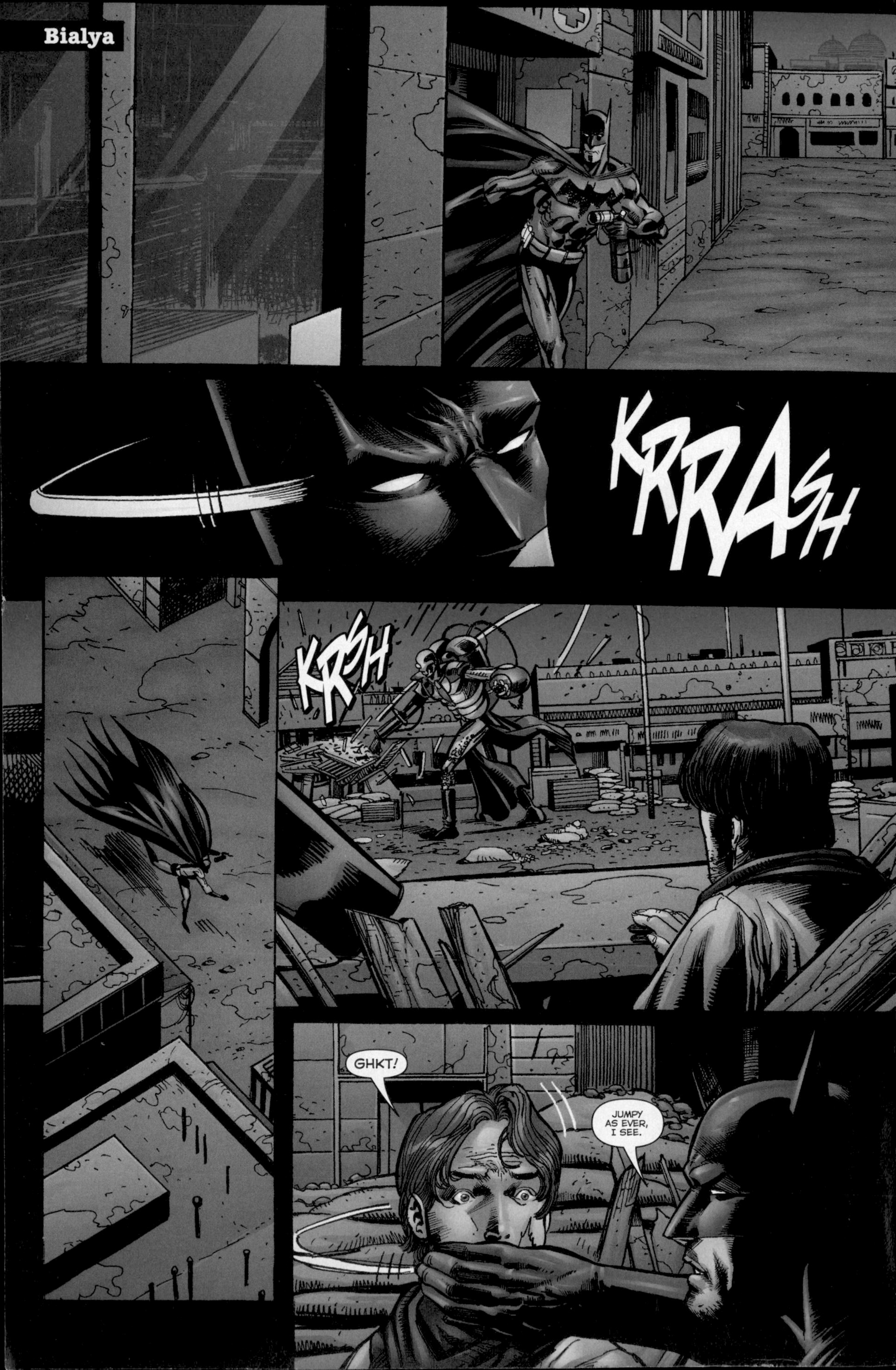
Bialya
KRRASH
KRSH
GHKT!
JUMPY AS EVER, I SEE.

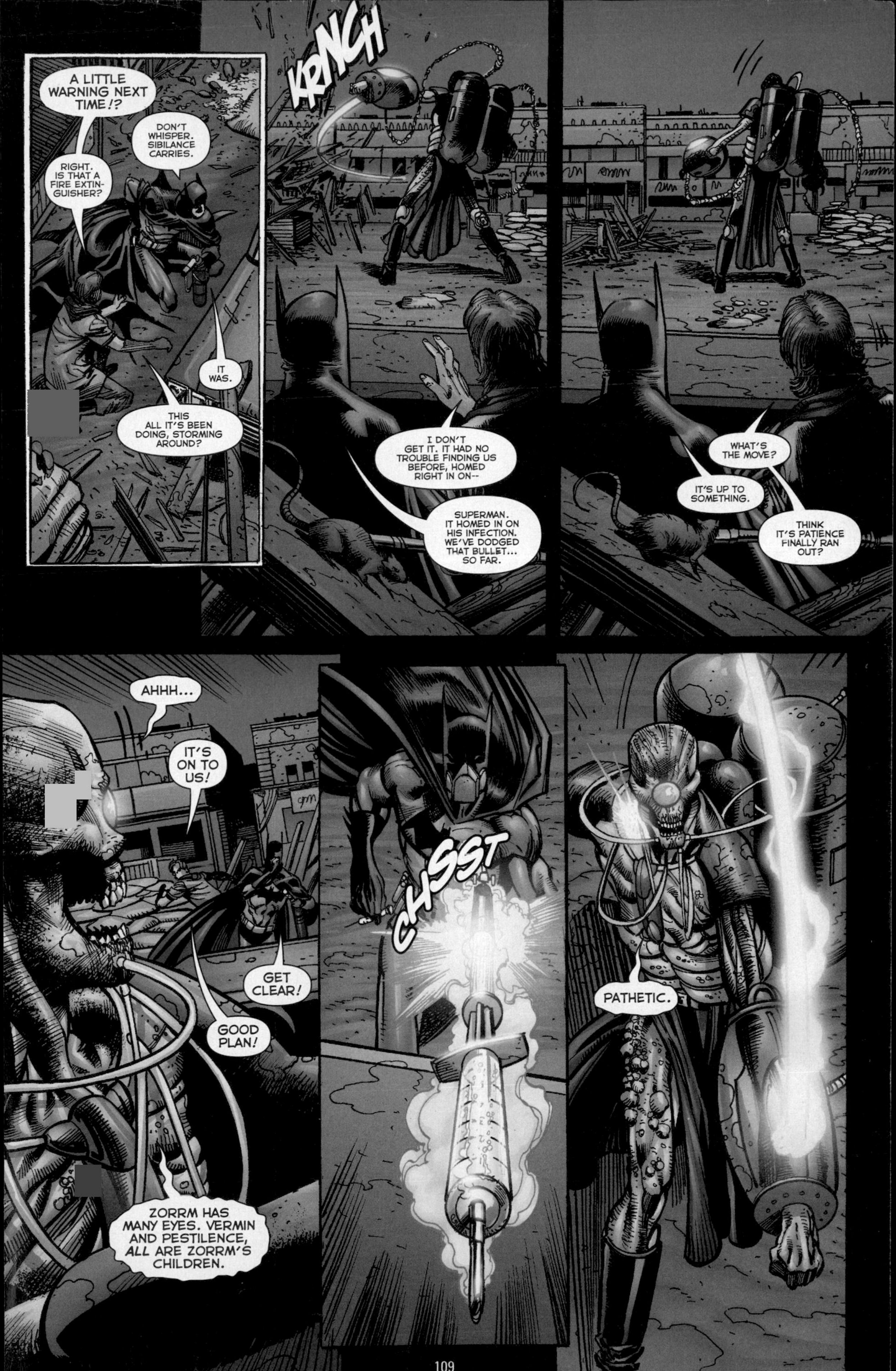
A LITTLE WARNING NEXT TIME!?
DON'T WHISPER. SIBILANCE CARRIES.
RIGHT. IS THAT A FIRE EXTIN-GUISHER?
IT WAS.
THIS ALL IT'S BEEN DOING, STORMING AROUND?
KRNCH
I DON'T GET IT. IT HAD NO TROUBLE FINDING US BEFORE, HOMED RIGHT IN ON--
SUPERMAN. IT HOMED IN ON HIS INFECTION. WE'VE DODGED THAT BULLET... SO FAR.
WHAT'S THE MOVE?
IT'S UP TO SOMETHING.
THINK IT'S PATIENCE FINALLY RAN OUT?
AHHH...
IT'S ON TO US!
GET CLEAR!
GOOD PLAN!
ZORRM HAS MANY EYES. VERMIN AND PESTILENCE, ALL ARE ZORRM'S CHILDREN.
CHSST
PATHETIC.

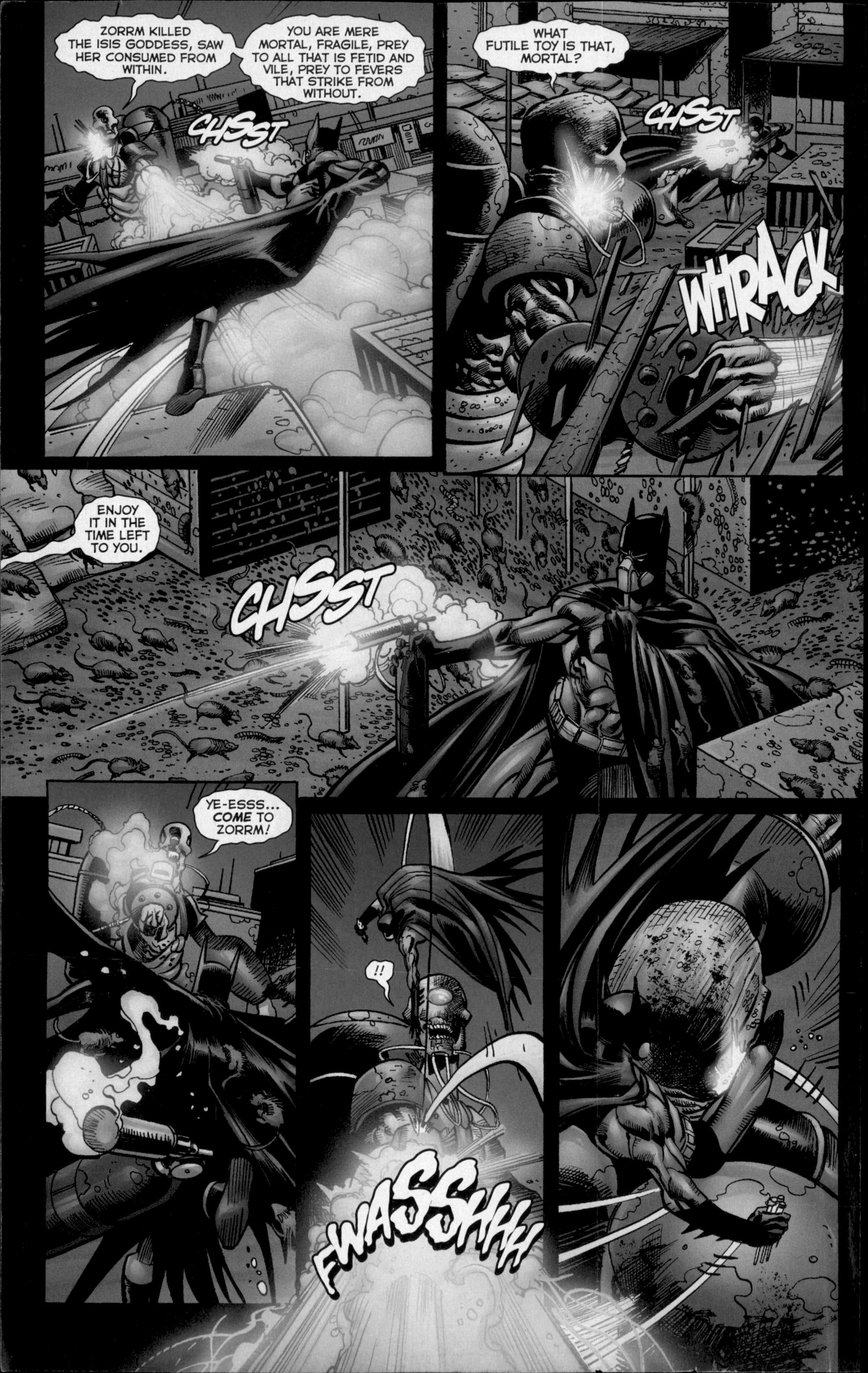

ZORRM KILLED THE ISIS GODDESS, SAW HER CONSUMED FROM WITHIN.
YOU ARE MERE MORTAL, FRAGILE, PREY TO ALL THAT IS FETID AND VILE, PREY TO FEVERS THAT STRIKE FROM WITHOUT.
CHSST
WHAT FUTILE TOY IS THAT, MORTAL?
CHSST
WHRACK
ENJOY IT IN THE TIME LEFT TO YOU.
CHSST
YE-ESSS... COME TO ZORRM!
!!
FWASSHHH

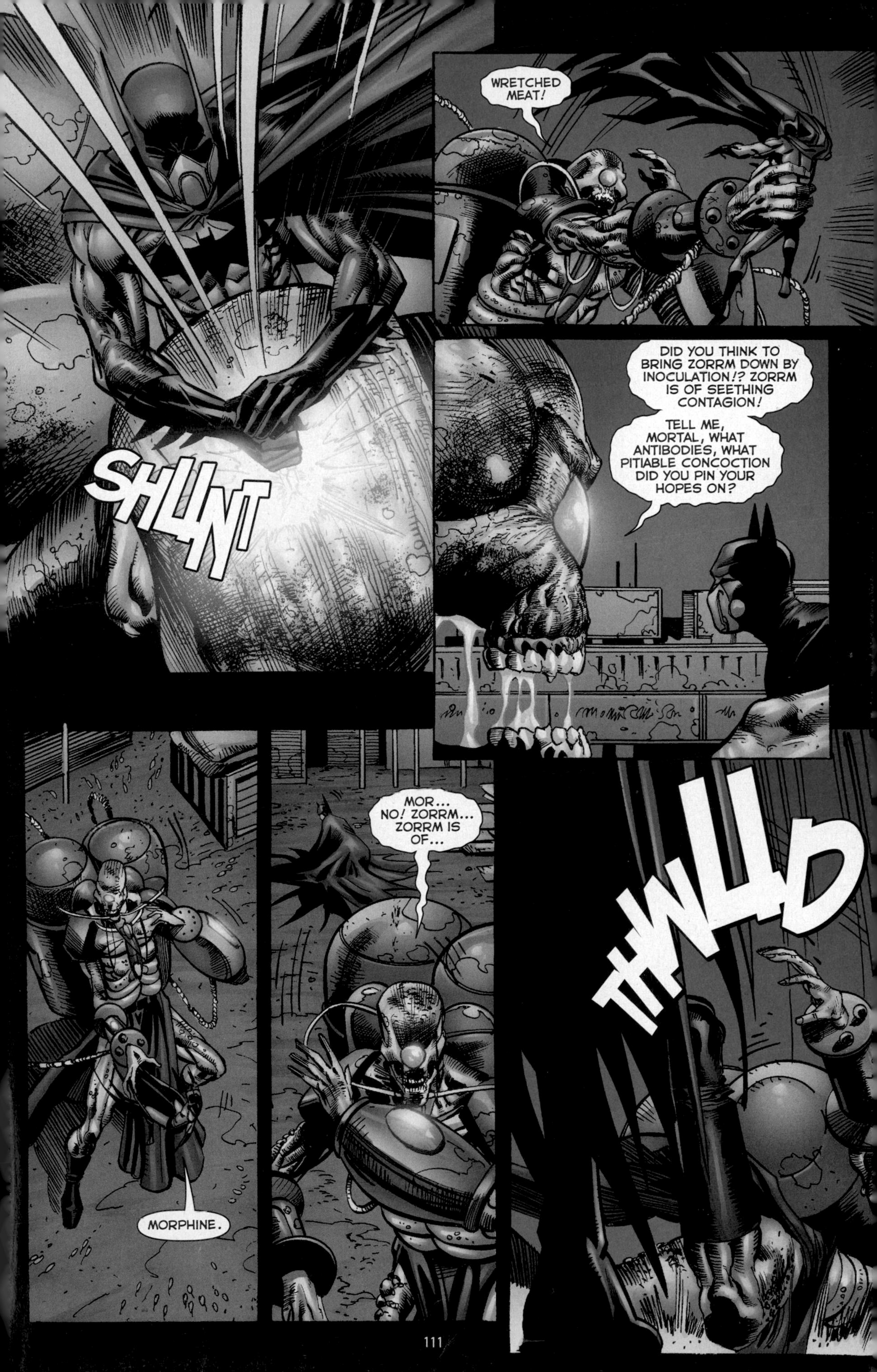
SHUNT
WRETCHED MEAT!
DID YOU THINK TO BRING ZORRM DOWN BY INOCULATION!? ZORRM IS OF SEETHING CONTAGION!
TELL ME, MORTAL, WHAT ANTIBODIES, WHAT PITIABLE CONCOCTION DID YOU PIN YOUR HOPES ON?
MORPHINE.
MOR... NO! ZORRM... ZORRM IS OF...
THWUD

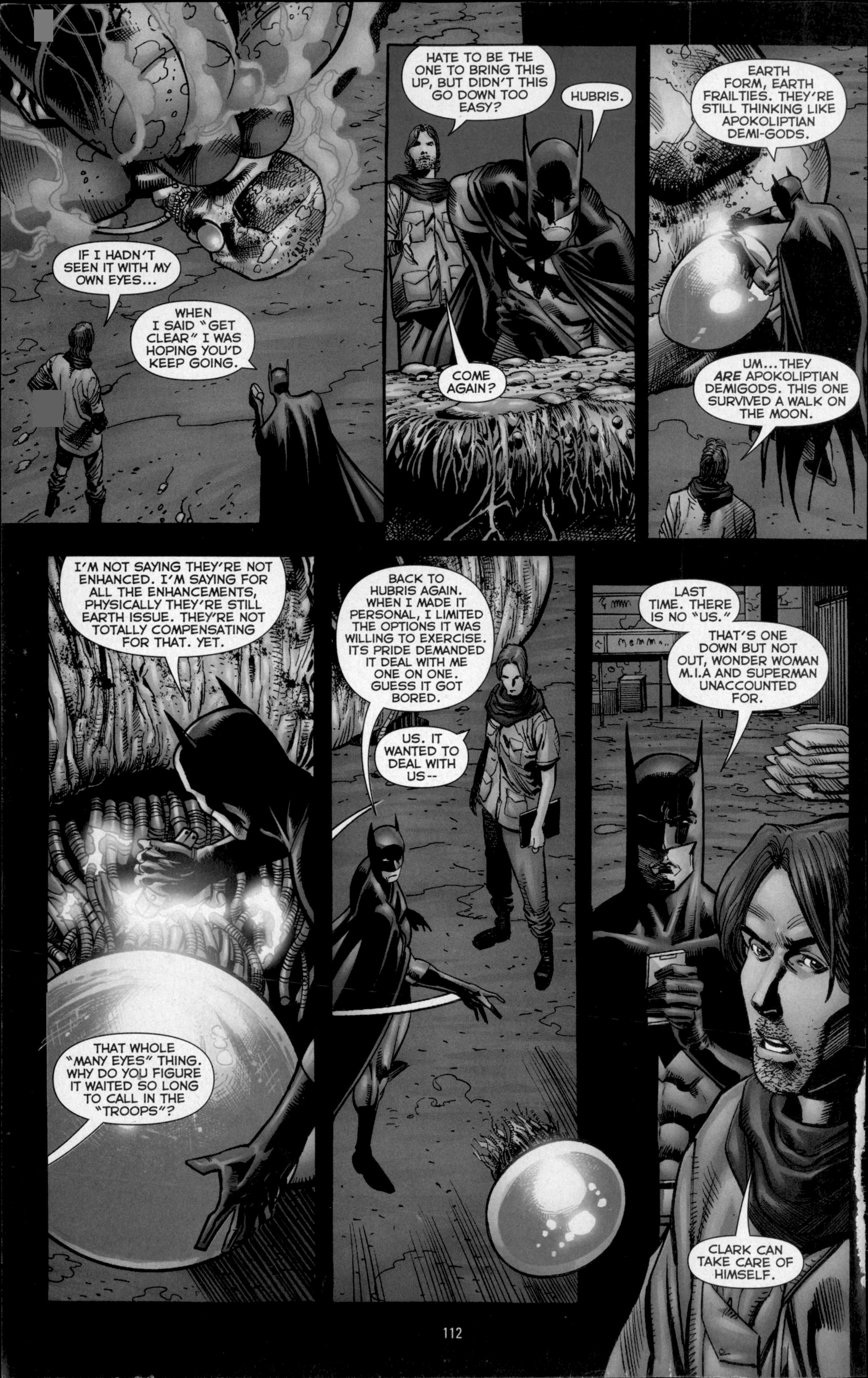
IF I HADN'T SEEN IT WITH MY OWN EYES...
WHEN I SAID "GET CLEAR" I WAS HOPING YOU'D KEEP GOING.
HATE TO BE THE ONE TO BRING THIS UP, BUT DIDN'T THIS GO DOWN TOO EASY?
HUBRIS.
COME AGAIN?
EARTH FORM, EARTH FRAILTIES. THEY'RE STILL THINKING LIKE APOKOLIPTIAN DEMI-GODS.
UM...THEY ARE APOKOLIPTIAN DEMIGODS. THIS ONE SURVIVED A WALK ON THE MOON.
I'M NOT SAYING THEY'RE NOT ENHANCED. I'M SAYING FOR ALL THE ENHANCEMENTS, PHYSICALLY THEY'RE STILL EARTH ISSUE. THEY'RE NOT TOTALLY COMPENSATING FOR THAT. YET.
THAT WHOLE "MANY EYES" THING. WHY DO YOU FIGURE IT WAITED SO LONG TO CALL IN THE "TROOPS"?
BACK TO HUBRIS AGAIN. WHEN I MADE IT PERSONAL, I LIMITED THE OPTIONS IT WAS WILLING TO EXERCISE. ITS PRIDE DEMANDED IT DEAL WITH ME ONE ON ONE. GUESS IT GOT BORED.
US. IT WANTED TO DEAL WITH US--
LAST TIME. THERE IS NO "US."
THAT'S ONE DOWN BUT NOT OUT, WONDER WOMAN M.I.A AND SUPERMAN UNACCOUNTED FOR.
CLARK CAN TAKE CARE OF HIMSELF.

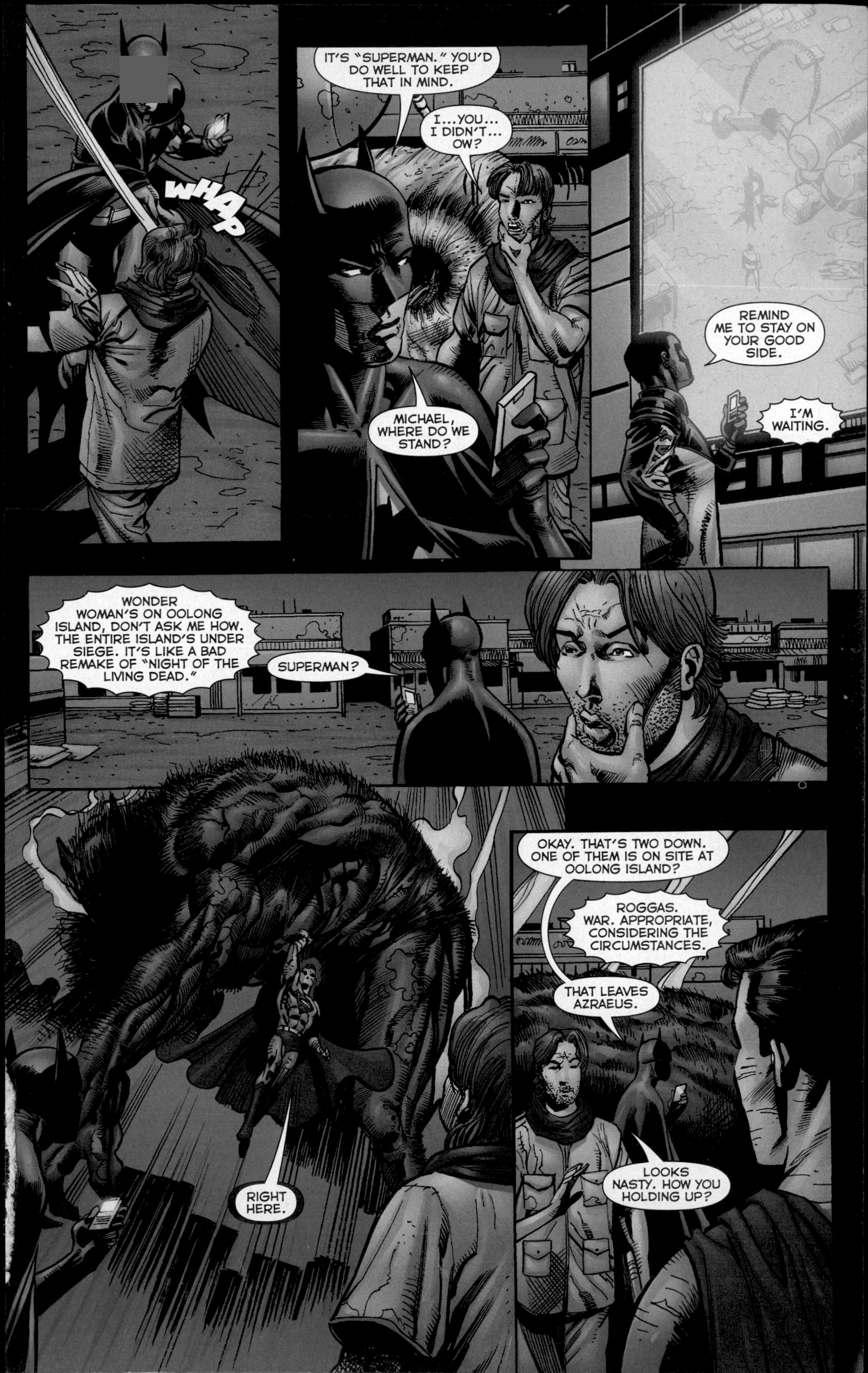
WHAP
IT'S "SUPERMAN." YOU'D DO WELL TO KEEP THAT IN MIND.
I...YOU... I DIDN'T... OW?
MICHAEL, WHERE DO WE STAND?
REMIND ME TO STAY ON YOUR GOOD SIDE.
I'M WAITING.
WONDER WOMAN'S ON OOLONG ISLAND, DON'T ASK ME HOW. THE ENTIRE ISLAND'S UNDER SIEGE. IT'S LIKE A BAD REMAKE OF "NIGHT OF THE LIVING DEAD."
SUPERMAN?
RIGHT HERE.
OKAY. THAT'S TWO DOWN. ONE OF THEM IS ON SITE AT OOLONG ISLAND?
ROGGAS. WAR. APPROPRIATE, CONSIDERING THE CIRCUMSTANCES.
THAT LEAVES AZRAEUS.
LOOKS NASTY. HOW YOU HOLDING UP?

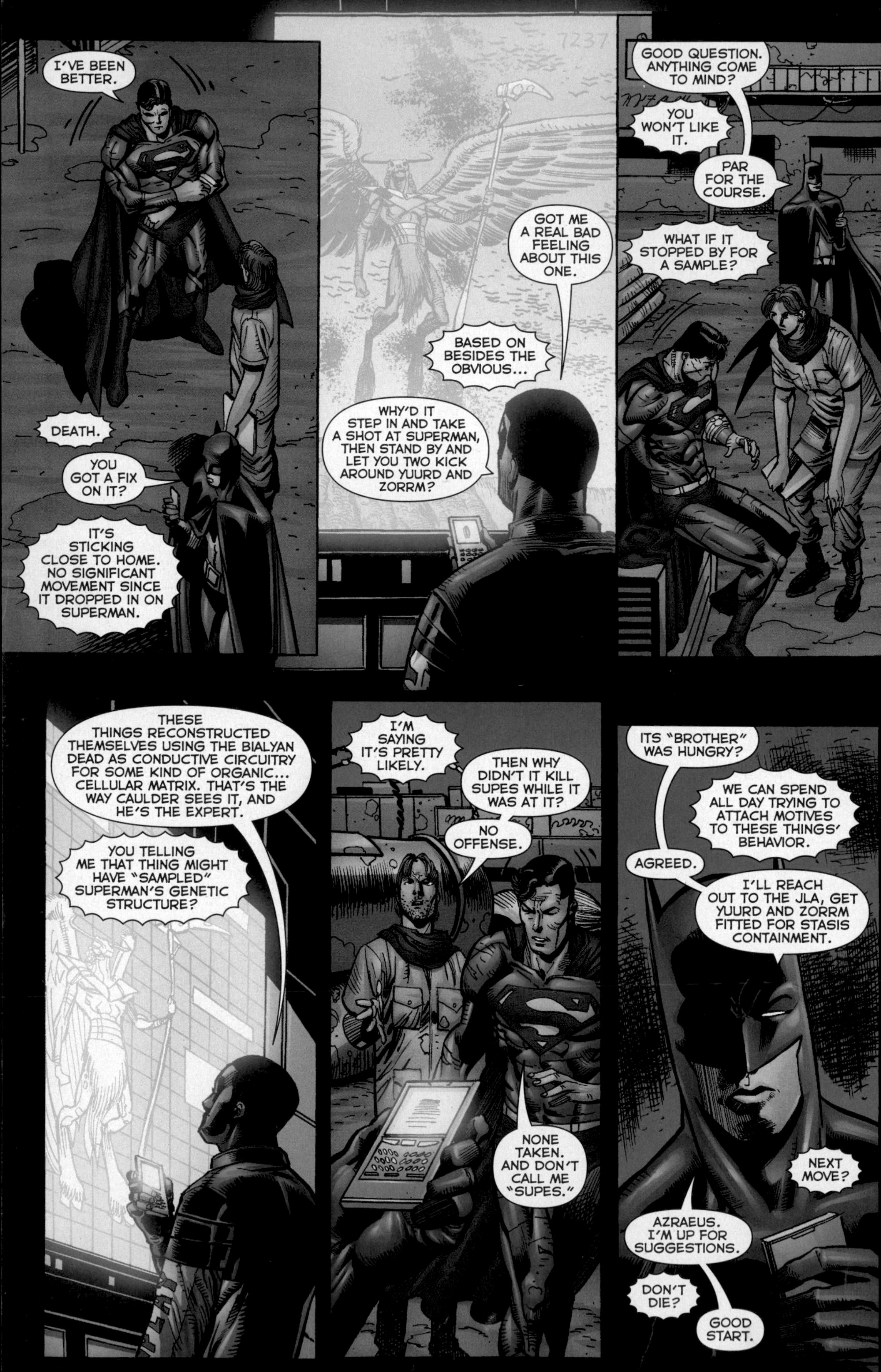
I'VE BEEN BETTER.
DEATH.
YOU GOT A FIX ON IT?
IT'S STICKING CLOSE TO HOME. NO SIGNIFICANT MOVEMENT SINCE IT DROPPED IN ON SUPERMAN.
GOT ME A REAL BAD FEELING ABOUT THIS ONE.
BASED ON BESIDES THE OBVIOUS...
WHY'D IT STEP IN AND TAKE A SHOT AT SUPERMAN, THEN STAND BY AND LET YOU TWO KICK AROUND YUURD AND ZORRM?
GOOD QUESTION. ANYTHING COME TO MIND?
YOU WON'T LIKE IT.
PAR FOR THE COURSE.
WHAT IF IT STOPPED BY FOR A SAMPLE?
THESE THINGS RECONSTRUCTED THEMSELVES USING THE BIALYAN DEAD AS CONDUCTIVE CIRCUITRY FOR SOME KIND OF ORGANIC... CELLULAR MATRIX. THAT'S THE WAY CAULDER SEES IT, AND HE'S THE EXPERT.
YOU TELLING ME THAT THING MIGHT HAVE "SAMPLED" SUPERMAN'S GENETIC STRUCTURE?
I'M SAYING IT'S PRETTY LIKELY.
THEN WHY DIDN'T IT KILL SUPES WHILE IT WAS AT IT?
NO OFFENSE.
NONE TAKEN. AND DON'T CALL ME "SUPES."
ITS "BROTHER" WAS HUNGRY?
WE CAN SPEND ALL DAY TRYING TO ATTACH MOTIVES TO THESE THINGS' BEHAVIOR.
AGREED.
I'LL REACH OUT TO THE JLA, GET YUURD AND ZORRM FITTED FOR STASIS CONTAINMENT.
NEXT MOVE?
AZRAEUS. I'M UP FOR SUGGESTIONS.
DON'T DIE?
GOOD START.

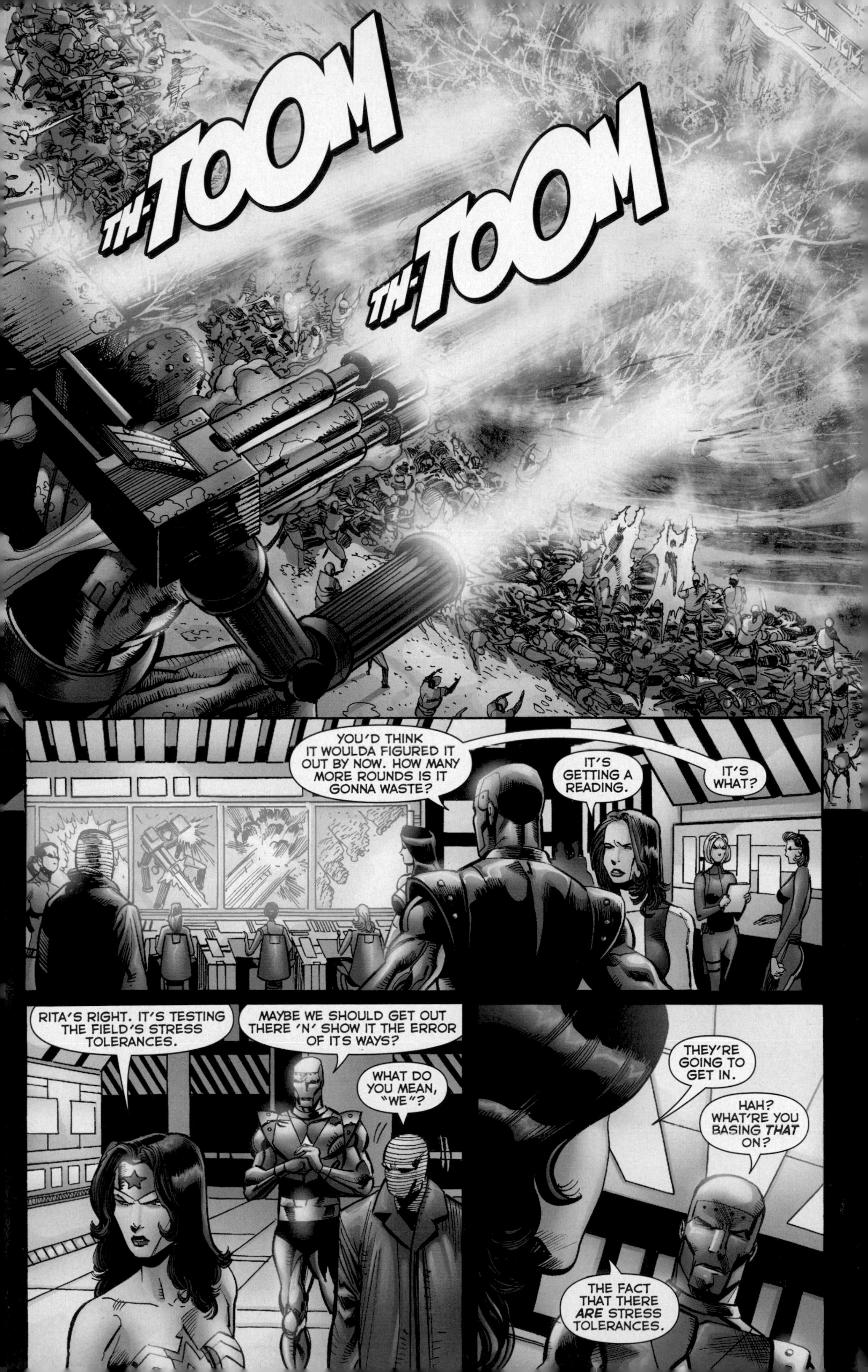
TH-TOOM
TH-TOOM
YOU'D THINK IT WOULDA FIGURED IT OUT BY NOW. HOW MANY MORE ROUNDS IS IT GONNA WASTE?
IT'S GETTING A READING.
IT'S WHAT?
RITA'S RIGHT. IT'S TESTING THE FIELD'S STRESS TOLERANCES.
MAYBE WE SHOULD GET OUT THERE 'N' SHOW IT THE ERROR OF ITS WAYS?
WHAT DO YOU MEAN, "WE"?
THEY'RE GOING TO GET IN.
HAH? WHAT'RE YOU BASING *THAT* ON?
THE FACT THAT THERE *ARE* STRESS TOLERANCES.

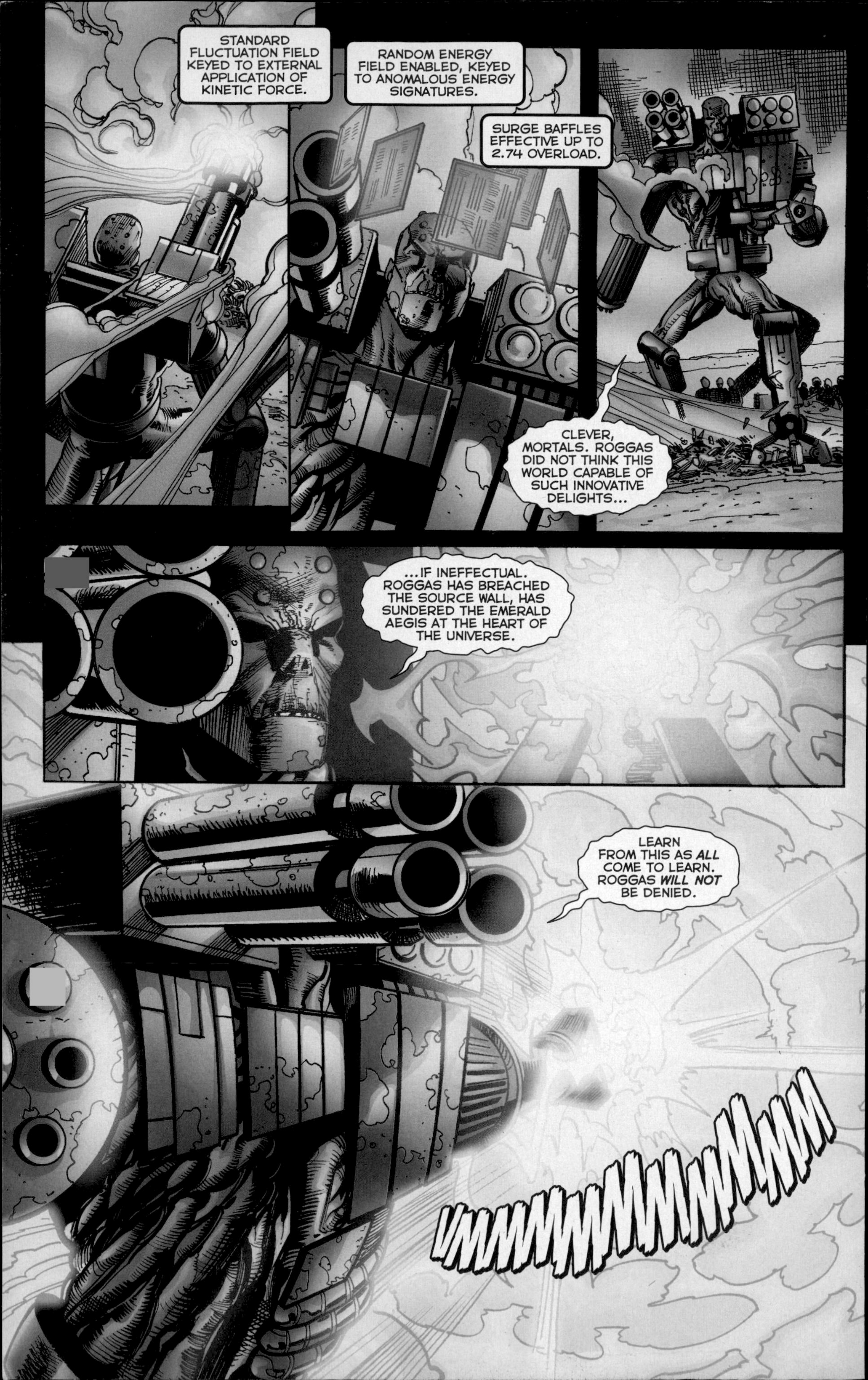
STANDARD FLUCTUATION FIELD KEYED TO EXTERNAL APPLICATION OF KINETIC FORCE.
RANDOM ENERGY FIELD ENABLED, KEYED TO ANOMALOUS ENERGY SIGNATURES.
SURGE BAFFLES EFFECTIVE UP TO 2.74 OVERLOAD.
CLEVER, MORTALS. ROGGAS DID NOT THINK THIS WORLD CAPABLE OF SUCH INNOVATIVE DELIGHTS...
...IF INEFFECTUAL. ROGGAS HAS BREACHED THE SOURCE WALL, HAS SUNDERED THE EMERALD AEGIS AT THE HEART OF THE UNIVERSE.
LEARN FROM THIS AS *ALL* COME TO LEARN. ROGGAS *WILL NOT* BE DENIED.
VMMMMMMMMMMMMMM

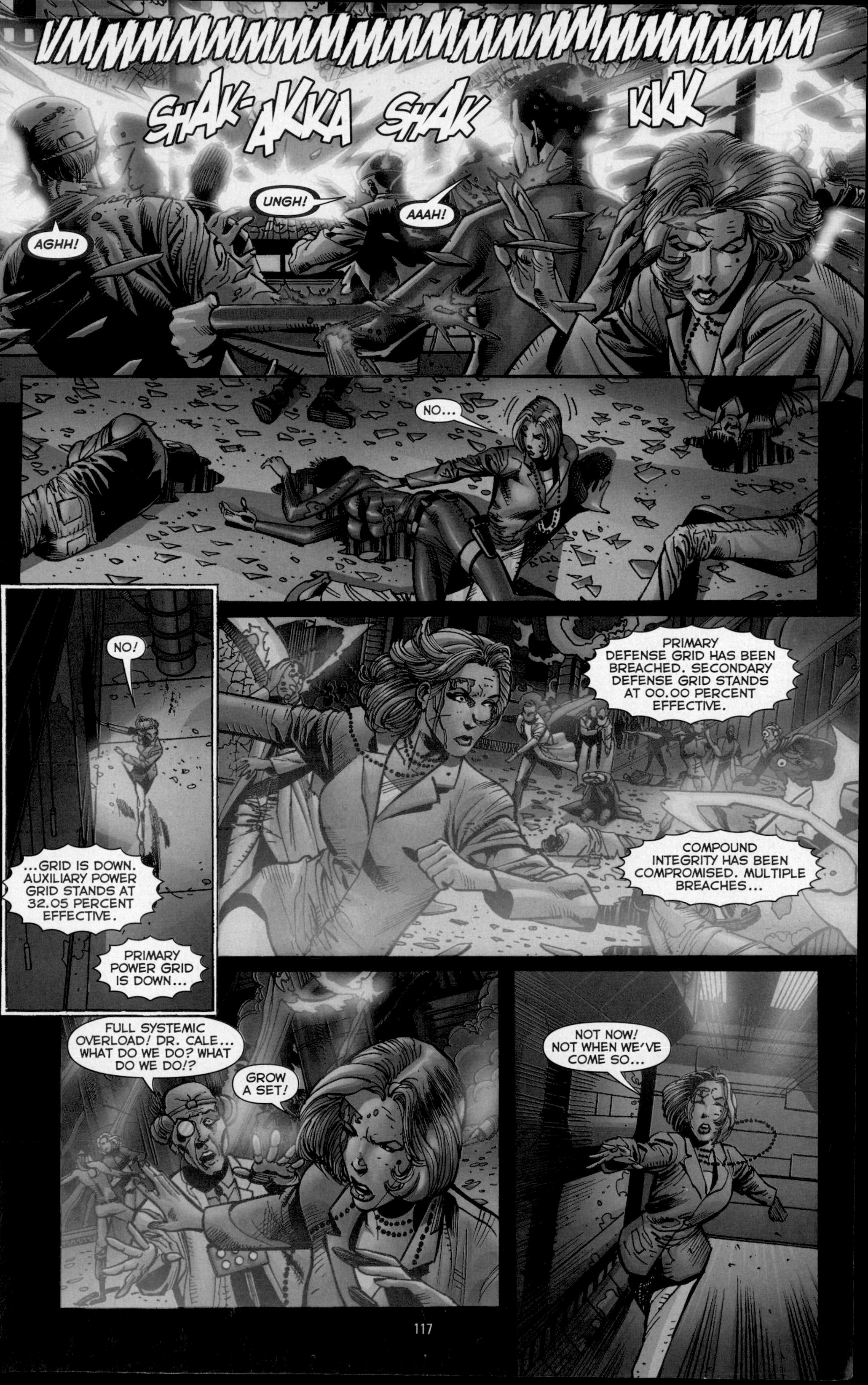

VMMMMMMMMMMMMMMMMMMMMMMM
SHAK-AKKA SHAK
KIKK
AGHH!
UNGH!
AAAH!
NO...
NO!
PRIMARY DEFENSE GRID HAS BEEN BREACHED. SECONDARY DEFENSE GRID STANDS AT 00.00 PERCENT EFFECTIVE.
COMPOUND INTEGRITY HAS BEEN COMPROMISED. MULTIPLE BREACHES...
...GRID IS DOWN. AUXILIARY POWER GRID STANDS AT 32.05 PERCENT EFFECTIVE.
PRIMARY POWER GRID IS DOWN...
FULL SYSTEMIC OVERLOAD! DR. CALE... WHAT DO WE DO? WHAT DO WE DO!?
GROW A SET!
NOT NOW! NOT WHEN WE'VE COME SO...

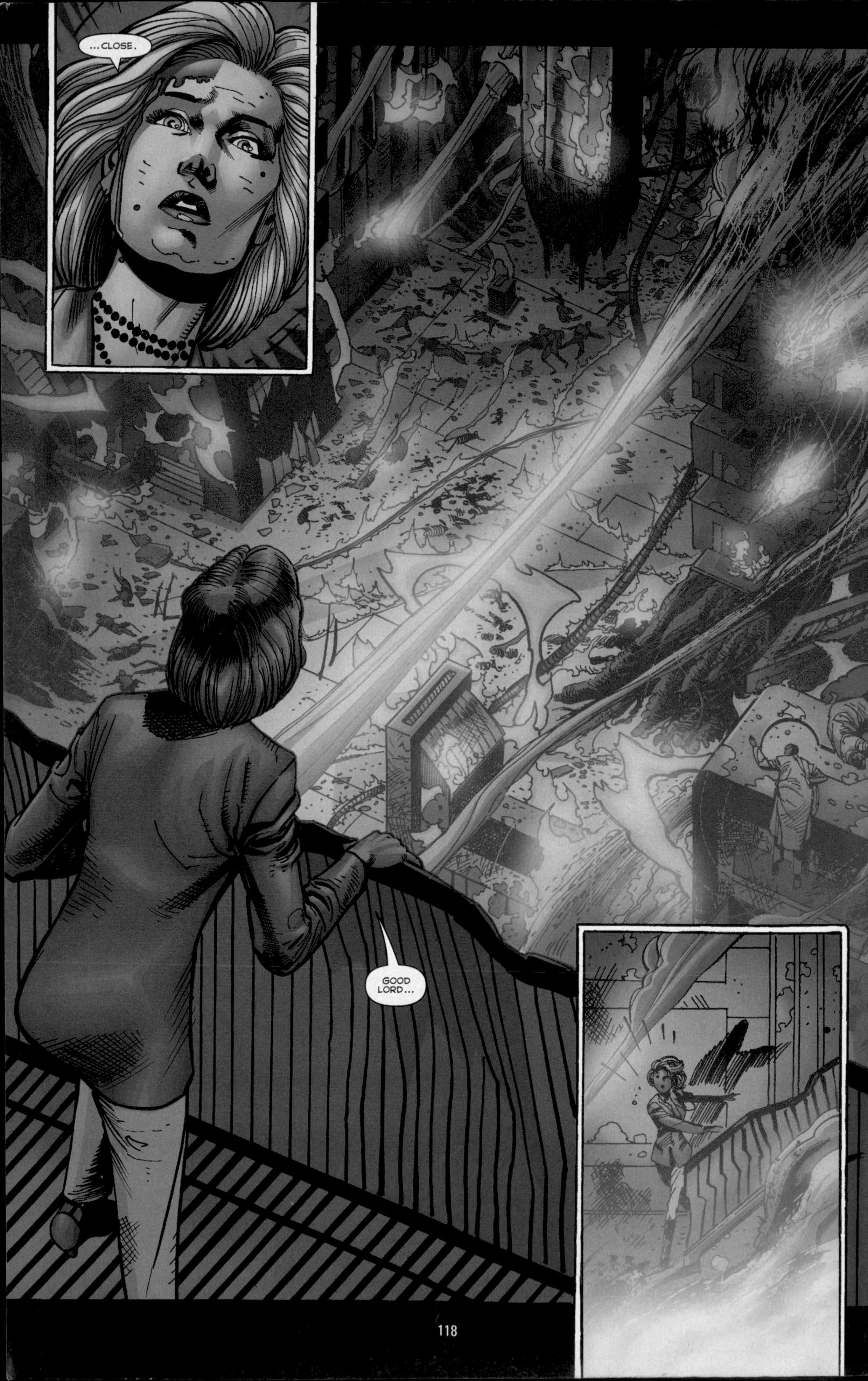
...CLOSE.
GOOD LORD...
!!

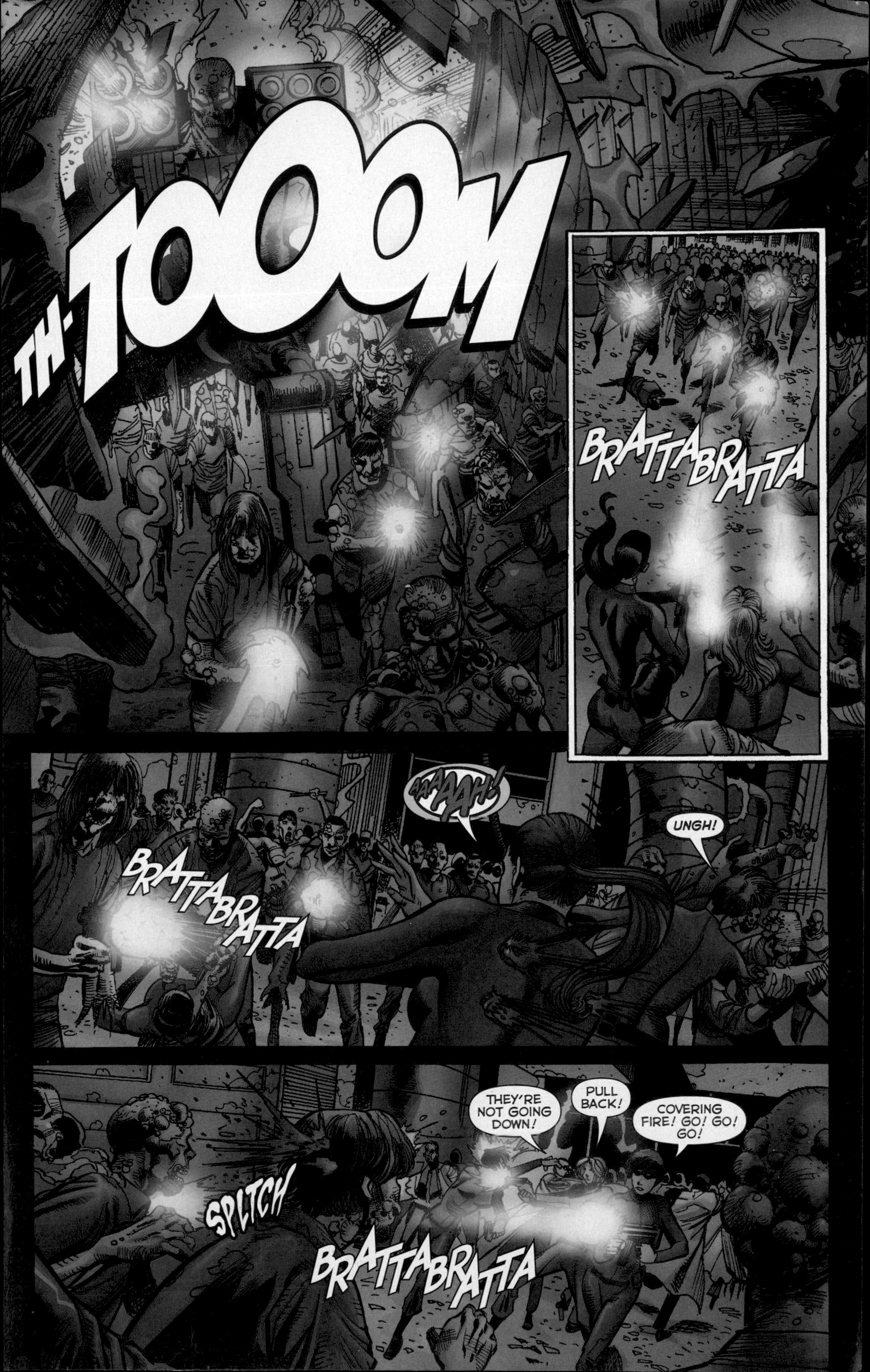
TH-TOOOM
BRATTABRATTA
AAAAAH!
UNGH!
BRATTABRATTA
THEY'RE NOT GOING DOWN!
PULL BACK!
COVERING FIRE! GO! GO! GO!
SPLTCH
BRATTABRATTA

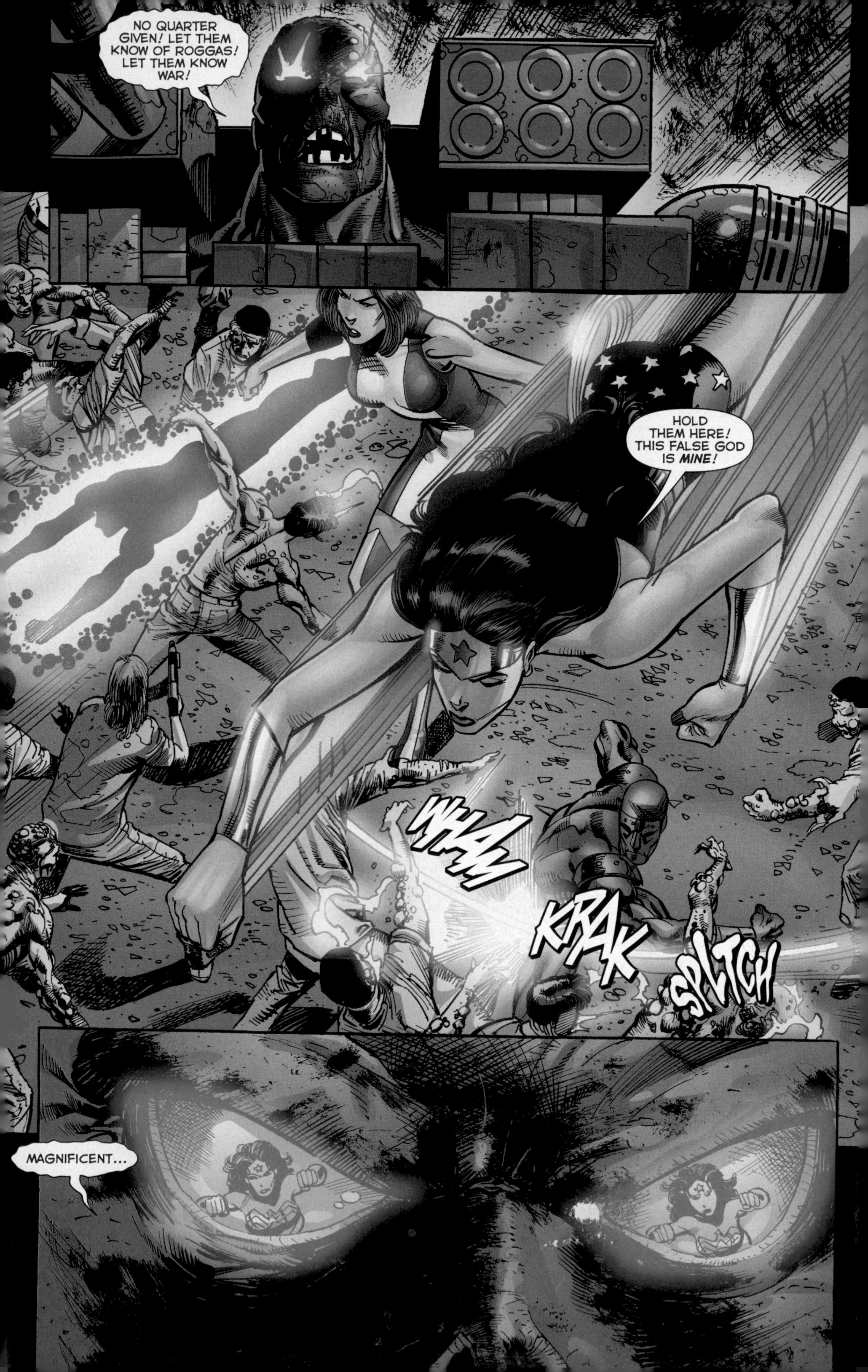
NO QUARTER GIVEN! LET THEM KNOW OF ROGGAS! LET THEM KNOW WAR!
HOLD THEM HERE! THIS FALSE GOD IS MINE!
WHAM
KRAK
SPLTCH
MAGNIFICENT...

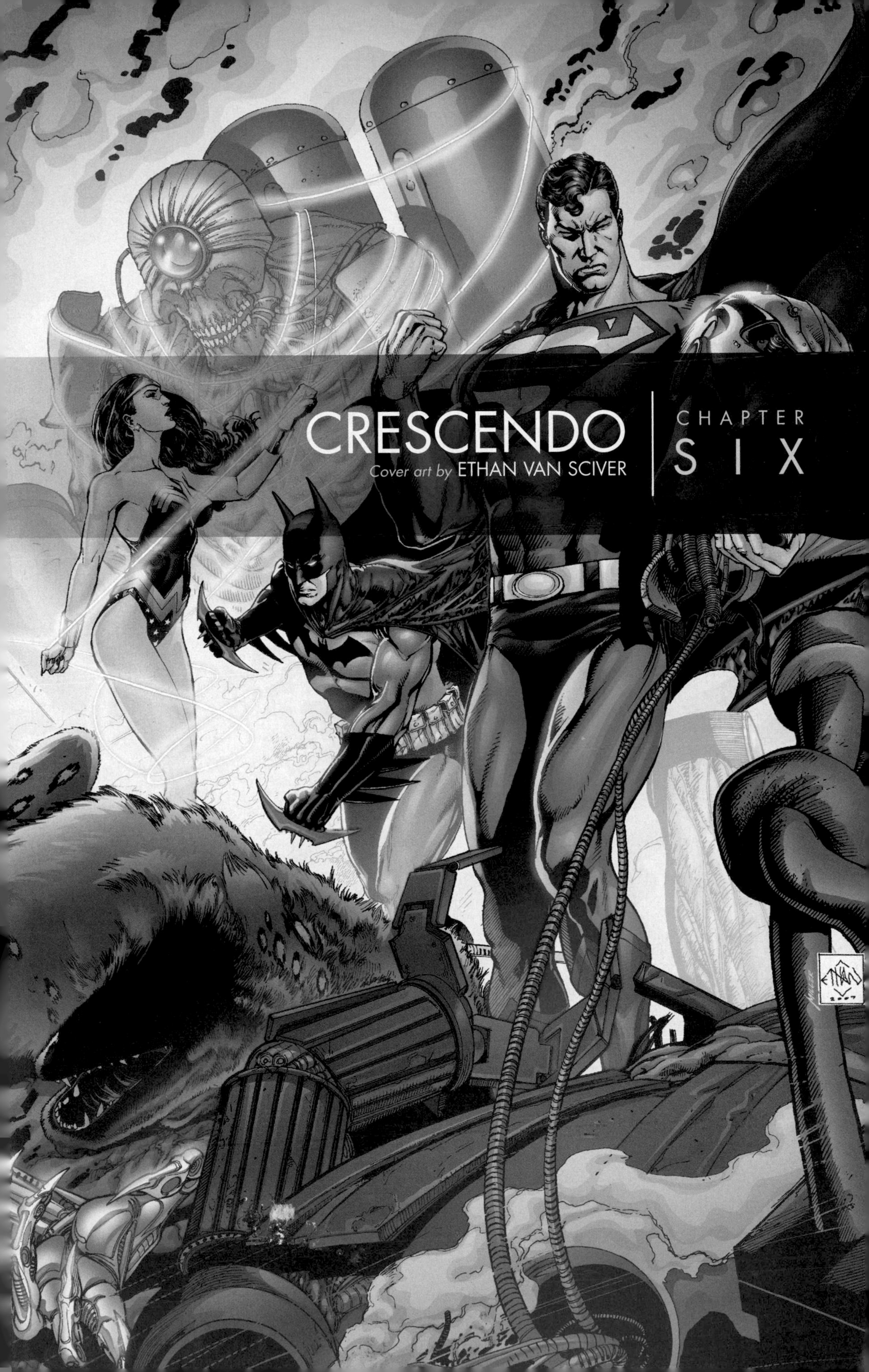

CRESCENDO

Cover art by ETHAN VAN SCIVER

CHAPTER SIX

DEATH
PESTILENCE
FAMINE
WAR

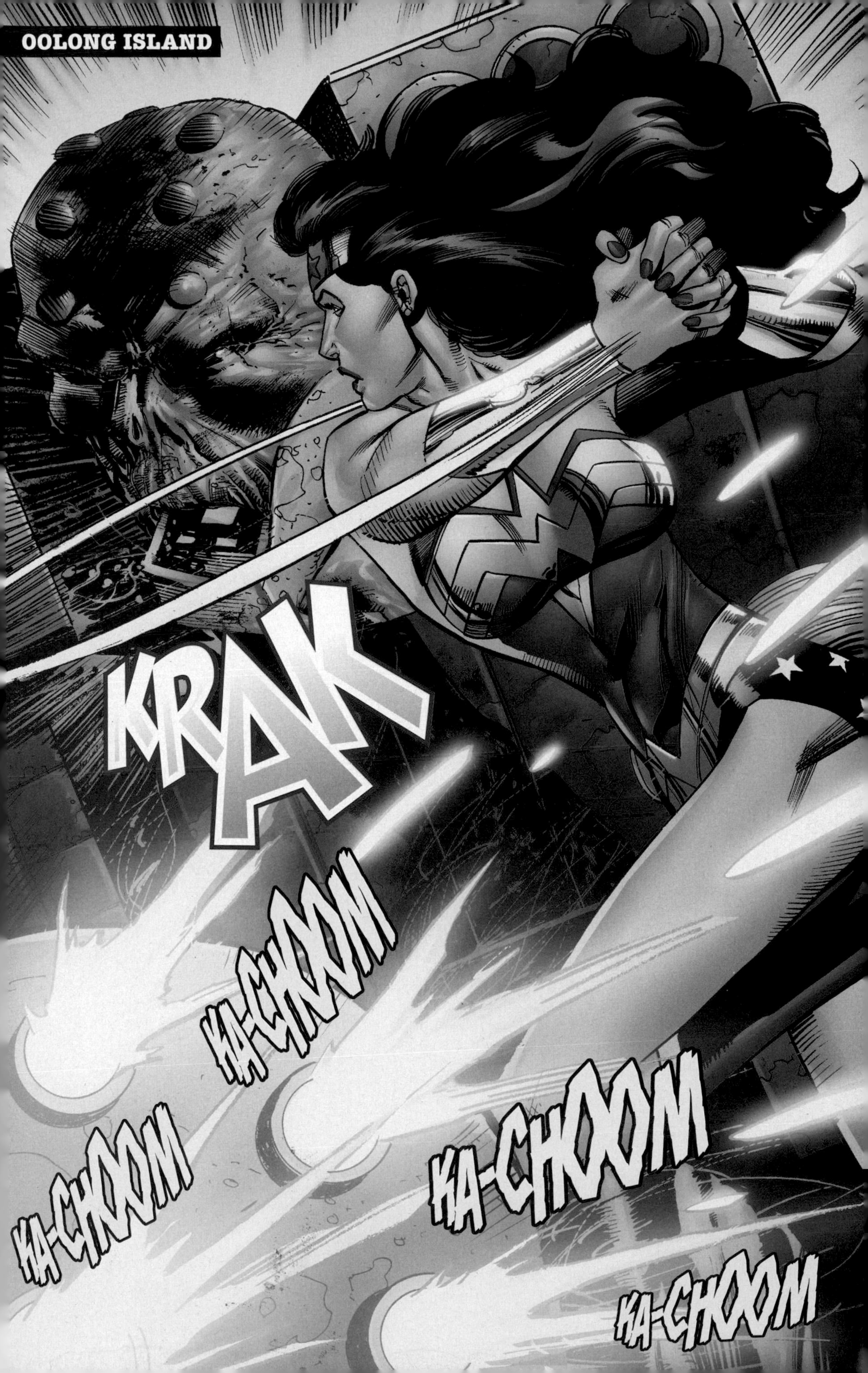
OOLONG ISLAND
KRAK
KA-CHOOM
KA-CHOOM
KA-CHOOM
KA-CHOOM

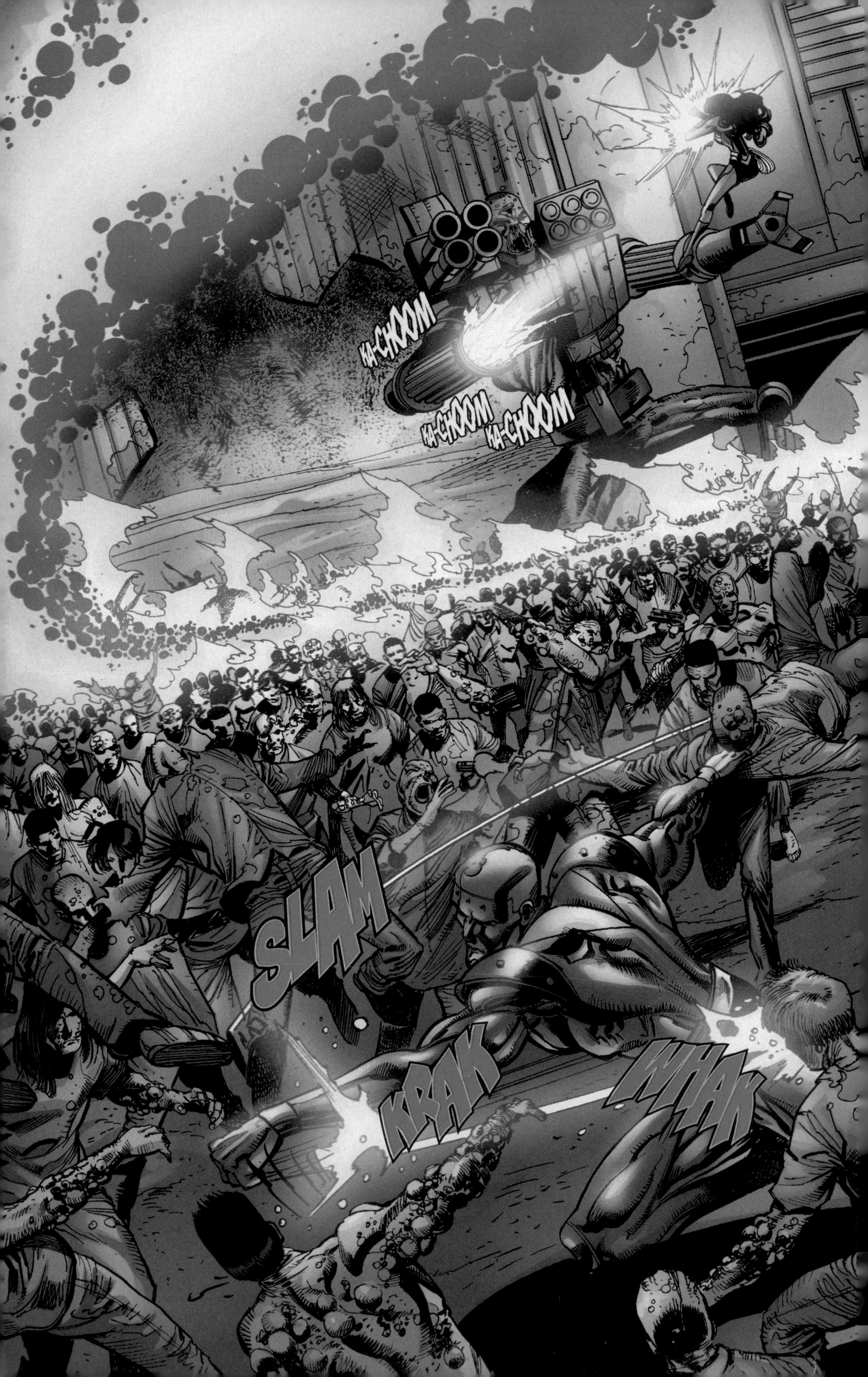
KA-CHOOM
KA-CHOOM
KA-CHOOM
SLAM
KRAK
WHAK

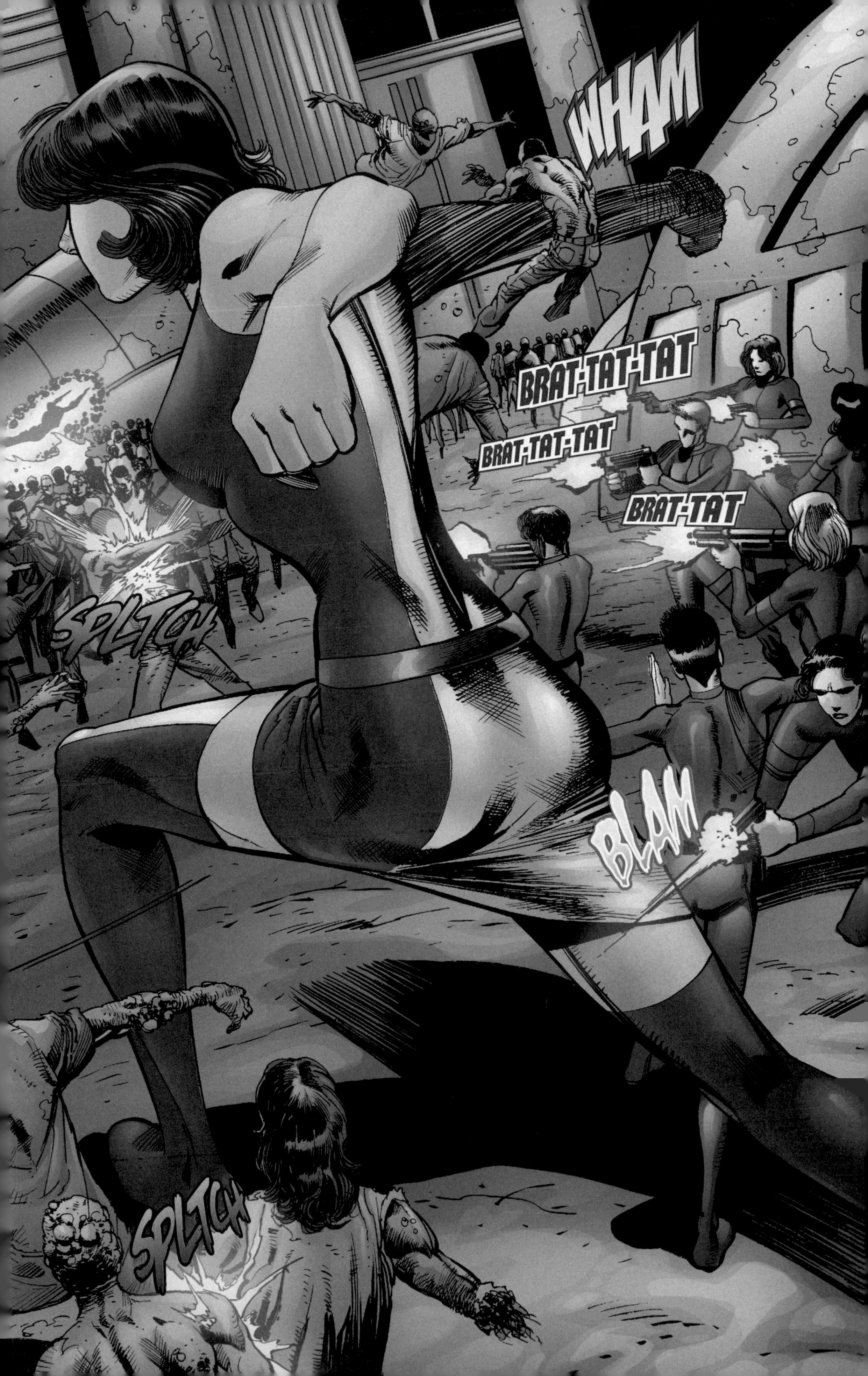
WHAM
BRAT-TAT-TAT
BRAT-TAT-TAT
BRAT-TAT
SPLTCH
BLAM
SPLTCH

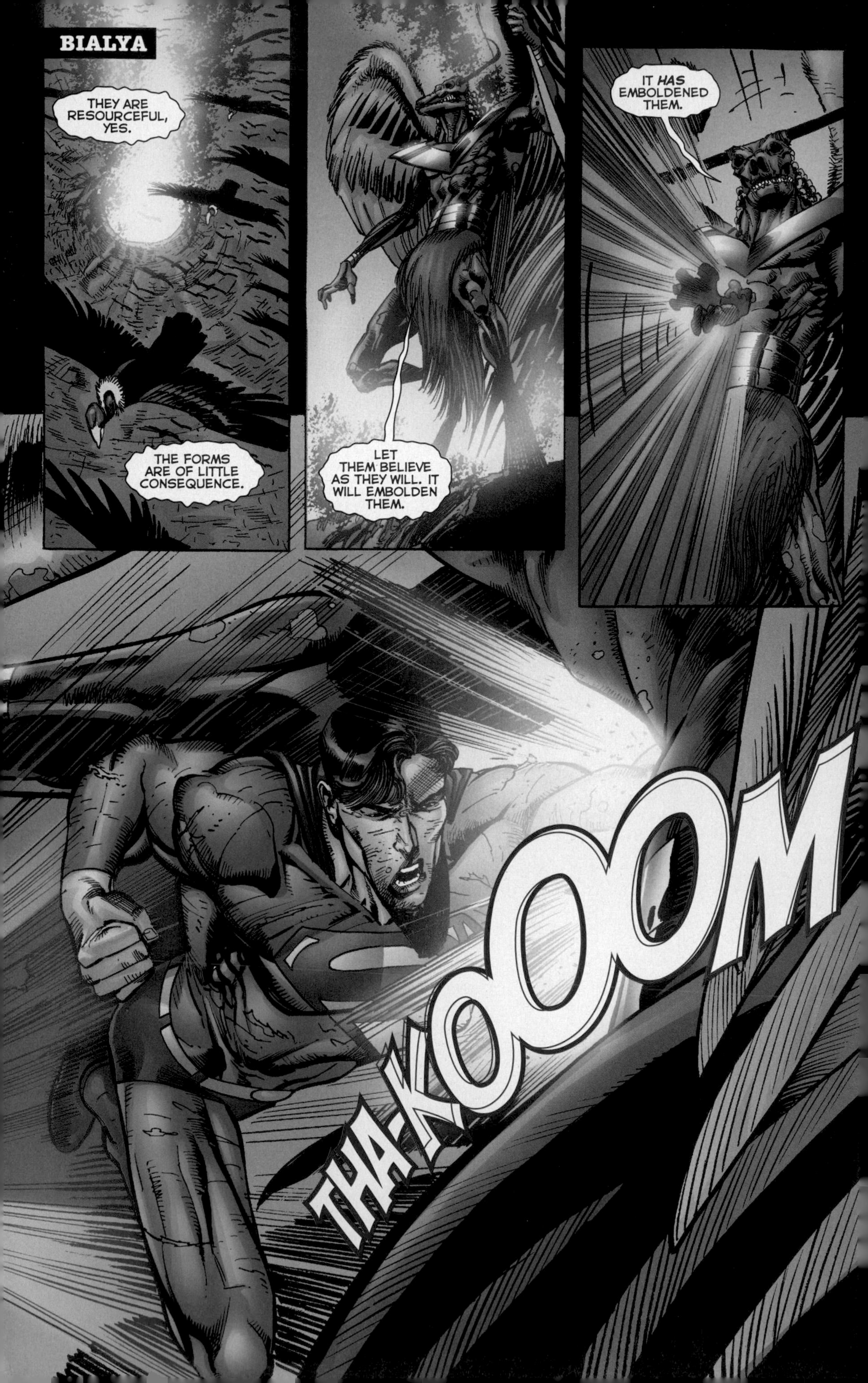
BIALYA
THEY ARE RESOURCEFUL, YES.
THE FORMS ARE OF LITTLE CONSEQUENCE.
LET THEM BELIEVE AS THEY WILL. IT WILL EMBOLDEN THEM.
IT HAS EMBOLDENED THEM.
THA-KOOOM

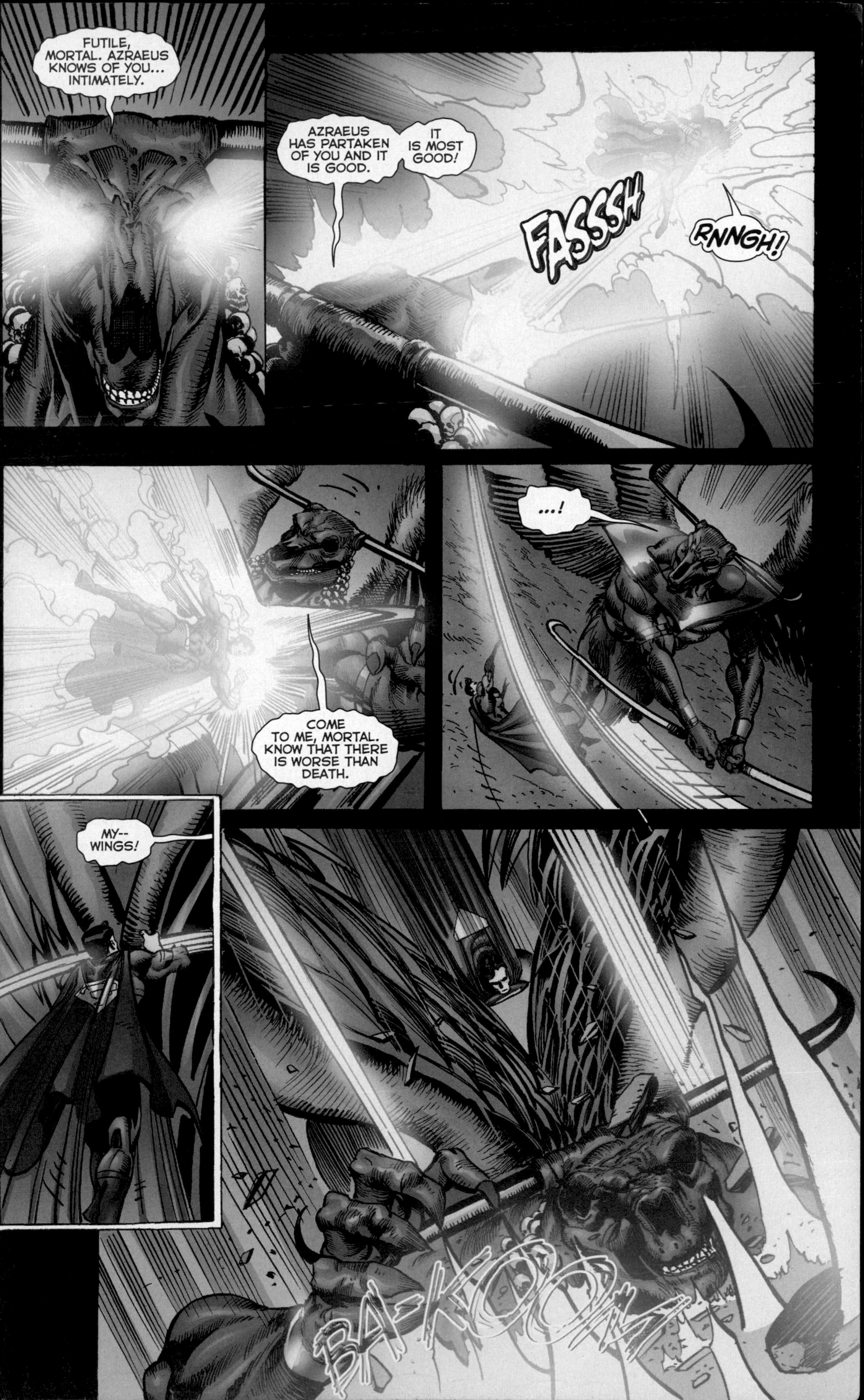
FUTILE, MORTAL. AZRAEUS KNOWS OF YOU... INTIMATELY.
AZRAEUS HAS PARTAKEN OF YOU AND IT IS GOOD.
IT IS MOST GOOD!
FASSSH
RNNGH!
COME TO ME, MORTAL. KNOW THAT THERE IS WORSE THAN DEATH.
...!
MY-- WINGS!
BA-KOOM

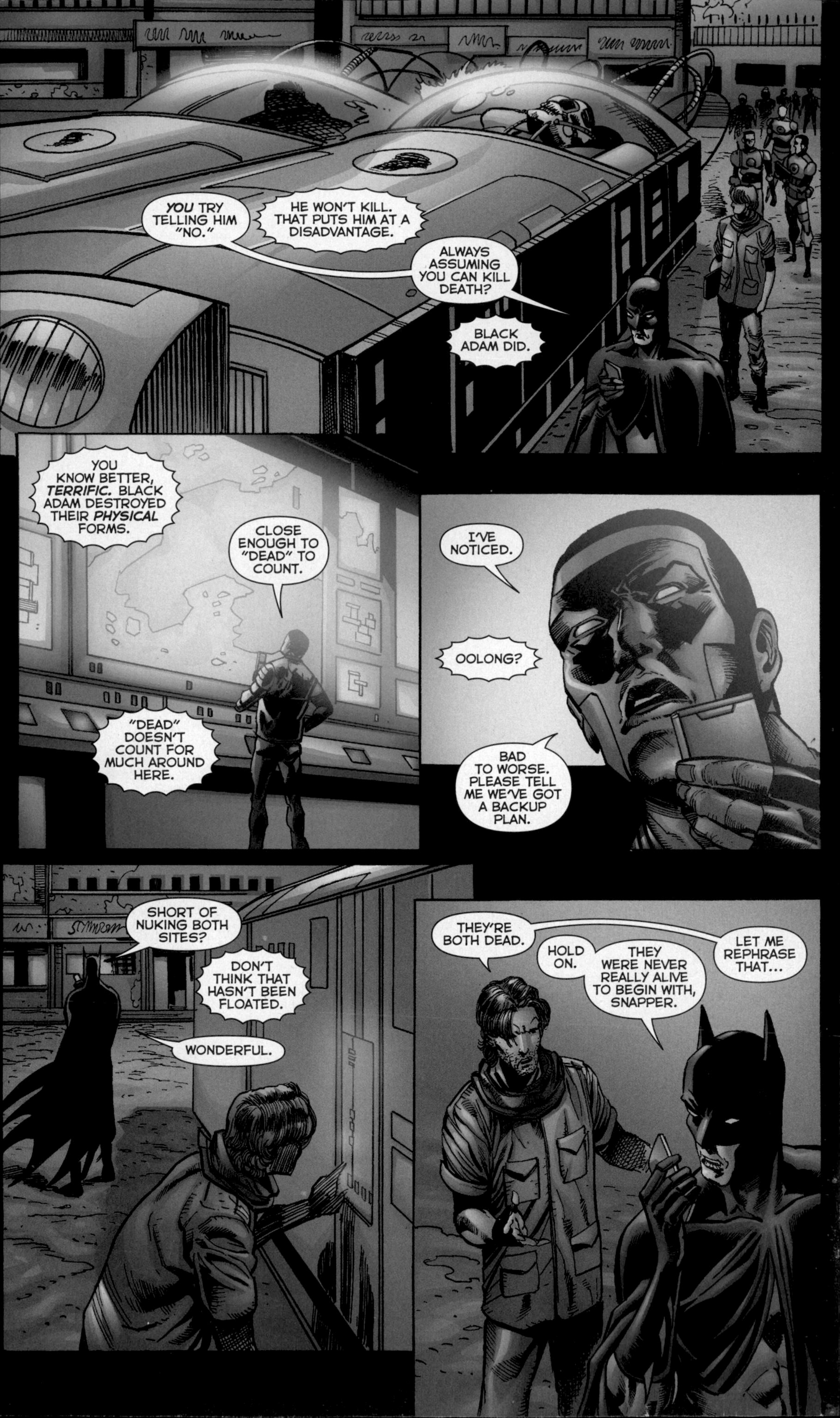
YOU TRY TELLING HIM "NO."
HE WON'T KILL. THAT PUTS HIM AT A DISADVANTAGE.
ALWAYS ASSUMING YOU CAN KILL DEATH?
BLACK ADAM DID.
YOU KNOW BETTER, TERRIFIC. BLACK ADAM DESTROYED THEIR PHYSICAL FORMS.
CLOSE ENOUGH TO "DEAD" TO COUNT.
"DEAD" DOESN'T COUNT FOR MUCH AROUND HERE.
I'VE NOTICED.
OOLONG?
BAD TO WORSE. PLEASE TELL ME WE'VE GOT A BACKUP PLAN.
SHORT OF NUKING BOTH SITES?
DON'T THINK THAT HASN'T BEEN FLOATED.
WONDERFUL.
THEY'RE BOTH DEAD.
LET ME REPHRASE THAT...
HOLD ON.
THEY WERE NEVER REALLY ALIVE TO BEGIN WITH, SNAPPER.

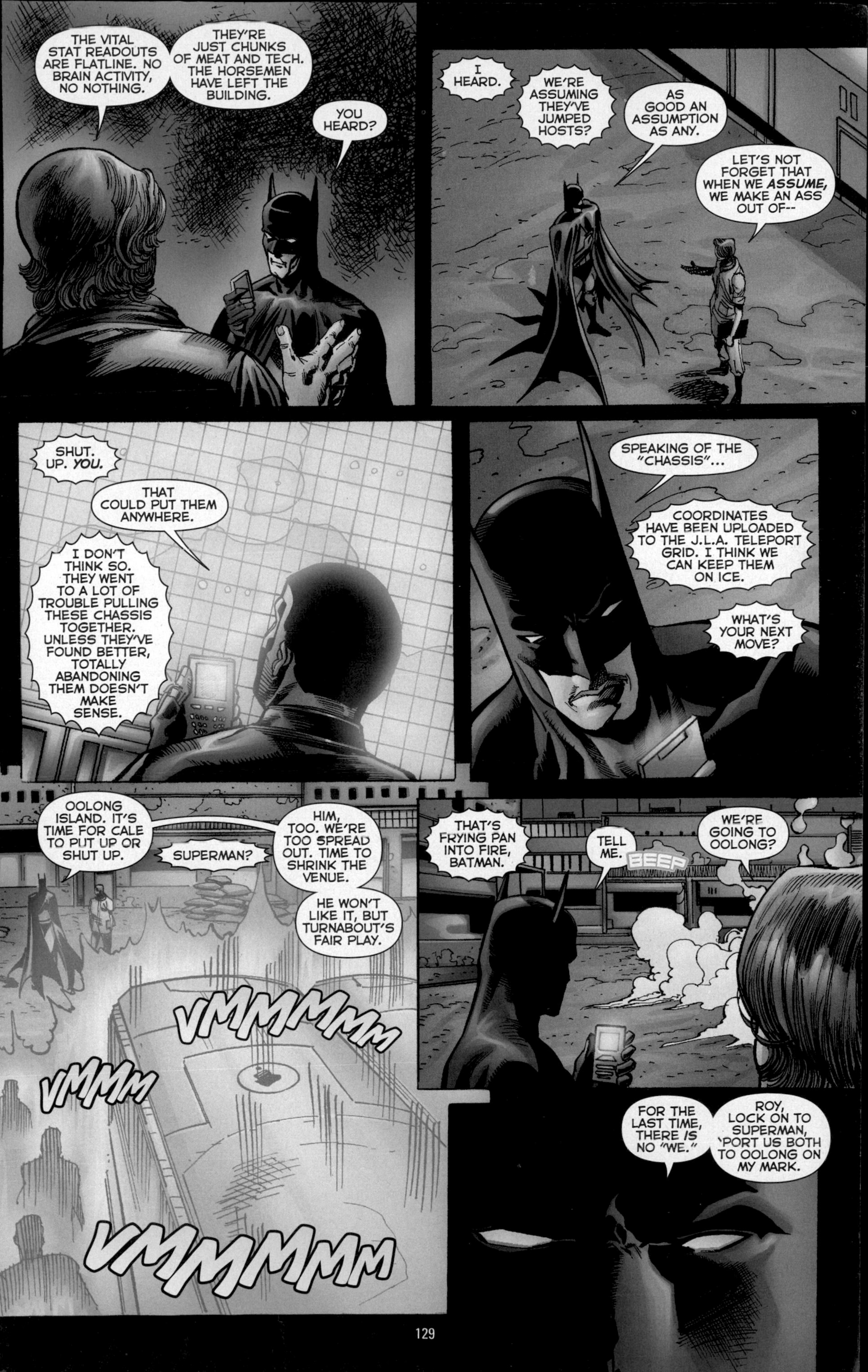
THE VITAL STAT READOUTS ARE FLATLINE. NO BRAIN ACTIVITY, NO NOTHING.
THEY'RE JUST CHUNKS OF MEAT AND TECH. THE HORSEMEN HAVE LEFT THE BUILDING.
YOU HEARD?
I HEARD.
WE'RE ASSUMING THEY'VE JUMPED HOSTS?
AS GOOD AN ASSUMPTION AS ANY.
LET'S NOT FORGET THAT WHEN WE ASSUME, WE MAKE AN ASS OUT OF--
SHUT. UP. YOU.
THAT COULD PUT THEM ANYWHERE.
I DON'T THINK SO. THEY WENT TO A LOT OF TROUBLE PULLING THESE CHASSIS TOGETHER. UNLESS THEY'VE FOUND BETTER, TOTALLY ABANDONING THEM DOESN'T MAKE SENSE.
SPEAKING OF THE "CHASSIS"...
COORDINATES HAVE BEEN UPLOADED TO THE J.L.A. TELEPORT GRID. I THINK WE CAN KEEP THEM ON ICE.
WHAT'S YOUR NEXT MOVE?
OOLONG ISLAND. IT'S TIME FOR CALE TO PUT UP OR SHUT UP.
SUPERMAN?
HIM, TOO. WE'RE TOO SPREAD OUT. TIME TO SHRINK THE VENUE.
HE WON'T LIKE IT, BUT TURNABOUT'S FAIR PLAY.
VMMMMMM
VMMM
VMMMMMM
THAT'S FRYING PAN INTO FIRE, BATMAN.
TELL ME.
BEEP
WE'RE GOING TO OOLONG?
FOR THE LAST TIME, THERE IS NO "WE."
ROY, LOCK ON TO SUPERMAN, 'PORT US BOTH TO OOLONG ON MY MARK.

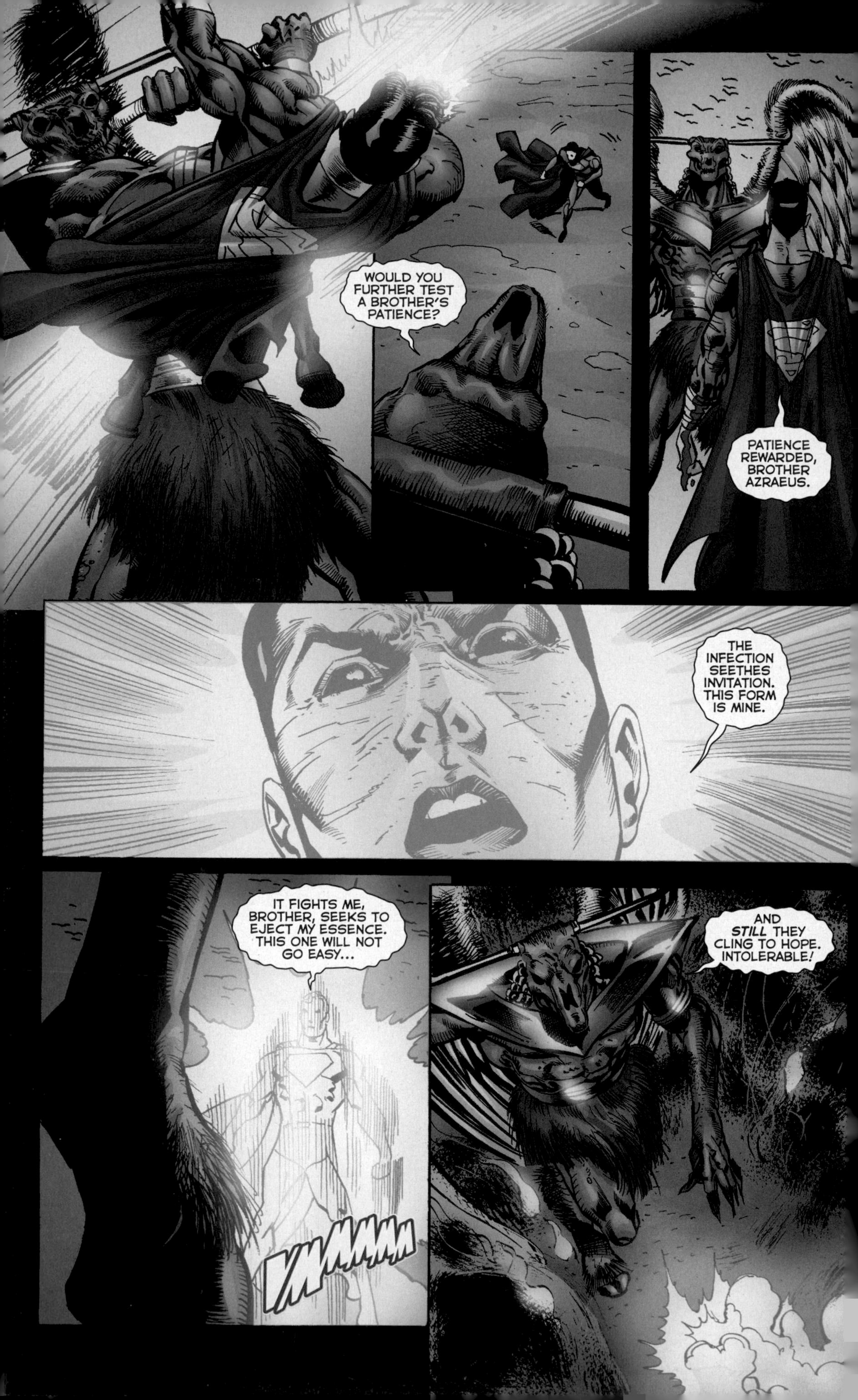
WOULD YOU FURTHER TEST A BROTHER'S PATIENCE?
PATIENCE REWARDED, BROTHER AZRAEUS.
THE INFECTION SEETHES INVITATION. THIS FORM IS MINE.
IT FIGHTS ME, BROTHER, SEEKS TO EJECT MY ESSENCE. THIS ONE WILL NOT GO EASY...
VMMMMM
AND *STILL* THEY CLING TO HOPE. INTOLERABLE!

"THE DEAD WERE ARRAYED... CONDUCTIVE CIRCUITRY. AN ORGANIC MATRIX..."

"KEYING THE GATE'S ENERGY SIGNATURE TO CELL STRUCTURE IS CRITICAL..."

"... APOKOLIPTIAN COMPONENTS ARE ORGANIC... LIVING TECH..."

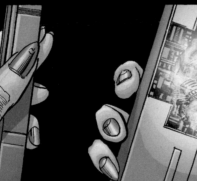

"... SEEN FIT TO RADICALLY ALTER THE CELLULAR MATRIX..."

"THE FOUR HORSEMEN ARE OF EARTH NOW..."

"KEY THE TECH TO A REVISED BIOLOGICAL IMPERATIVE..."

"... LIVING TECHNORGANIC COMPONENTS..."

"I MADE THE THINGS THAT KILLED YOUR FAMILY..."

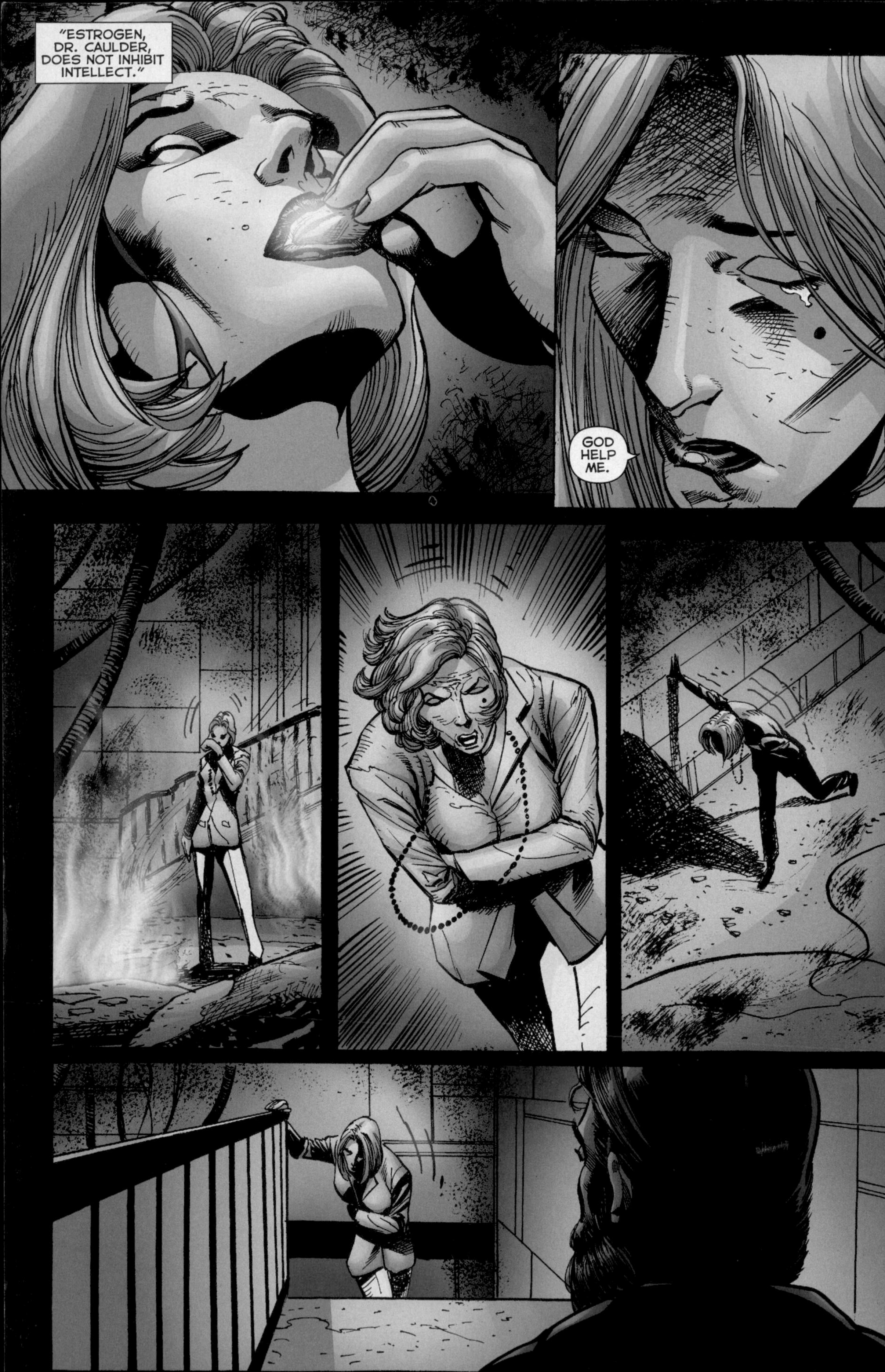
"ESTROGEN, DR. CAULDER, DOES NOT INHIBIT INTELLECT."
GOD HELP ME.

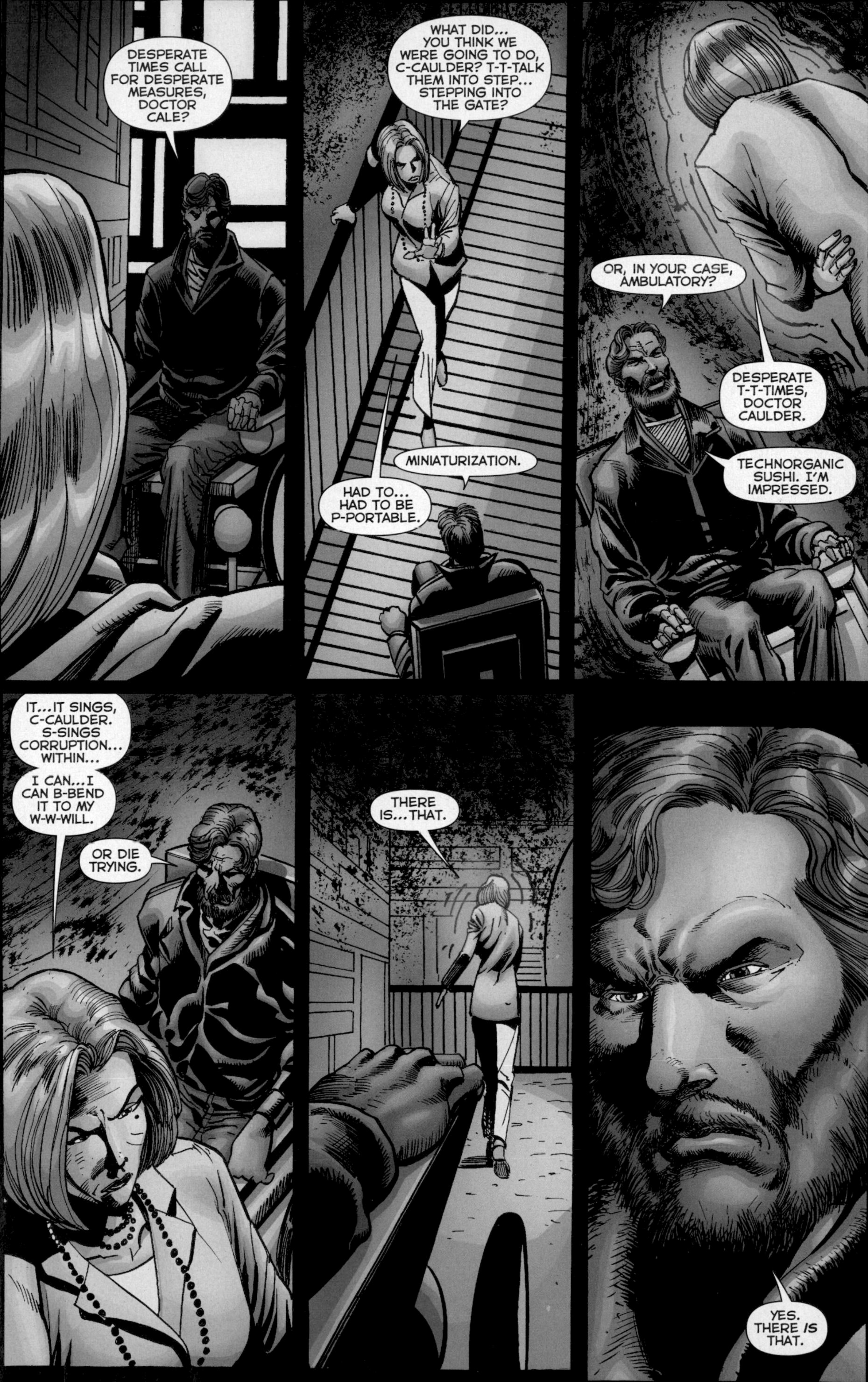
DESPERATE TIMES CALL FOR DESPERATE MEASURES, DOCTOR CALE?
WHAT DID... YOU THINK WE WERE GOING TO DO, C-CAULDER? T-T-TALK THEM INTO STEP... STEPPING INTO THE GATE?
MINIATURIZATION.
HAD TO... HAD TO BE P-PORTABLE.
OR, IN YOUR CASE, AMBULATORY?
DESPERATE T-T-TIMES, DOCTOR CAULDER.
TECHNORGANIC SUSHI. I'M IMPRESSED.
IT...IT SINGS, C-CAULDER. S-SINGS CORRUPTION... WITHIN...
I CAN...I CAN B-BEND IT TO MY W-W-WILL.
OR DIE TRYING.
THERE IS...THAT.
YES. THERE *IS* THAT.

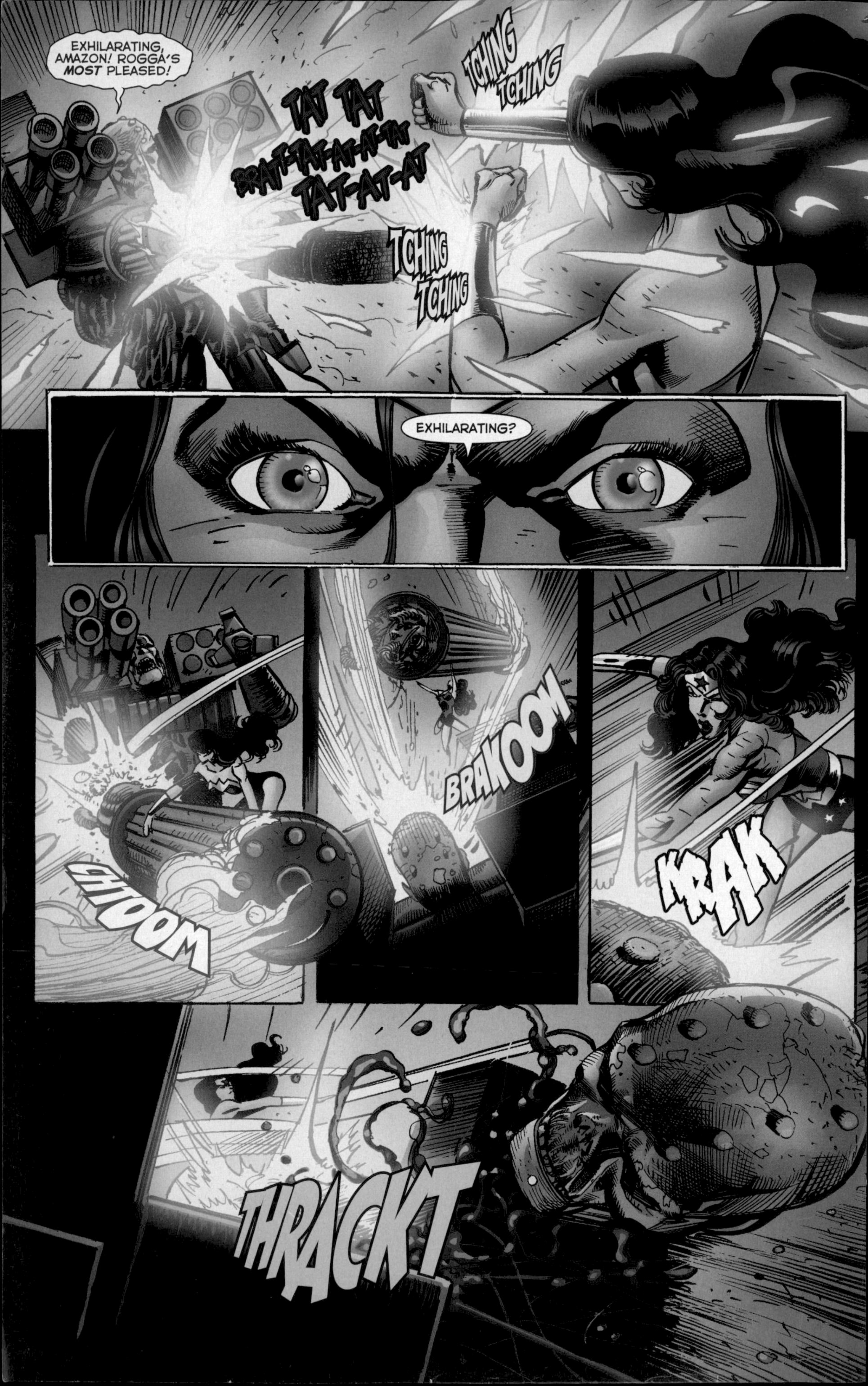

EXHILARATING, AMAZON! ROGGA'S MOST PLEASED!
TAT TAT
BRATT-TAT-AT-AT-TAT
TAT-AT-AT
TCHING TCHING
TCHING TCHING
EXHILARATING?
CHOOM
BRAKOOM
KRAK
THRACKT

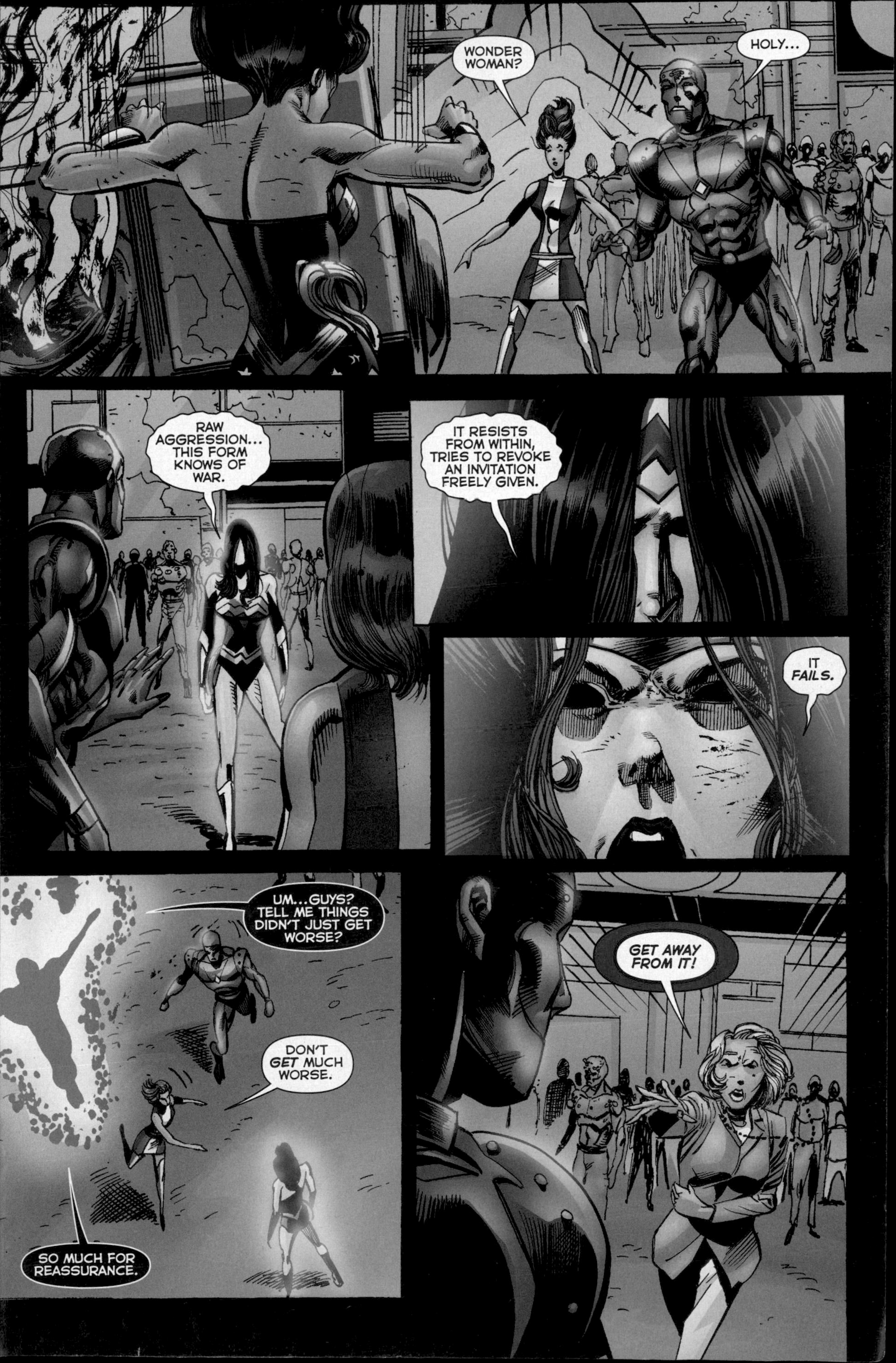
WONDER WOMAN?
HOLY...
RAW AGGRESSION... THIS FORM KNOWS OF WAR.
IT RESISTS FROM WITHIN, TRIES TO REVOKE AN INVITATION FREELY GIVEN.
IT FAILS.
UM...GUYS? TELL ME THINGS DIDN'T JUST GET WORSE?
DON'T GET MUCH WORSE.
SO MUCH FOR REASSURANCE.
GET AWAY FROM IT!

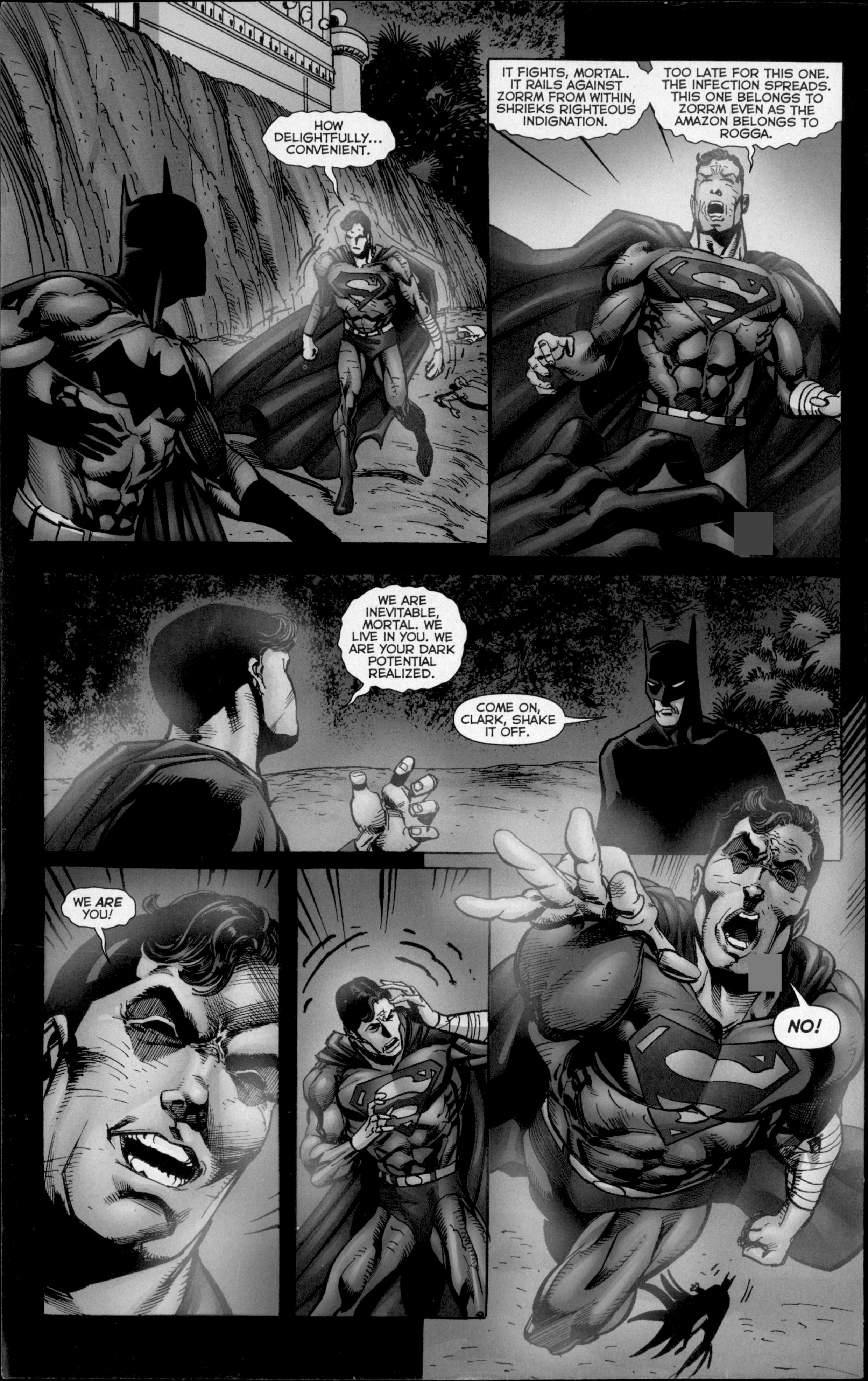
HOW DELIGHTFULLY... CONVENIENT.
IT FIGHTS, MORTAL. IT RAILS AGAINST ZORRM FROM WITHIN, SHRIEKS RIGHTEOUS INDIGNATION.
TOO LATE FOR THIS ONE. THE INFECTION SPREADS. THIS ONE BELONGS TO ZORRM EVEN AS THE AMAZON BELONGS TO ROGGA.
WE ARE INEVITABLE, MORTAL. WE LIVE IN YOU. WE ARE YOUR DARK POTENTIAL REALIZED.
COME ON, CLARK, SHAKE IT OFF.
WE ARE YOU!
NO!

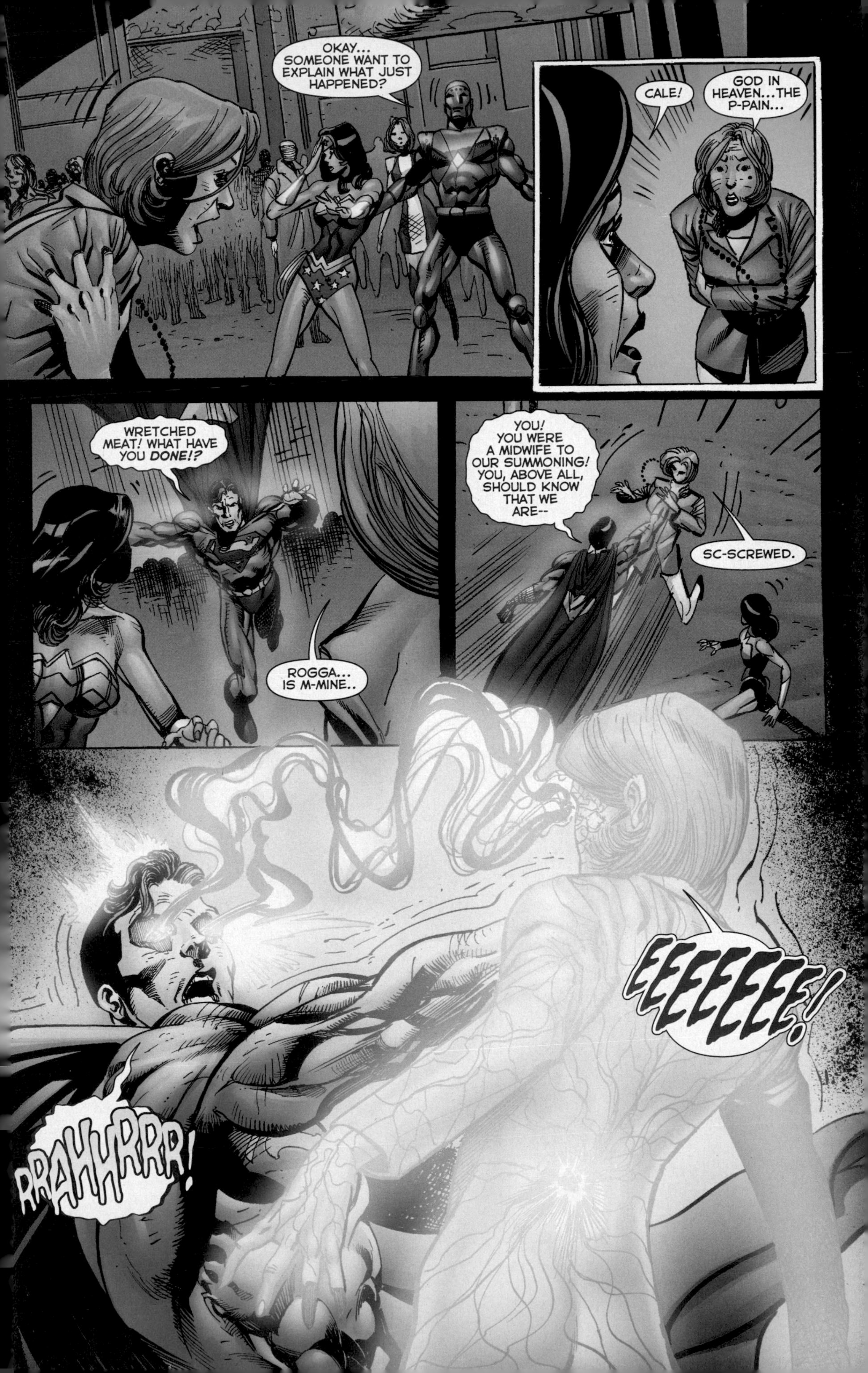
OKAY... SOMEONE WANT TO EXPLAIN WHAT JUST HAPPENED?
CALE!
GOD IN HEAVEN...THE P-PAIN...
WRETCHED MEAT! WHAT HAVE YOU DONE!?
ROGGA... IS M-MINE..
YOU! YOU WERE A MIDWIFE TO OUR SUMMONING! YOU, ABOVE ALL, SHOULD KNOW THAT WE ARE--
SC-SCREWED.
EEEEEEE!
RRAHHRRR!

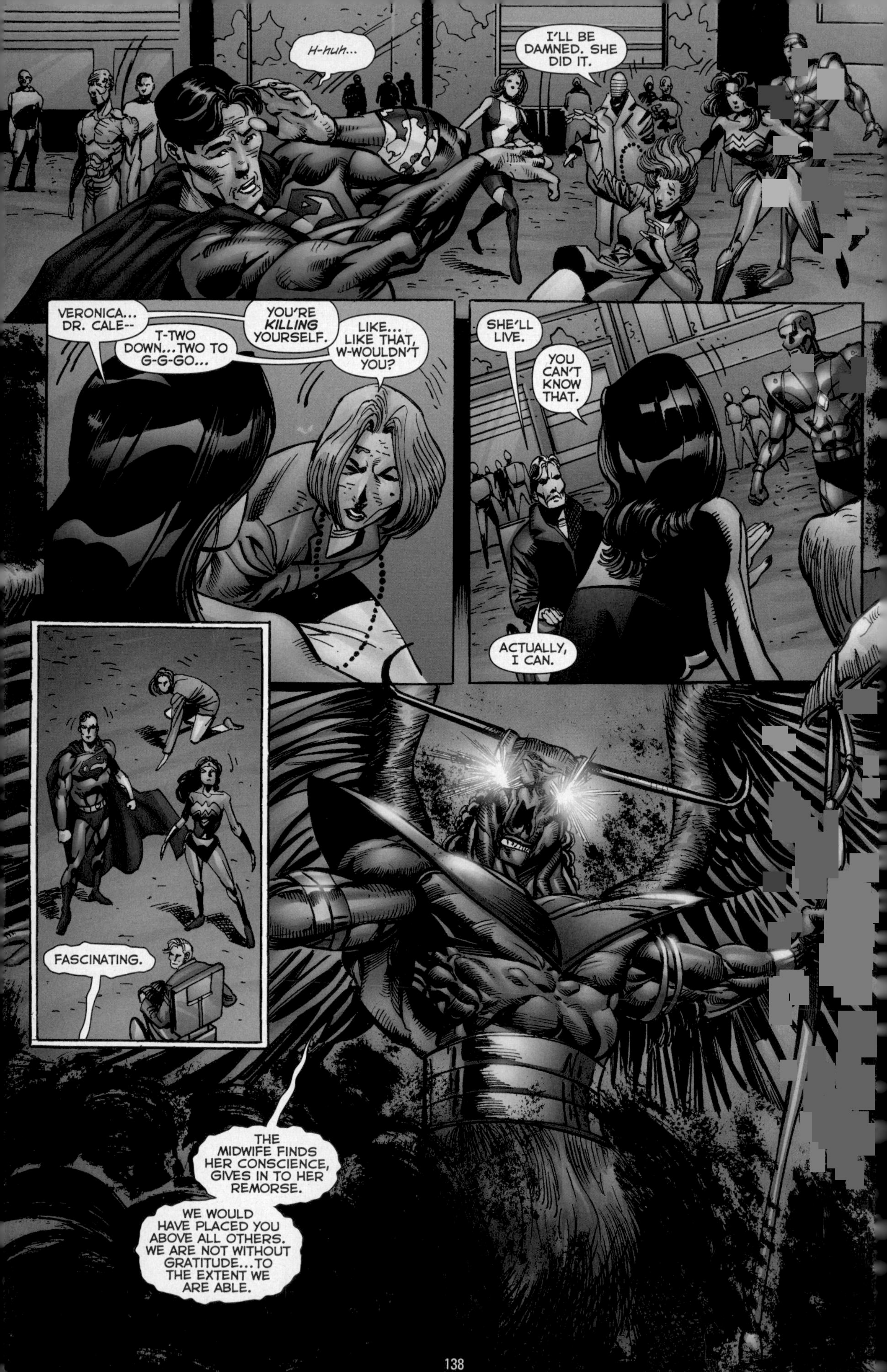
H-huh...
I'LL BE DAMNED. SHE DID IT.
VERONICA... DR. CALE--
T-TWO DOWN...TWO TO G-G-GO...
YOU'RE KILLING YOURSELF.
LIKE... LIKE THAT, W-WOULDN'T YOU?
SHE'LL LIVE.
YOU CAN'T KNOW THAT.
ACTUALLY, I CAN.
FASCINATING.
THE MIDWIFE FINDS HER CONSCIENCE, GIVES IN TO HER REMORSE.
WE WOULD HAVE PLACED YOU ABOVE ALL OTHERS. WE ARE NOT WITHOUT GRATITUDE...TO THE EXTENT WE ARE ABLE.

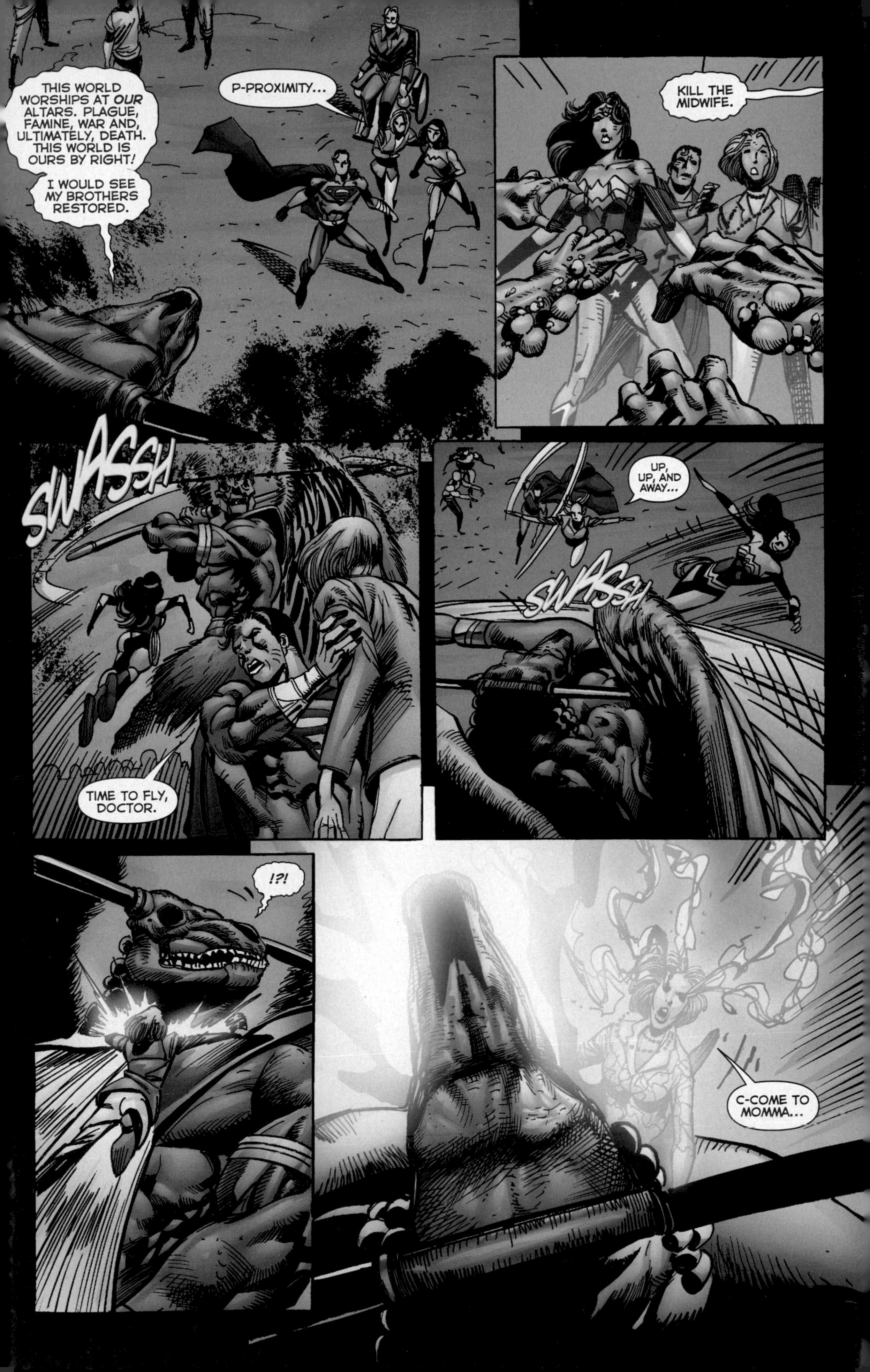
THIS WORLD WORSHIPS AT OUR ALTARS. PLAGUE, FAMINE, WAR AND, ULTIMATELY, DEATH. THIS WORLD IS OURS BY RIGHT!
I WOULD SEE MY BROTHERS RESTORED.
P-PROXIMITY...
KILL THE MIDWIFE.
SWASSH
TIME TO FLY, DOCTOR.
UP, UP, AND AWAY...
SWASSH
!?!
C-COME TO MOMMA...

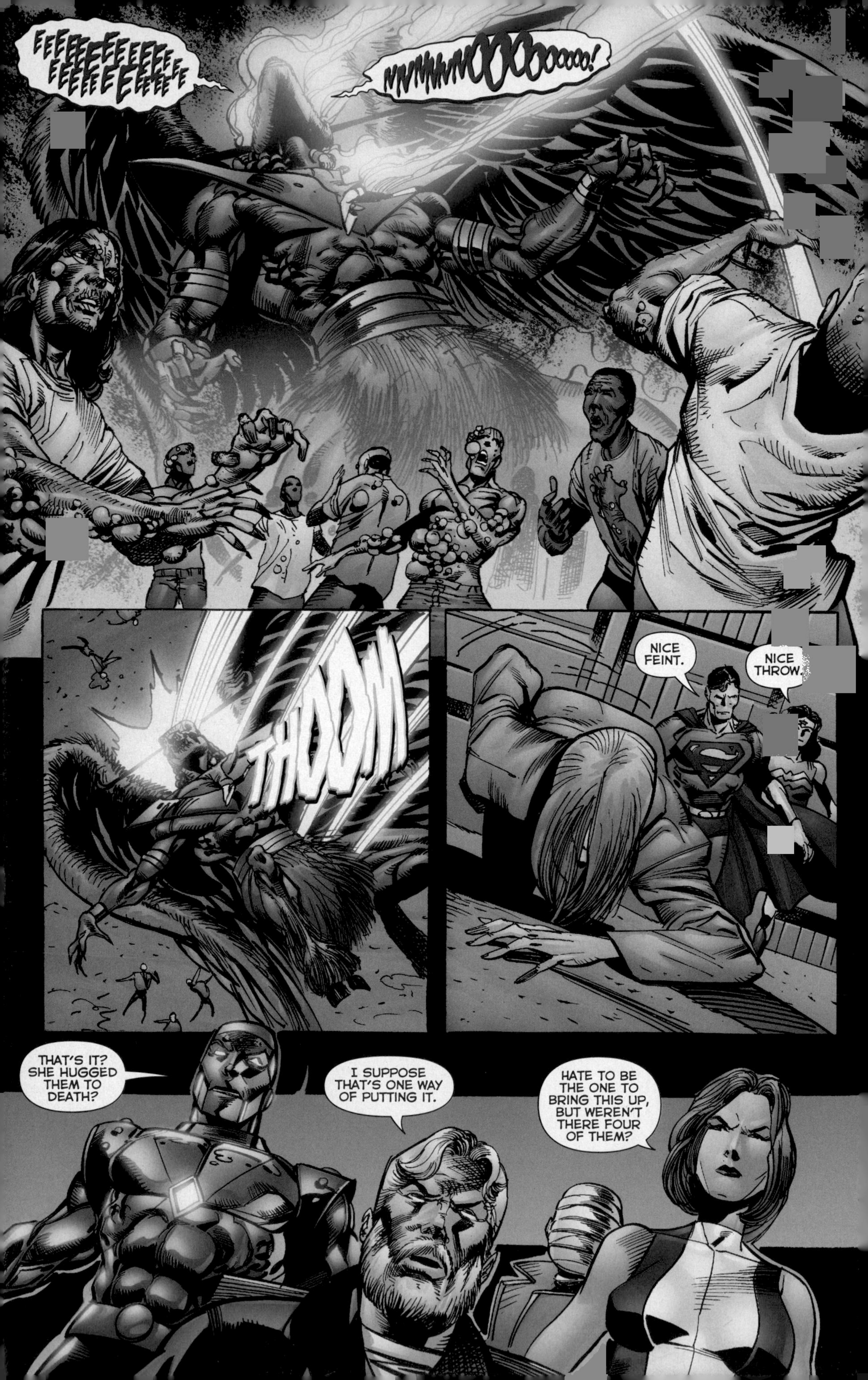
EEEEEEEEEEEEEEEEEEEEEEEEEEE
NNNNNNOOOOooooo!
THOOM
NICE FEINT.
NICE THROW.
THAT'S IT? SHE HUGGED THEM TO DEATH?
I SUPPOSE THAT'S ONE WAY OF PUTTING IT.
HATE TO BE THE ONE TO BRING THIS UP, BUT WEREN'T THERE FOUR OF THEM?

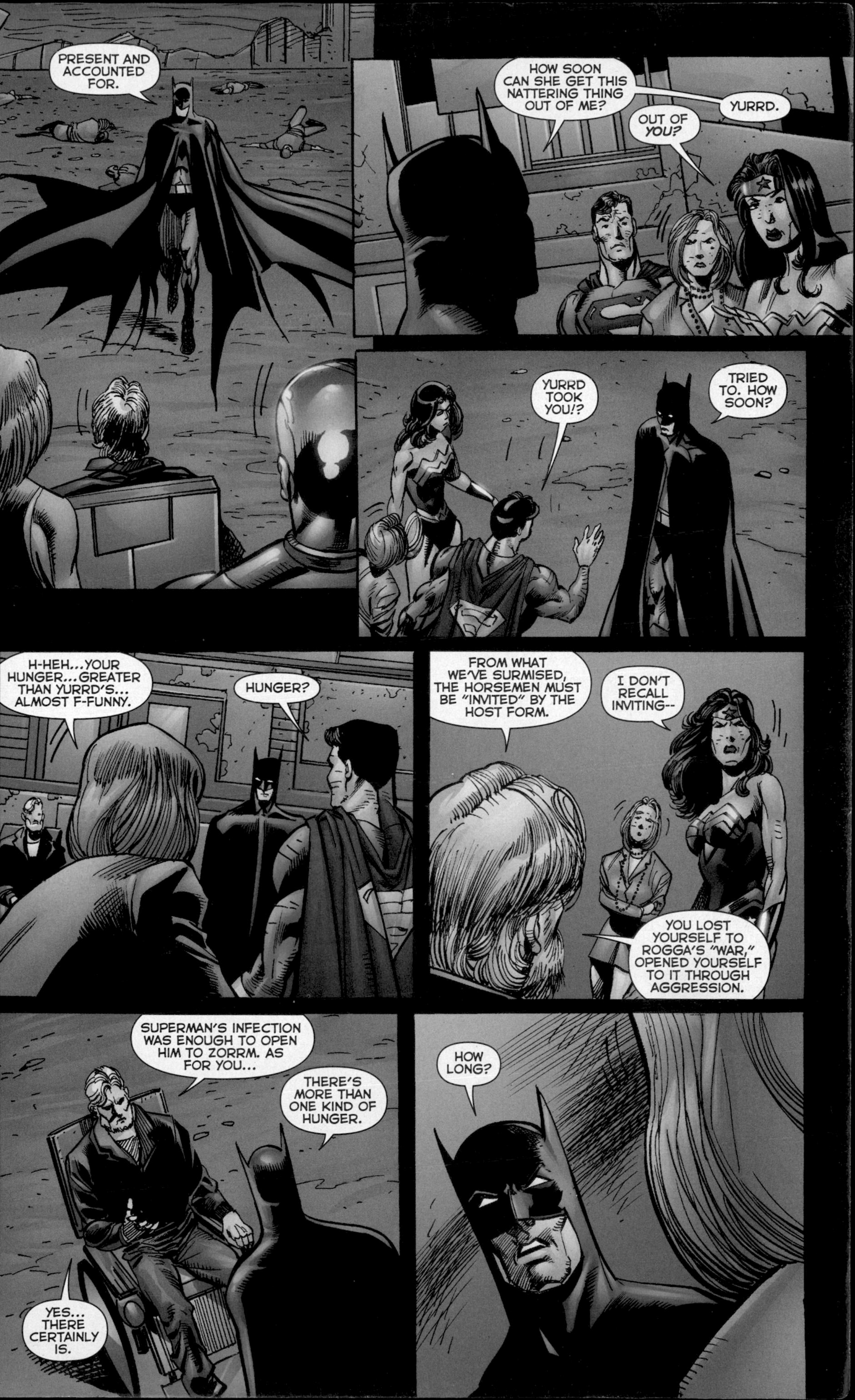
PRESENT AND ACCOUNTED FOR.
HOW SOON CAN SHE GET THIS NATTERING THING OUT OF ME?
YURRD.
OUT OF YOU?
YURRD TOOK YOU!?
TRIED TO. HOW SOON?
H-HEH...YOUR HUNGER...GREATER THAN YURRD'S... ALMOST F-FUNNY.
HUNGER?
FROM WHAT WE'VE SURMISED, THE HORSEMEN MUST BE "INVITED" BY THE HOST FORM.
I DON'T RECALL INVITING--
YOU LOST YOURSELF TO ROGGA'S "WAR," OPENED YOURSELF TO IT THROUGH AGGRESSION.
SUPERMAN'S INFECTION WAS ENOUGH TO OPEN HIM TO ZORRM. AS FOR YOU...
THERE'S MORE THAN ONE KIND OF HUNGER.
YES... THERE CERTAINLY IS.
HOW LONG?

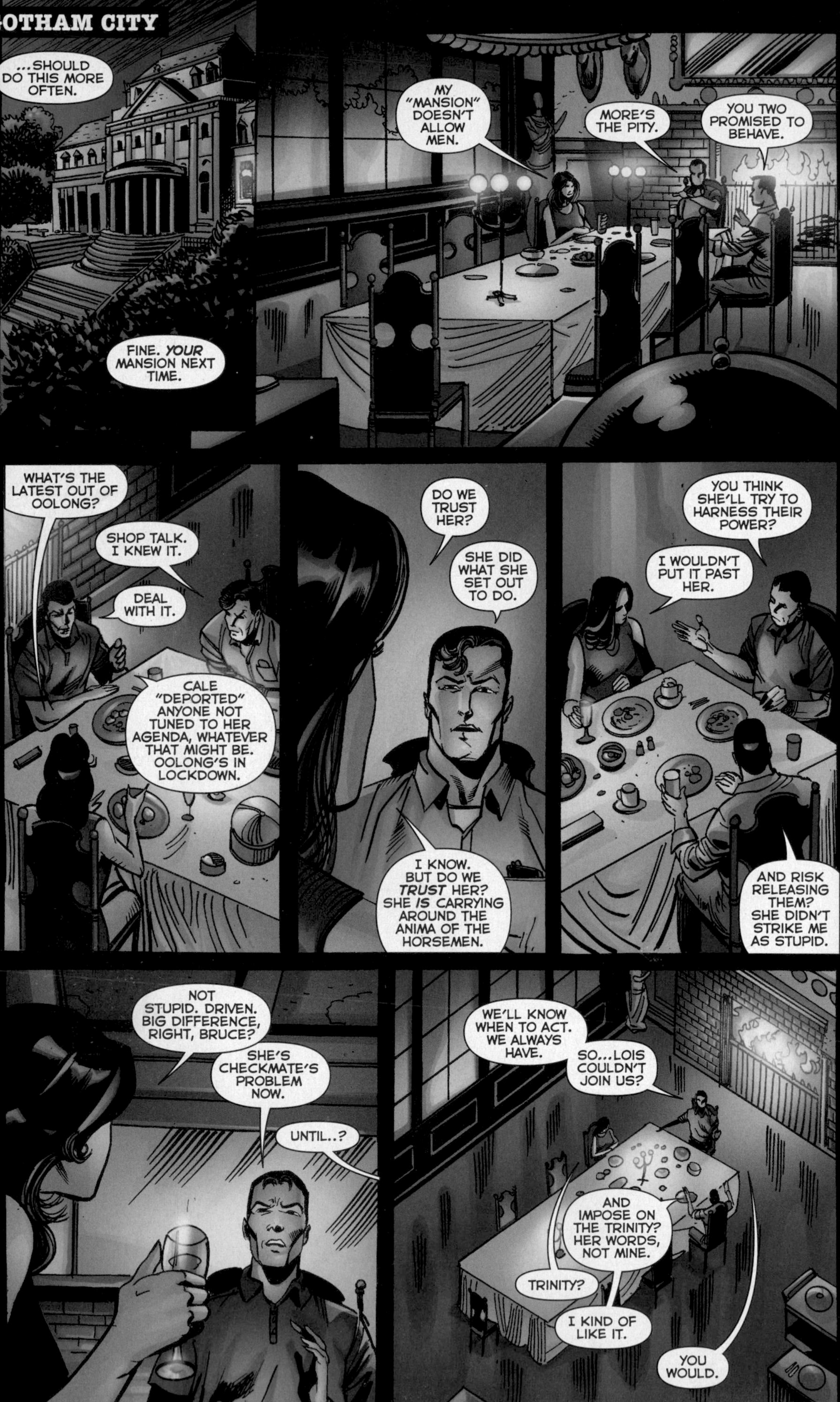
GOTHAM CITY
...SHOULD DO THIS MORE OFTEN.
MY "MANSION" DOESN'T ALLOW MEN.
MORE'S THE PITY.
YOU TWO PROMISED TO BEHAVE.
FINE. *YOUR* MANSION NEXT TIME.
WHAT'S THE LATEST OUT OF OOLONG?
SHOP TALK. I KNEW IT.
DEAL WITH IT.
CALE "DEPORTED" ANYONE NOT TUNED TO HER AGENDA, WHATEVER THAT MIGHT BE. OOLONG'S IN LOCKDOWN.
DO WE TRUST HER?
SHE DID WHAT SHE SET OUT TO DO.
I KNOW. BUT DO WE *TRUST* HER? SHE *IS* CARRYING AROUND THE ANIMA OF THE HORSEMEN.
YOU THINK SHE'LL TRY TO HARNESS THEIR POWER?
I WOULDN'T PUT IT PAST HER.
AND RISK RELEASING THEM? SHE DIDN'T STRIKE ME AS STUPID.
NOT STUPID. DRIVEN. BIG DIFFERENCE, RIGHT, BRUCE?
SHE'S CHECKMATE'S PROBLEM NOW.
UNTIL..?
WE'LL KNOW WHEN TO ACT. WE ALWAYS HAVE.
SO...LOIS COULDN'T JOIN US?
AND IMPOSE ON THE TRINITY? HER WORDS, NOT MINE.
TRINITY?
I KIND OF LIKE IT.
YOU WOULD.

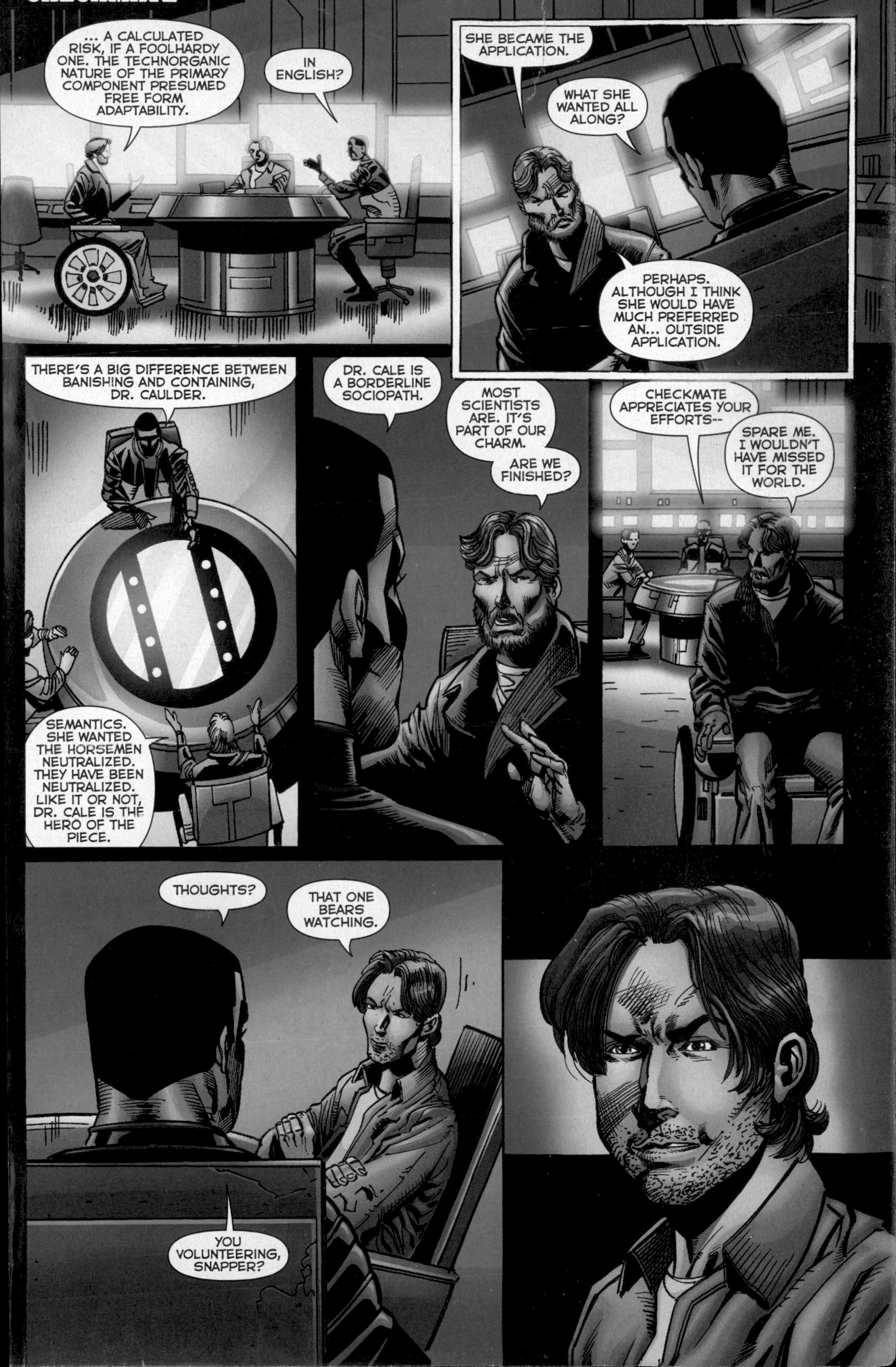
... A CALCULATED RISK, IF A FOOLHARDY ONE. THE TECHNORGANIC NATURE OF THE PRIMARY COMPONENT PRESUMED FREE FORM ADAPTABILITY.
IN ENGLISH?
SHE BECAME THE APPLICATION.
WHAT SHE WANTED ALL ALONG?
PERHAPS. ALTHOUGH I THINK SHE WOULD HAVE MUCH PREFERRED AN... OUTSIDE APPLICATION.
THERE'S A BIG DIFFERENCE BETWEEN BANISHING AND CONTAINING, DR. CAULDER.
SEMANTICS. SHE WANTED THE HORSEMEN NEUTRALIZED. THEY HAVE BEEN NEUTRALIZED. LIKE IT OR NOT, DR. CALE IS THE HERO OF THE PIECE.
DR. CALE IS A BORDERLINE SOCIOPATH.
MOST SCIENTISTS ARE. IT'S PART OF OUR CHARM.
ARE WE FINISHED?
CHECKMATE APPRECIATES YOUR EFFORTS--
SPARE ME. I WOULDN'T HAVE MISSED IT FOR THE WORLD.
THOUGHTS?
THAT ONE BEARS WATCHING.
YOU VOLUNTEERING, SNAPPER?

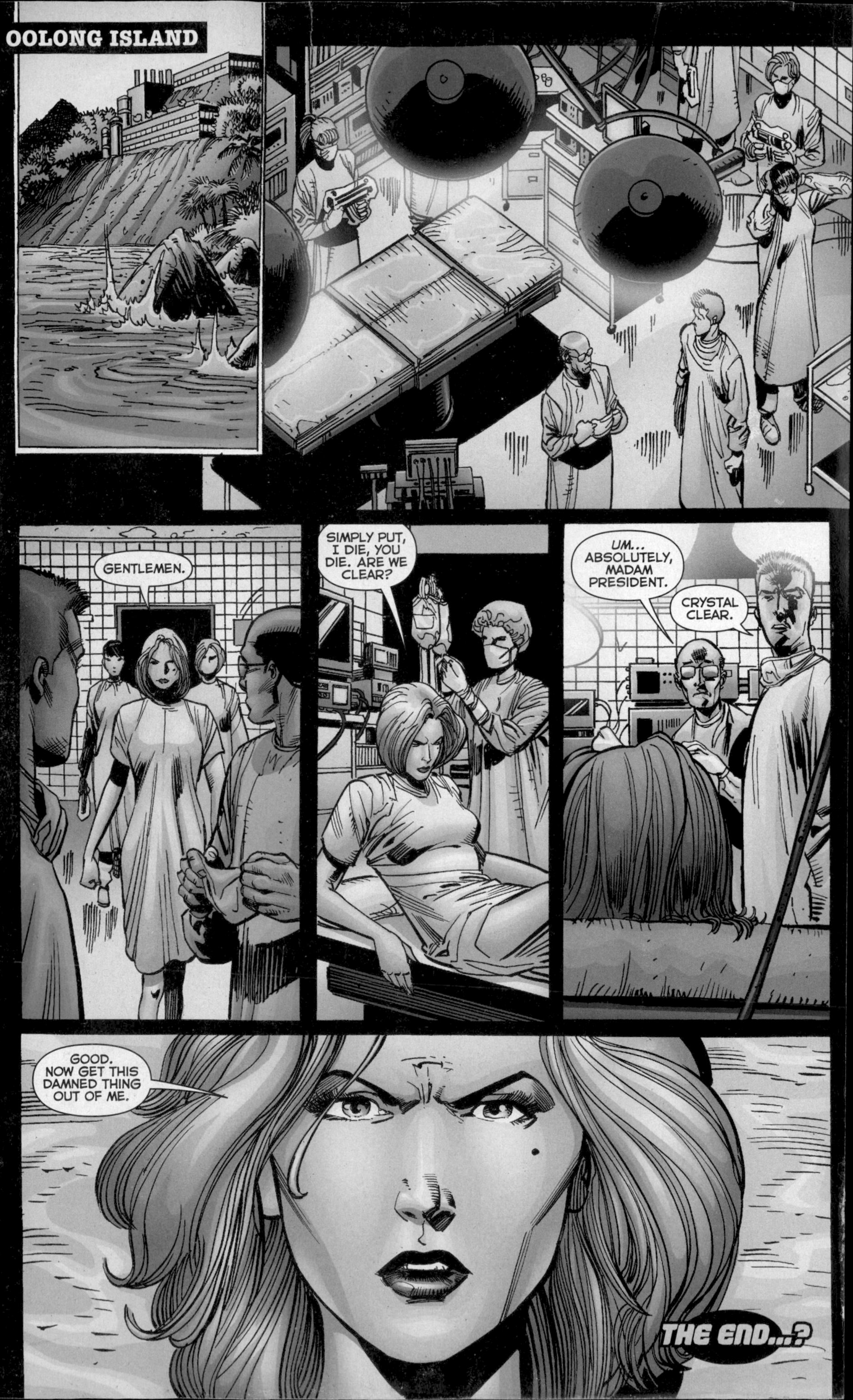
OOLONG ISLAND
GENTLEMEN.
SIMPLY PUT, I DIE, YOU DIE. ARE WE CLEAR?
UM... ABSOLUTELY, MADAM PRESIDENT.
CRYSTAL CLEAR.
GOOD. NOW GET THIS DAMNED THING OUT OF ME.
THE END...?